Abraham Lincoln

ABRAHAM LINCOLN

Sources and Style of Leadership

Edited by
FRANK J. WILLIAMS,
WILLIAM D. PEDERSON,
and VINCENT J. MARSALA

Contributions in American History, Number 159
Sponsored by the Abraham Lincoln Association

GREENWOOD PRESS
Westport, Connecticut · London

Library of Congress Cataloging-in-Publication Data

Abraham Lincoln—sources and style of leadership / edited by Frank J.
   Williams, William D. Pederson, and Vincent J. Marsala.
        p.   cm. — (Contributions in American history, ISSN 0084–9219;
   no. 159)
      Includes bibliographical references and index.
      ISBN 0–313–29359–7 (alk. paper)
        1. Lincoln, Abraham, 1809-1865.   2. Political leadership—United
   States—History—19th century.   I. Williams, Frank J.
   II. Pederson, William D.   III. Marsala, Vincent John.
   IV. Series.
   E457.2A146   1994
   973.7'092—dc20   94–12321

British Library Cataloguing in Publication Data is available.

Library of Congress Catalog Card Number: 94-12321
ISBN: 0–313–29359–7
ISSN: 0084–9219

First published in 1994

Greenwood Press, 88 Post Road West, Westport, CT 06881
An imprint of Greenwood Publishing Group, Inc.

Printed in the United States of America

♾™

The paper used in this book complies with the
Permanent Paper Standard issued by the National
Information Standards Organization (Z39.48–1984).

10 9 8 7 6 5 4 3 2

To

James Chowning Davies
Eugene, Oregon

Peggy and Norman Kinsey
Shreveport, Louisiana

Contents

Preface

Only one American, Abraham Lincoln, has earned a special classification by the Library of Congress because of the enormous amount of material written on him. Though his leadership has inspired the public and leaders at home and abroad from his time until today, little systematic analysis of it has been done. This volume explores the style and sources of Lincoln's leadership that political theorists consider were essential in making him so effective. The focus is on his personality and the culture that shaped his unique political style. The essays present new research, assess the state of current knowledge, and suggest the relevance of this material for understanding Lincoln's political achievement in the development of democratic leadership.

The book grew out of papers delivered at the first academic conference on America's sixteenth president ever held in the Deep South, 17–18 September 1992. It was a propitious time for such a national gathering, for it took place during the 2,500th anniversary of the world's first democracy in Athens and during the bicentennial of the White House, as well as a century after the death of Walt Whitman, "the poet of Lincoln." James Madison, "the father of the United States Constitution," had the audacity to challenge the accepted wisdom of classical political theory by his application of federalism to the world's first large republic, as immortalized in the *Federalist Papers*. Abraham Lincoln's contribution to Western political thought is found in his equally audacious leadership style, which combined liberal and conservative, as well as democratic and autocratic, elements. Though unable to prevent a civil war, he ultimately contributed to broadening the base of democracy as established in Athens by upholding the moral equality of human beings in the American experiment in self-government.

The conference was held on the campus of Louisiana State University in Shreveport during its twenty-fifth anniversary as a spin-off from the Land-Grant College Act that Lincoln signed into law. The setting of the conference was most appropriate, for Lincoln had developed special ties to Louisiana. From his two trips down the Mississippi River to New Orleans as a youth until his opportunity to steer the ship of state, Louisiana remained a part of his southern and western heritage. He closely followed events in the state, wished to extend the elective franchise there, and recognized the state's potential upon its return to the Union. The state became a linchpin in his plan for Reconstruction. His last public words from the White House dealt with Louisiana's future.

It was both fitting and ironic that the conference took place in Shreveport, the final capital of the Confederacy and the only one militarily undefeated during the Civil War. The city is located on Louisiana's "other" river, which flows near its western border; the Red River in Shreveport links southern tradition to the western democratic hopes epitomized in Lincoln's life. During the nineteenth century, navigation on the Red River was impossible due to the Great River Raft—a major logjam near Shreveport. Ironically, it took federal resources to open the river to navigation, just as it took Lincoln's leadership during the war to begin the long-term effort to break down racial and social barriers among U.S. citizens.

As part of the Louisiana Purchase, Shreveport is also linked to the Midwest. The Abraham Lincoln Association, headquartered in Lincoln's hometown of Springfield, Illinois, co-sponsored the conference with Louisiana State University in Shreveport and is the sponsor of this volume. First known as the Lincoln Centennial Association, it was organized in 1908 to celebrate the hundredth anniversary of Lincoln's birth the following 12 February. The association's charter requires it to promote the study of Lincoln, and its sponsorship of the conference and this volume represents the ongoing fulfillment of its mission to bring new information about Lincoln to people beyond the precincts of Springfield. Early in its history, the association discovered and made accessible unknown facts about the life of Lincoln. Since 1940, with the publication of the *Abraham Lincoln Quarterly* and later, the *Journal of the Abraham Lincoln Association*, the organization has emphasized interpretation of facts already accumulated. It is hoped that this volume may further break down the mystery about Lincoln's leadership.

The volume is divided into three parts. The first part focuses on the impact that others had on Lincoln and how he transformed these ideas into his own political vision. The second part deals with Lincoln's political style during the Civil War and how he influenced others. The third part is a comparative chapter that puts Lincoln's political style in the perspective of the world leaders of his age.

The editors wish to express appreciation to Louisiana State University in Shreveport for organizing and hosting the conference, as well as to the support extended by the Abraham Lincoln Association. We thank the following three talents at Greenwood Press: Cynthia Harris, the Executive Editor of Reference Books; Penny Sippel, Senior Production Editor, and Susan Winslow, the copyeditor. We owe a major debt to the secretarial skills of Donna J. Saffel and the editing expertise of Anne King as well as the technical services of Laser King (Hal and Elaine King). Our deepest thanks are extended to the participants at the conference. These essays suggest the liveliness of the endeavor to identify the sources and style of Abraham Lincoln's leadership.

Introduction: Sources and Style of Abraham Lincoln's Leadership

Frank J. Williams and William D. Pederson

Toward the end of her life, the American historian Barbara Tuchman raised the question of why government seemed to produce the least successful leaders compared to the arts and sciences.[1] She suggested that most political leaders lack what she termed "fitness of character." Though Abraham Lincoln's leadership has been praised along with federalism as the two greatest gifts of American democracy in the world,[2] comparatively little work has been done to understand his character and its relationship to leadership. As a result, several popular schools of thought have developed that view Lincoln as a racial bigot without a commitment to emancipation and as belonging to "the American pragmatic tradition."

Perhaps the primary reason for the lack of work on Lincoln's political leadership is that his style is unique. It defies classification since it contained conservative and liberal values, active and passive elements, and democratic and autocratic tendencies. Moreover, he went suddenly from one of America's most heavily criticized presidents during his administration to virtual sainthood following his assassination.

Most scholars agree today that leadership involves a relationship between the leader and the followers. This relationship may be limited to a power dimension or involve a more subtle dimension reflecting the psychological needs of both parties. Building on the pioneering work of Abraham Maslow, Lawrence Kohlberg, and James Chowning Davies, the political scientist and historian James McGregor Burns argues that great leaders engage in a democratic dialogue with their followers and often are able to inspire their higher psychological needs. The dialogue between them often changes both parties.[3] Because Lincoln's leadership contained both Machiavellian and magnanimous dimensions, it often misleads critics and even supporters. He was a conservative Whig who gradually emerged as the leader of America's second revolution. What accounts for his transformation?

ACTIVITY, VISION, AND FLEXIBILITY:
KEYS TO CHARACTER

Though difficult to classify, Lincoln's leadership demonstrates several consistent patterns. Similar to other great leaders, he epitomized an individual with extraordinary energy that permitted him to have careers in both law and politics. A key to his intense activity was his psychological marginality (a sense of not belonging, or being an outsider). He was the most marginal U.S. president. With illegitimate relatives, physically too tall and too skinny, born in the frontier West, and possessing less than one year of formal schooling, Lincoln epitomizes physical, social, and intellectual marginality. Fortunately, he was able to resolve his marginality in a positive direction through a successful legal and political career.

In contrast to his immediate predecessor, James Buchanan, America's sixteenth president was willing to act. Lincoln internalized the democratic values derived from his frontier upbringing and those of the framers of the U.S. Constitution. Though he went far beyond traditional presidential restraints, he always sought and received congressional backing after taking bold steps to preserve the Union. He understood the Lockean notion expressed by Alexander Hamilton in *Federalist Paper* no. 70 that "Energy in the Executive is a leading character in the definition of good government."

Lincoln's vision is a second key to understanding his leadership style.[4] Initially, his conservative Whig goal was merely to preserve the Union that had allowed individuals like himself to improve socially and to find psychological fulfillment. That middle-class desire was gradually transformed during the war into a larger democratic vision that sought equality for all. The stress on equality and human dignity reflected his frontier experience and the way he related to others in concrete terms.

Both in private and public, he captured the democratic imagination. His heroes were democratic ones—George Washington and Thomas Jefferson. His vision reflected his personal treatment of others and the way he wanted to be treated himself. Both personal friends and the American public responded to his ability to relate to them as individuals rather than abstractions. He knew how to communicate both informally and formally.

A third key to Lincoln's leadership is his flexibility. Though a traditional conservative Whig, he changed with the times, evolving into a prudent and magnanimous democrat. Never an ideologue, he favored prudent solutions that sought to reconcile principle to circumstance. His flexible methods in dealing with political problems in self-government extended even to his private life. He recognized mental health and sought medical advice for his "manic depression." Moreover, he experimented in treating himself through developing friendships and his sense of humor.

Lincoln was flexible in adapting to change and to the needs of those around him. His "active-flexible" personality made him a delight to be around. In fact, one American psychologist suggests this quality is the essence of mental health:

flexibility, the freedom to learn through experience, the freedom to change with changing internal and external circumstances, to be influenced by reasonable argument, admonitions, exhortation, and the appeal to emotions; the freedom to respond appropriately to a stimulus of reward and punishment, and especially the freedom to cease when sated. The essence of normality is flexibility in all of these vital ways.[5]

Lincoln's character determined his leadership style, which developed on the frontier. Active-flexible personalities need democratic environments to develop fully.[6] Lincoln's performance in the White House is better understood within this context and in contrast to foreign leaders, who were the products of other traditions.

LINCOLN AS AN ACTIVE-FLEXIBLE LEADER

The essays that follow contain variations on the theme of Lincoln as a magnanimous political leader with an "active-flexible" personality who rejected both moral idealism and cynicism and tried to adapt principle to circumstance. The first four chapters deal with influences on Lincoln's leadership. Ethan Fishman in "Under the Circumstances: Abraham Lincoln and Classical Prudence," places Lincoln in the classical mode of Aristotle, Thomas Aquinas, and Edmund Burke. Lincoln strove to avoid moral extremes. Fishman shows how this effort was reflected in Lincoln's position on slavery before the war, on Fort Sumter, on emancipation, and on Reconstruction. Fishman rejects revisionist historians such as James G. Randall, Richard Hofstadter, and David Donald, who argue that Lincoln belonged to American pragmatic tradition. According to Fishman, Lincoln belongs to the tradition of classical prudence—reconciling principle and circumstance. He was a principled man who could seek realistic solutions in extenuating circumstances.

Ronald D. Rietveld in "Lincoln's View of the Founding Fathers" presents a guide to the young Lincoln's study of the framers and shows how he became a master of "argumentative analysis." According to Rietveld, Thomas Jefferson was the primary founder who meant most to Lincoln. The Declaration of Independence was the source of all of Lincoln's basic beliefs, especially moral equality and human dignity. Lincoln continued the work of Jefferson's generation by reestablishing the Union on those founding principles. He did not break with the framers.

Joseph R. Fornieri in "Abraham Lincoln and the Declaration of Independence: The Meaning of Equality" argues that Lincoln viewed the Declaration as a "founding document" whose precepts committed the new American system to equality and the consent of the governed, and thus to the end of slavery. "Indeed," Fornieri writes, "the substance of Lincoln's political thought consists in his prudential discernment of the incompatibility between slavery and a regime that purported to be founded upon the self-evident truth of human equality." Fornieri rejects conservative revisionists such as M. E. Bradford and Garry Wills, who contend that the Declaration was not a "founding document" and that Lincoln's efforts to make it so went against the framers and led to the "imperial presidency." Fornieri points out that Lincoln's interpretation was in fact that of Thomas Jefferson and John Adams.

The problem with conservative revisions is their failure to acknowledge the role of equality in the American political tradition. Fornieri asserts that Lincoln "harmonized the universal principles of the Declaration within the concrete framework of the Constitution." As a result, he embodies the prudential statesman *par-excellence.*

An effective leader must be able to communicate his vision to others. James A. Stevenson in "Lincoln's Poetry and Prose" discusses the painstaking craftsmanship in Lincoln's voice and how his apprenticeship to poetry profoundly influenced his prose. Though everyone praises the eloquence and literary quality of Lincoln's speeches and state papers, few have explained why those documents have such power. Stevenson argues that Lincoln was influenced by Shakespeare and the early nineteenth-century Romantic poets in his 1840s poems about his boyhood home in Indiana. His poetry apprenticeship honed his skill in the use of metaphor, imagery, and rhythm. This experience prevented him from using the overblown rhetoric of the day and allowed him to develop a prose that was "precise, vernacular, rhythmic, melodic, and elegant." In short, Lincoln was a poetic person whose speeches hummed with the cadences of verse.

The four essays in the middle of this volume illustrate the style and quality of Abraham Lincoln's leadership during the Civil War. David E. Long in "I Shall Never Recall a Word" disposes the notion that Lincoln was a bigot who used emancipation as an expedient while the slaves freed themselves. Long demonstrates that the Emancipation Proclamation was "an act of staggering importance" in the context of its time and place, one that put "a moral blockade" around the Confederacy. He argues that Lincoln never seriously considered retracting the promise of emancipation, even during his lowest ebb in the summer of 1864, and would never have restored the rebellious states with slavery intact. He analyzes Henry J. Raymond's peace plan and Lincoln's handling of it, as well as "the illogic of the speculation" that Lincoln would have dropped emancipation if Jefferson Davis would have opened a dialogue with him about peace. Long considers the 1864 election as "the most important electoral event in American history," since the Union electorate guaranteed a second term for Lincoln, an end to slavery, and that the United States would "enter the twentieth century undivided."

Brooks D. Simpson in "Lincoln and Grant: A Reappraisal of a Relationship" treats Lincoln's leadership style in dealing with his best commander, as well as the Grant-Lincoln relationship, since little has been said about Grant's handling of Lincoln. Simpson disputes the traditional view that Lincoln believed in Grant early in the war, that he waited patiently for him to evolve into a great commander, that he protected him from criticism, and that after appointing him to supreme command, he interfered in Grant's plans only to save the general from error. Simpson shows that Lincoln did nothing unusual to promote Grant; his promotions stemmed from battlefield accomplishments rather than Lincoln's foresight. On several occasions Lincoln considered replacing Grant. Presidential politics often determined and even impaired Grant's military planning. For example, during the spring offensive in 1864, Grant had to find places for two political generals, Franz Sigel and Benjamin F. Butler, and the failure of their operations deprived him of the chance to "crush" Lee in "a campaign of maneuver." Though political considerations often constrained Grant, he did not complain. His cautious, judicious, and uncomplaining behavior with his commander-in-chief encouraged "a warm personal relationship" of mutual trust and respect.

Another crucial Lincoln relationship is explored by William C. Harris, in "Abraham Lincoln and Southern White Unionism"; it also sheds further light on Lincoln's style of leadership, which sought to accommodate principle to circumstance. In his efforts to restore loyal governments to the conquered South and in outlawing slavery there, Lincoln displayed considerable empathy for the predicament of Southern white Unionists. At the start of hostilities, his oft-stated hatred of slavery set him apart from these Unionists, and his Emancipation Proclamation "complicated" his early Reconstruction efforts. But in the end most Southern white Unionists came around to Lincoln's position. Though his Reconstruction efforts stalled during the summer of 1864, he enjoyed greater support among Southern Unionists than among their Northern counterparts. Indeed, Southern white Unionists "overwhelmingly" endorsed the Lincoln-Johnson ticket that year. In essence, Harris says Lincoln followed a policy of nonintervention in restoring civilian rule, a policy that derived from his strong belief in self-government.

David H. Leroy in "Lincoln and Idaho: A Rocky Mountain Legacy" delves into the way Lincoln developed and maintained permanent friendships. Though he made no speaking tours of the North and delivered few speeches in Washington, he developed a network of loyal friends during his Illinois years through his ability to communicate directly with people. In addition to his public letters, proclamations, congressional messages, and inaugural addresses, he continually met the public individually in the White House during his "public opinion baths." Leroy sketches Lincoln's dealings with Idaho politicos during the creation of that western territory. A master of patronage appointments, he cemented the friendships that his life inspired. The chapter also serves to remind readers of the inherently western outlook beneath many of his friendships. Lincoln took a particular interest in the Idaho Territory and exercised a special "guardianship" over it. On the last day of his life, Abraham and Mary took a carriage drive and talked about their future. He thought their sons might have a better life in California. His own life illustrated the centuries-old struggle of the common person in Western civilization and the U.S. West offered possibilities of a society based on equality and opportunity.[7] His success as a western lawyer and politician, as well as his personal concern and treatment of others, were magnets that drew people to him. Lincoln was the self-made individual of all times and regions, a man whom others enjoyed and wanted to emulate.

In contrast to "The Last Best Hope of Earth," the final chapter of the book illustrates the limitations of the Old World, indeed the rest of the world in the mid-nineteenth century. Frank J. Williams in "Lincoln and Leadership: An International Perspective" compares Lincoln's style and achievements to those of other world leaders and nation builders of his time. Constrained by tradition, these leaders fixated on Machiavellian methods to stay in power. By contrast, Lincoln's personality and political heritage encouraged responsible democratic rule. He was a leader who would not be an autocratic or a naive idealist; he acted to preserve and promote the democratic values of the framers. Classical prudence and magnanimity were part of his democratic character.[8]

Overall, this collection of essays contributes to understanding the sources, quality, and style of Lincoln's leadership. The contributors present variations on the theme of a magnanimous "active-flexible" personality, which rejected moral idealism and cynicism and tried to adopt principle to circumstance. The portrait that emerges is of a principled leader who could seek practical solutions in extenuating circumstances, a poetic personality whose speeches captured the democratic vision from classical times, an informed politician who was inspired by Thomas Jefferson, and a moral and generous statesman who was a master of "argumentative analysis" and was "an effective persuader" without equal in his day.

NOTES

1. Barbara Tuchman, "An Inquiry into the Persistence of Unwisdom in Government, "in *The Rating Game in American Politics,* ed. William D. Pederson and Ann M. McLaurin (New York: Irvington Publishers, 1987), 197–212.

2. James C. Davies, *Human Nature in Politics* (New York: John Wiley & Sons, 1963), 320.

3. James McGregor Burns, *Leadership* (New York: Harper & Row, 1978).

4. Warren Bennis and Burt Nanus, *Leaders: The Strategies for Taking Charge* (New York: Harper & Row, 1985).

5. Lawrence S. Kubie, *Neurotic Distortion of the Creative Process* (Lawrence: University of Kansas Press, 1958), 20.

6. William D. Pederson, ed., *The "Barberian" Presidency* (New York: Peter Lang, 1989); and William D. Pederson and Kenneth G. Kuriger, Jr., "A Comparative Test of Jimmy Carter's Character," in *The Presidency and Domestic Policies of Jimmy Carter,* ed. Herbert D. Rosenbaum and Alexej Ugrinsky (Westport, Conn.: Greenwood Press, 1994), 243–257.

7. James C. Davies, "Lincoln: The Saint and the Man," in *The Rating Game in American Politics,* ed. William D. Pederson and Ann M. McLaurin (New York: Irvington Publishers, 1987), 297–335.

8. See Larry Arnhart, "Statesmanship as Magnanimity: Classical, Christian, and Modern," *Polity* 16, no. 2 (winter 1983): 263–283.

Part I

Sources of Leadership: Influences on Lincoln

1 Under the Circumstances: Abraham Lincoln and Classical Prudence

Ethan Fishman

When historical figures achieve mythological status, it becomes much harder to accurately examine their lives and thoughts. There is a natural tendency to view them as icons rather than complex human beings facing complicated situations. Such is the case with Abraham Lincoln. Descriptions of him have ranged from the biblical "Father Abraham" to a self-serving politician with an extraordinary passion for fame and power.

Contrary to myth, my own view is that Lincoln was a political moderate, in general, and an adherent of classical Western prudence in particular. Since, by the middle of the nineteenth century, classical prudence already had lost the popularity it once enjoyed, Lincoln might be considered remarkable in adapting its tenets. In every other respect, however, Lincoln's prudence represented the epitome of moderation, a conscious effort to avoid extremes, especially those of moral idealism and moral cynicism in politics.

In this chapter I will attempt to defend my thesis by demonstrating the relationship between the classical concept of prudence and the ideas Lincoln expressed during his political career as well as the decisions he made during the American Civil War. First I will discuss classical Western prudence in its original Aristotelian form and later interpretations by Thomas Aquinas, Edmund Burke, and Jacques Maritain. Then I will explain the fundamental prudential character of Lincoln's attitudes towards such issues as slavery, its spread to the territories, the impending dissolution of the Union, the Emancipation Proclamation, and Reconstruction. I will close with an analysis of the views of certain contemporary revisionist Lincoln historians who have confused classical prudence with moral cynicism and pragmatism.

CLASSICAL PRUDENCE

Aristotle, who developed the first theory of prudence (*phronesis*), based his arguments on a distinctive view of human nature. Human beings possess a soul, Aristotle maintained, that permits us both to comprehend the differences between right and wrong and freely choose between good and evil courses of action. Aristotle realized, however, that our souls often are seduced by powerful material temptations. He thus offered prudence, which he called "calcula(tion) . . . for the attainment of a particular end of a fine sort," as a resource to help us make moral decisions under constantly changing and often very difficult circumstances.[1]

In Book VI of his *Ethics* Aristotle distinguished between theoretical and practical reason and the intellectual and moral virtues that these forms of reason employ. Theoretical reason and the intellectual virtues apply to subjects that deal exclusively with abstractions. Metaphysics, physics, and mathematics involve knowledge for the sake of knowledge and yield universal truths that cannot be affected by human volition. Politics represents another matter altogether, Aristotle observed, precisely because it exists in the material world and is subject to human fallibility. Here only practical reason and the moral virtues that yield contingent truths learned from life experiences are relevant.

Aristotle considered politics to be the preeminent form of practical reason because it involves an understanding of the noblest human motives for the sake of noble action. He concluded that prudence is the archetypal moral virtue because its "knowledge of the correct ends or values as well as the calculation of the correct means to these ends"[2] enables us to do the right thing to the right person at the right time.

Aristotle's approach to tyranny illustrates what he meant by prudence. He acknowledged that success at accumulating and maintaining power theoretically has nothing to do with virtuous political leadership. He also realized that the theory of good governance alone was not going to convince tyrants to renounce their dictatorships. In order to achieve genuine reform he sought to exploit their greed by warning them that excessive abuse can lead to revolution and forfeiture of total control. Through this method Aristotle did not expect to create virtuous rulers out of tyrants. He did not even expect them to become "half good" or "half bad." As he contended in Book V of his *Politics*, the most we can expect of an entrenched tyrannical regime is that it becomes no longer "*wholly bad.*"[3]

In the thirteenth century Thomas Aquinas converted Aristotelian prudence into one of the cardinal virtues of Christian theology. For Aquinas prudence serves a three-fold purpose: it reminds Christians what God expects of them in their personal and political lives; it identifies the obstacles that they inevitably will confront in an imperfect world; and it counsels them about what reasonably can be done to overcome these obstacles. It functions, in other words, "to regulate the specific means toward the end of love and makes it effective in action."[4]

In view of the obstacles, Aquinas's advice to rulers is not to expect too much in the way of virtuous behavior from citizens. Prudent rulers simultaneously must set their sights on the natural-law standards of political justice and adjust human law to the capacity of the populace to observe those standards. "Now human law is framed for a number of human beings, the majority of whom are not perfect in virtue," Aquinas wrote. "Wherefore human laws do not forbid all vices from which the virtuous abstain, but only the more grievous vices from which it is possible for the majority to abstain and chiefly those that are to the hurt of others, without the prohibition of which society could not be maintained: thus human law prohibits murder, theft, and suchlike."[5]

Five hundred years later Edmund Burke interpreted Aristotle's and Aquinas's lessons for modern Western civilization. Burke admonished the French *philosophes* for neglecting to realize that all nations do not arrive at the same level of historical development at the same time. "I flatter myself that I love a manly, moral, regulated liberty as well as any gentleman of that society, be he who he will," he wrote.

But I cannot stand forward and give praise or blame to anything which relates to human actions, and human concerns, on a simple view of the object, as it stands stripped of every relation, in all the nakedness and solitude of metaphysical abstraction. Circumstances (which with some gentlemen pass for nothing) give in reality to every political principle its distinguishing color and discriminating effect. The circumstances are what render every civil and political scheme beneficial or noxious to mankind.[6]

To Burke, prudence is indispensable to politics because it allows us to think creatively on the one plane that politics will admit—"on the more or the less, the earlier or the later, and on a balance of advantage and inconvenience, of good and evil."[7] By formulating a metaphysical doctrine of natural rights, Burke warned, the French misplaced that creativity and imprudently jeopardized their future as a democratic republic.

Then as now, scholars have experienced difficulty reconciling Burke's opposition to the French Revolution with his support for the American one. The way Burke himself explained this apparent paradox was by differentiating between American prudence and French radical idealism. While the latter expected successfully to adopt ideals that had never existed before in French society, he observed, the former had the much more moderate goal of transplanting traditional English political standards to native grounds.

The neo-Thomist Jacques Maritain was one of the few distinguished twentieth-century political theorists to realize the worth of classical prudence. Aristotle recommended prudential means to reform entrenched unjust regimes—even totally evil totalitarian dictatorships. Maritain, who lived and wrote during the Nazi Holocaust, took Aristotle one step further. He located in classical prudence justification for the temporary use of otherwise unjust methods by otherwise just people to overthrow Hitler. "The application of moral rules immutable to themselves takes lower and lower forms as the social environment declines," Maritain argued.

In utterly barbarized societies like a concentration camp, or even in quite particular conditions like those of clandestine resistance in an occupied country, many things which were, as to their moral nature, objectively fraud or murder or perfidy in ordinary civilized life cease, now, to come under the same definition and become . . . objectively permissible or ethical things.[8]

Despite the clarity of Aristotle's, Aquinas's, Burke's, and Maritain's statements, prudence obviously is easier to define than attain, and it is not hard to see why the concept often has been misunderstood. On the one hand, because prudence involves a healthy component of moral principle, pragmatists and cynics have tended to identify it with idealism. On the other hand, because prudence also emphasizes material circumstances, it has been described by some idealists as a form of moral cynicism.

Actually, through its recognition of humankind's capacity for both moral and evil decisions, classical prudence is able to avoid the limitations of moral idealism and cynicism. Classical prudence neither denies moral principles nor considers them sufficient to meet the demands of practical politics. It considers moral principles to be necessary because of their immutability: they provide consistent civilized goals towards which human beings can strive. In this sense classical prudence represents the antithesis of cultural relativism. Yet classical prudence considers moral principles to be insufficient because of their inflexibility: they are incapable of adjusting fixed rules to new situations. The function of classical prudence represents the rejection of ideology in politics. Its refusal to compress unprecedented policy issues into preordained dogmas resembles realism much more than any other form of political orientation.

For the past few centuries acceptance of classical prudence has significantly decreased. A full discussion of the reasons for this decrease is beyond the scope of the present chapter, but some observations are appropriate to my thesis, as they may help to explain the quality of Lincoln's vision.

One of the recognizable trends in modern Western history is that we seem to have developed a more sanguine view of human nature than our ancestors possessed. Hobbes's and Locke's social-contract theories and Marxian anthropology are cases in point. Aristotle, Aquinas, Burke, and Maritain had argued that government is natural in the sense that we require it to reach our potential as human beings. "All associations aim at some good," Aristotle thus argued. "And we may also hold that the particular association which is the most sovereign of all, and includes all the rest, will pursue this aim most, and will be directed to the most sovereign of all goods. This most sovereign and inclusive association is the polis, as it is called, or the political association."[9]

By positing a state of nature antecedent to society and government, however, Hobbes and Locke implied that we are essentially self-sufficient creatures who can take government or leave it according to our needs and capabilities. Marx's prediction that an apolitical advanced stage of communism eventually will emerge in which machines will do all the work and human frustrations will disappear embodies a similar implication. Prudence was designed by Aristotle, Aquinas, Burke, and

Maritain to help fallible human beings confront what sometimes appear to be insuperable dilemmas. Yet the impression we get from contractarians and Marxists is that nothing is impossible for us. From the perspective of classical prudence, therefore, much of modern Western thought represents a serious underestimation of our liability to err.

LINCOLN'S PRUDENCE

As the record demonstrates, Lincoln was unequivocal. "I am naturally anti-slavery," he wrote in 1864. "If slavery is not wrong, nothing is wrong. I can not remember when I did not so think, and feel."[10] Lincoln's position on this issue echoed that of his predecessors. Even Aristotle, who supported the institution, opposed race slavery based on conquest. Adherents of classical prudence always have assumed that human beings with souls require at least some significant degree of political freedom in order to exercise their humanity. As Lincoln put it: "If the negro *is* a man, is it not to that extent, a total destruction of self-government, to say that he too shall not govern *himself.*"[11]

On the question of using the power of the national government to end slavery in the South, Lincoln was similarly adamant. By the middle of the nineteenth century, slavery had existed in the Southern states for two hundred years. It would be imprudent to compel them to overturn ingrained social, political, and economic practices overnight, he reasoned after the fashion of Burke. The resulting chaos would be worse than the status quo for all parties concerned. Since future economic realities most likely would render such repellent practices anachronistic, he predicted, it made more sense to follow the route of reform and let them die a natural death over time.

Lincoln could not countenance the spread of slavery to the territories, however, where the South's "peculiar institution" had not taken root. Under these entirely different circumstances it would be unconscionable to justify its existence there. During his famous debates with Stephen Douglas, Lincoln said:

The Republican party . . . looks upon [slavery] as being a moral, social, and political wrong; and while they contemplate it as such, they nevertheless have due regard for its actual existence among us, and the difficulties of getting rid of it in any satisfactory way. . . . Yet having a due regard for these, they desire a policy in regard to it that looks to its not creating any more danger. They insist that it should as far as may be, *be treated* as a wrong, and one of the methods of treating it as a wrong is to *make provision that it shall grow no larger.*[12]

The reaction to Lincoln's moderate policies predictably was anything but moderate. Despite his explicit opposition to slavery, Radical Republicans condemned him as a "slave-hound." Despite his pledge to leave the South alone, Southern Democrats denounced him as an abolitionist. Perhaps the unkindest cut came from Stephen Douglas, who characterized Lincoln as an enemy of popular sovereignty. In his masterful study of the Lincoln-Douglas debates, the political scientist Harry

Jaffa explained the misguided nature of these charges. According to Jaffa, Lincoln fit neatly into none of the mainstream categories of modern political thought. In large part it was the novelty of Lincoln's position that increased the ranks of his critics and fanned the flames of their vituperation. The position to which Jaffa referred is that "changing circumstances might reasonably elicit constructive interpretations of old principles."[13]

To Southerners Lincoln invoked the principle of the Declaration of Independence that all human beings are equal in God's eyes. To abolitionists he pointed out two centuries of slavery in the Southern states. To Douglas he retold the Lincoln clan saga of a frontier family desperately seeking equal opportunity on free soil. In the territories, under conditions immediately favorable to the achievement of the Declaration's ideals, Lincoln maintained, the power of the franchise did not extend to denying others their basic rights. Once the precedent for the enslavement of blacks was set in these areas, he warned, within a short time xenophobes like the "Know-Nothings" would subject immigrant white workers to similar discrimination. "Anyone who defends the moral right of slavery creates an ethic by which his own enslavement may be justified," he said.[14]

Our progress in degeneracy appears to me to be pretty rapid. As a nation, we began by declaring that "*all men are created equal.*" We now practically read it "all men are created equal, *except negroes.*" When the "Know-Nothings" get control, it will read "all men are created equal, except negroes, *and foreigners, and catholics.*" When it comes to this I should prefer emigrating to some country where they make no pretence of loving liberty—to Russia, for instance, where despotism can be taken pure, and without the base alloy of hypocracy.[15]

When South Carolina laid siege to Fort Sumter, Lincoln's prudence again was put to the test. The secessionists claimed that they were acting merely to protect themselves against the hostility of the national government. Lincoln, thinking ahead about how important public opinion would be to the Northern war effort, immediately sought to shift the burden of aggression over to the rebels in no uncertain terms. Toward that end he formally announced his intention to send medicine and food by barge to the besieged troops. When the rebels fired on the unarmed convoy, as Lincoln knew they would, his public relations ploy succeeded. Here again principle and circumstance, coming to the aid of injured and starving men as a pretext to war, achieved their necessary balance.

With the outbreak of full-scale hostilities, Lincoln felt obliged to explain why Northern soldiers should risk their lives in battle. Saving the Union may have been an effective war cry, but it did not meet the standards of classical prudence. Unadulterated nationalism, which smacks of fighting for the "fatherland," is insufficiently principled. Lincoln solved this dilemma by connecting the Union to the ideals it represented, namely freedom and equality under the law. To attack the Union, he maintained, was to attack its most basic ideals. To save the Union was to preserve these ideals for the rest of the world to emulate. Lincoln first articulated this view in 1854 while opposing the Kansas-Nebraska Act.

This *declared* indifference, but as I must think, covert *real* zeal for the spread of slavery, I can not but hate. I hate it because of the monstrous injustice of slavery itself. I hate it because it deprives our republican example of its just influence in the world—enables the enemies of free institutions, with plausibility, to taunt us as hypocrites—causes the real friends of freedom to doubt our sincerity, and especially because it forces so many really good men amongst ourselves into an open war with the very fundamental principles of civil liberty— criticizing the Declaration of Independence, and insisting that there is no right principle of action but *self-interest*.[16]

Without denying his repugnance for slavery and his desire to see it eradicated as soon as possible, Lincoln now became committed to winning the war as his number one priority. New circumstances warrant new policies, he explained to Horace Greeley in 1862. "My paramount object in this struggle *is* to save the Union, and is *not* either to save or to destroy slavery. If I could save the Union without freeing *any* slave I would do it; and if I could save it by freeing *all* the slaves I would do it; and if I could save it by freeing some and leaving others alone I would also do that."[17]

Fearful of losing the loyalty of the border states at a time when Union war prospects appeared dim, Lincoln countermanded a 1861 order by General John C. Fremont to free slaves in Missouri. Two years later, however, when the course of events started to take an upward turn, Lincoln considered a new strategy. On 1 January 1863, he issued the Emancipation Proclamation, which had the practical effect of freeing Confederate slaves alone. True to his prudential purposes, he wanted to espouse the nation's opposition to slavery in dramatic terms while keeping the border states on his side and encouraging Confederate slaves to take up arms against their masters.

Was it not inconsistent for Lincoln to abolish slavery in the South now when he had opposed that course of action before the North started winning battles? His prior argument had been that overturning a long-established institution too quickly would lead to societal chaos reminiscent of France after their revolution. But once the Southern states had brought chaos upon themselves, and the border states chose to side with a winner, extreme caution was no longer necessary. The principles remained the same, freedom and equality under the law. When historical circumstances changed, new, less conciliatory, policies became possible.

Throughout the war Lincoln resorted to methods that led some to charge him with being a "presidential dictator." Among the extra-legal powers he assumed were to raise an army without congressional consent, suspend the writ of habeas corpus, permit government tampering with private correspondence, and declare martial law behind the lines. While admitting the unconstitutionality of these measures, Lincoln claimed that they were necessitated by an extraordinary challenge to the Constitution itself. "I did understand," he argued in 1864,

that my oath to preserve the constitution to the best of my ability, imposed upon me the duty of preserving, by every indispensable means, that government—that nation of which that constitution was the organic law. Was it possible to lose the nation, and yet preserve the

constitution? By general law life *and* limb must be protected; yet often a limb must be am-
putated to save a life; but a life is never wisely given to save a limb. I felt that measures,
otherwise unconstitutional, might become lawful, by becoming indispensable to the preservation of the constitution, through the preservation of the nation. Right or wrong, I assumed this ground, and now avow it.[18]

The ferocity with which Lincoln pursued victory in war was tempered by the
prospects for peace. Once the danger subsided, he announced during his 1865 inaugural address, it would be appropriate to reconstruct the country according to a
program emphasizing "malice toward none . . . charity for all."[19] Against congressional opposition, he proposed a "10 percent plan" that would restore any Confederate state to the Union once one-tenth of its citizens who voted in the 1860
presidential election pledged their loyalty to the Constitution. After Appomattox,
indeed, Lincoln did not order the execution of any rebels and only briefly imprisoned a few, including Jefferson Davis. Moreover, he expressly supported the
passage of the Thirteenth Amendment and the efforts of groups such as the Freedmen's Bureau to aid former slaves.

In each of these instances Lincoln displayed the aversion to moralism and cynicism in politics characteristic of classical prudence. As with Aristotle, Aquinas,
Burke, and Maritain, he based his conclusions on a view of human nature that ne-
glects neither our capacity for good nor our propensity for evil. He was allied with
them also in that his understanding of political justice, to quote Harry Jaffa,
"pointed simultaneously in two directions: one, towards the philosopher's understanding of the universal, transpolitical dimension of human experience; the other,
towards the political man's understanding of the particular experiences of particular peoples in particular regimes." Lincoln, in short, "undertook to guide political
men, who need to know what is right here and now, but to guide them in the light
of what is just everywhere and always."[20]

Of course what differentiates Lincoln from his predecessors is that, in addition to
appreciating prudence in theory, he also was able to practice it successfully during
some of the most trying times in human history. Herein lies the true measure of his
greatness.

LINCOLN REVISIONISM

The problem with interpreting Lincoln accurately in the twentieth century involves
the optimism that has had such a significant impact on modern thought. Moral idealists tend to ignore extenuating circumstances. Nothing can convince them that there
are impediments to the complete and immediate achievement of their ideals that cannot be overcome. They are suspicious of attempts to balance principles and circumstances because such balancing acts threaten to interfere with their burning desire to
do the theoretically right thing, right here, right now. Their inclination, therefore, is
to view proponents of classical prudence as cynics at worst and pragmatists at best.

A number of twentieth-century histories of Lincoln's life and thought have taken a consciously revisionist approach based on this sanguine view of human nature. In his important two-volume study, *Lincoln the President*, for example, James G. Randall offered a blunt critique of the Lincoln-Douglas debates. As we know, Lincoln opposed interference with slavery in the Southern states but refused to support its spread to the territories on the principle that popular sovereignty does not extend to denying another person's humanity. Randall found Lincoln's argument to be hollow and essentially unsubstantive. Since Lincoln knew that the history and geography of most of the territories were not conducive to a slave economy, Randall maintained, he could give the false impression of being principled and gain votes from a variety of factions in the process. Because Douglas also was aware of these unfavorable conditions, Randall concluded, it "would be a perversion of history" to take the "difference between the two men" seriously.[21]

Assuming that popular sovereignty would have led to the same result in the territories that Lincoln favored, does it really make sense to so thoroughly disparage his logic in the debates? From Randall's perspective, Lincoln was not above stooping to self-serving half-truths to win the 1858 Illinois U.S. senatorial election. Is it really a half-truth to claim that popular sovereignty is not an end in itself but a means to the end of just government? Proponents of classical prudence define the public interest contextually, in terms of a nation's present and future. Moral idealists are less patient with contextual analyses. From their perspective, a strategy toward American slavery in 1861 that took the eighteenth and twentieth centuries seriously would indeed appear to be the equivalent of political cynicism.

Another prime example of Lincoln revisionism is Richard Hofstadter's "Abraham Lincoln and the Self-Made Myth" contained in his *American Political Tradition*. As we have seen, Lincoln represents a variety of things to a variety of people. Hofstadter chose to concentrate on his political ambition, which Lincoln's law partner William Herndon called "a little engine that knew no rest."[22] Hofstadter contended that Lincoln was the originator of the mythology that continues to rank him among the elite heroes of world history. In fact, Hofstadter argued, Lincoln was less like a demigod than a demagogue as well as being a "deliberate and responsible" opportunist, a courtier of "influential and financial friends," a world class "political propagandist," a "professional politician looking for votes," and a "follower . . . not a leader of public opinion."[23] The Emancipation Proclamation, Hofstadter added, had "all the moral grandeur of a bill of lading."[24]

What would cause Hofstadter to paint such an unflattering portrait? We know from the positive things he had to say about Wendell Phillips elsewhere in *The American Political Tradition* that his sympathies lay somewhere in the vicinity of radical abolitionism. We also know that no one gets to be president of the United States without being ambitious. The key question is what a president does after he takes office. Lincoln's presidency led to the preservation of the Union, as well as its ideals, and to the eventual passage of the Thirteenth, Fourteenth, and Fifteenth amendments. According to Jaffa, "Lincoln understood the task of statesmanship . . . to know what is good or right, to know how much of that good is attainable, and to act to secure that much good but not to abandon the attainable good by grasping for more."[25] To a moral idealist, however, all of this would not be enough.

A much less caustic but nevertheless inaccurate interpretation is found in David Donald's *Lincoln Reconsidered*. Donald ascribed to Lincoln all of the aforementioned qualities of classical prudence yet located him within what he called "the American pragmatic tradition."[26] In so doing Donald mistakenly equated divergent political views. Cynics are people like Hitler who deny moral reality. While pragmatists are not amoral, they do allow material circumstances to play a preponderant role in their decisions. University presidents, who comprehend and accept the traditional mission of higher learning yet abandon core curricula in favor of vocational education to increase enrollments, are pragmatists. Proponents of classical prudence seek to reconcile principle and circumstance. They do not compromise ideals but adjust them to the sometimes nasty facts of life. They are eternal balancers and authentic realists, according to the ancient definition of the term. University presidents, who require all students to learn how to think critically about their nation, their culture, and the world, at the same time that they are taught a trade, are proponents of classical prudence. So was Abraham Lincoln.

Fortunately not every Lincoln historian has been captured by the revisionist imagination. Because he sought political power for noble purposes, Richard Current classified Lincoln as a statesman.[27] Because he adhered to venerable Western conceptions of reality and human nature, Current also characterized him as a conservative.[28] Lincoln "has been described as essentially a politician's politician, as a pragmatist, a man more interested in immediate, practical advantages than in underlying principles." Current wrote:

He has been characterized as a flexible man rather than one of fixed determination. In fact, however, he was flexible and pragmatic only in his choice of means and in his sense of timing. Though no doctrinaire, Lincoln was a man of deep conviction and settled purpose. Only by compromising with the necessities of his time could he hope to gain and hold political power. And only by holding political power could he hope to give reality, even in part, to his concept of the Union and its potentialities.[29]

In a similar vein T. Harry Williams observed:

Lincoln would not have been able to comprehend the attempts of modern writers to classify his ideas into an ideology. Indeed, he would not have known what an ideology was. Although he believed deeply in certain principles which might be called his philosophy of politics, those principles were at the opposite pole of what is termed ideology today. . . . Lincoln distrusted deep theoretical thinkers and their slick assurance that they knew what the world needed. He was too conscious of the realities in every situation to be an ideologue. One of the keys to his thinking is his statement that few things in the world were wholly good or wholly evil. . . . As somebody has remarked, Lincoln was not the kind of man who is ready to do what God would do if God had all the facts.[30]

SUMMARY AND CONCLUSION

There is a certain irony in describing Abraham Lincoln as a moderate. From his physical appearance to his rhetoric to the reactions he elicited during his lifetime and since his death, there was nothing average about the man. Popular mythology rates him "the greatest character since Christ, "[31] "the martyred Christ of democracy's passion play."[32] Historical revisionists tend to agree with Wendell Phillips that he was a "huckster in politics . . . a first-rate *second-rate* man."[33] Of course, the moderation to which he subscribed has nothing to do with taking the middle of the road. He was a proponent of classical prudence, which is sober but certainly not average.

The first and foremost philosopher of classical prudence, Aristotle based his ideas on a view of human nature that takes seriously both our capacity for justice and our potential for evil. Reinhold Niebuhr neatly captured that view when he located the human condition as "standing in the paradoxical situation of freedom and finiteness."[34] Like Niebuhr, Aristotle believed that each time we congratulate ourselves for a job well done and come to the conclusion that we are essentially good, we fall prey to the sin of pride. Each time we question our intentions and consider ourselves to be essentially evil, our ability to reach such a judgment "would seem to negate its context."[35]

In order to be consistent with his interpretation of human existence as inherently paradoxical, Aristotle sought to create a political philosophy that refused to simplify contradictions. He advocated only that we strive honestly and intelligently to do our very best under invariably complex circumstances. His strategy, in short, was to strike a balance between expecting too much and accepting too little justice in politics. He thus advised extracting some degree of decency from entrenched tyrants by manipulating their fear of revolution.

Aquinas, Burke, and Maritain adapted this strategy for subsequent generations. Aquinas admonished legislators about passing laws that citizens cannot obey. Burke criticized the *philosophes* for asking more of French society than French history could bear. Maritain counseled the use of otherwise indecent means by otherwise decent people against the forces of tyranny.

The evidence indicates that Lincoln followed a similar strategy throughout his political career. Southern planters were his tyrants, radical abolitionists his *philosophes*. Against the former he posited the conscience of a moral man in an immoral society. Against the latter he prescribed caution to oppose both groups successfully and save the Union. Jaffa has written that Lincoln was required to combine the virtue of Shakespeare's Brutus, who, "although a man of purest intentions, was a guileless bungler," and the shrewdness of Shakespeare's Cassius, "who possessed the wisdom of the serpent."[36] In the final analysis, it is this reconciliation of principle and circumstance that defines classical prudence and describes Lincoln's politics.

"In his own distinctly American way," Donald has argued, "Abraham Lincoln possessed what John Keats called the quality [that] went to form a Man of Achievement, that quality which Shakespeare possessed so enormously—. . . *Negative Capability*, that is when a man is capable of being in uncertainties. Mysteries, doubts, without any irritable reaching after fact and reason."[37] Lincoln undeniably was such a man and the American people will continue to benefit from his achievement as long as the Union and its ideals prevail.

NOTES

1. Aristotle, *The Ethics*, trans. by J. A. K. Thomson (Baltimore: Penguin Books, 1966), 176.
2. R. G. Mulgan, *Aristotle's Political Theory* (New York: Oxford University Press, 1977), 9.
3. Aristotle, *The Politics*, trans. by Ernest Barker (New York: Oxford University Press, 1962), 250.
4. Clarke Cochran, *Religion in Public and Private Life* (New York: Routledge, 1990), 121.
5. Dino Bigonqiari, ed., *The Political Ideas of St. Thomas Aquinas* (New York: Hafner Press, 1953), 68.
6. Edmund Burke, *Reflections on the Revolution in France*, ed. by Thomas Mahoney (Indianapolis: Bobbs-Merrill, 1955), 8.
7. Francis Canavan, *The Political Reason of Edmund Burke* (Durham, N.C.: Duke University Press, 1960), 14.
8. Jacques Maritain, *Man and the State* (Chicago: University of Chicago Press, 1951), 73.
9. Aristotle, *Politics*, 1. All italics in the chapter trans. by Ernest Barker.
10. Richard N. Current, ed. *The Political Thought of Abraham Lincoln* (Indianapolis: Bobbs-Merrill, 1967), 297.
11. Ibid., 72.
12. Ibid., 110.
13. Harry V. Jaffa, *Crisis of the House Divided* (Chicago: University of Chicago Press, 1982), 12.
14. Current, *Political Thought*, 378.
15. Ibid., 83.
16. Ibid., 326–327.
17. Ibid., 215.
18. Ibid., 298.
19. Ibid., 316.
20. Jaffa, *Crisis*, 1.
21. James G. Randall, *Lincoln the President*, (New York: Dodd, Mead, 1945), 1: 127.
22. Richard Hofstadter, *The American Political Tradition* (New York: Vintage Books, 1961), 93.
23. Ibid., 100, 116, and 133.
24. Ibid., 132.
25. Jaffa, *Crisis*, 371.
26. David Donald, *Lincoln Reconsidered* (New York: Vintage Books, 1961), 128.
27. Richard N. Current, *The Lincoln Nobody Knows* (New York: Hill & Wang, 1963), 188.
28. Current, *Political Thought*, xxix.
29. Ibid., xxix.

30. T. Harry Williams, "Abraham Lincoln: Principle and Pragmatism in Politics," *Mississippi Valley Historical Review* 40 (1953): 96–97.

31. Hofstadter, *American Political Tradition*, 93.

32. Jaffa, *Crisis*, 232.

33. Donald, *Lincoln Reconsidered*, 3.

34. Reinhold Niebuhr, *The Nature and Destiny of Man* (New York: Charles Scribner's Sons, 1941), 182.

35. Ibid., 2.

36. Jaffa, *Crisis*, 215.

37. Donald, *Lincoln Reconsidered*, 143.

2 Lincoln's View of the Founding Fathers

Ronald D. Rietveld

Abraham Lincoln's memories of his childhood and early youth were at times painful for him—even as an adult. Lincoln's first biographer, John Locke Scripps, wrote that when he had interviewed Lincoln the man seemed to be painfully impressed with the poverty of his early surroundings—"the utter absence of all romantic and heroic elements."[1]

Lincoln's memories, which seemed so difficult for him to share, were about hard labor, storms, and frequent death—among them were his own mother, who had died of the "milk sick" when he was nine, and his sister, who had died in childbirth ten years later. The land was difficult. The winters were brutal. Lincoln said to Scripps on one occasion: "It is a great piece of folly to attempt to make anything out of my early life. It can all be condensed into a single sentence and that sentence you will find in Gray's Elegy: 'the short and simple annals of the poor.' That's my life, and that's all you or any one else can make of it."[2]

In the midst of the chores of survival, young Lincoln learned to read and discovered his lifetime heroes—George Washington, Benjamin Franklin, Thomas Jefferson, James Madison, and those other patriots of the Revolutionary War generation.

Many years later, president-elect Lincoln publicly testified to the impact "all the accounts . . . given of the battlefields, and struggles for the liberties of the country" had on him during those difficult years. All fixed themselves on his memory, he told the New Jersey senators on 21 February 1861: "You all know, for you have all been boys, how these early impressions last longer than any others." He then continued:

I recollect thinking then, boy even though I was, that there must have been something more than common that those men struggled for. I am exceedingly anxious that that thing which they struggled for; that something that held out a great promise to all the people of the world to all time to come; I am exceedingly anxious that this Union, the Constitution, and the liberties of the people shall be perpetuated in accordance with the original idea for which that struggle was made, and I shall be most happy indeed if I shall be a humble instrument in the hands of the Almighty, and of this, his almost chosen people, for perpetuating the object of that great struggle.[3]

Young Lincoln's ambition was fired by the accounts of these heroes, and as he labored in the fields of Indiana, he dreamed of Washington and Jefferson, whom he came to idolize. The theme of the founding fathers became an integral part of Lincoln's entire life, political career, and even his own death and funeral.

LINCOLN'S EARLY YEARS: KENTUCKY AND INDIANA

Far from the turmoil of Europe at war, and the unrest in New England, across the Appalachian Mountains, Abraham Lincoln was born on 12 February 1809, on the unproductive Sinking Spring farm owned by Thomas and Nancy Hanks Lincoln, who, according to an eyewitness at their wedding, "were just steeped of . . . notions about the wrong of slavery and the rights of man as explained by Thomas Jefferson and Thomas Paine."[4]

When Lincoln was born, Daniel Webster was twenty-eight years old and had not yet entered Congress; Henry Clay was in the United States Senate and well on the way to a brilliant career at thirty-two; John C. Calhoun was serving in the South Carolina legislature at twenty-seven; Robert E. Lee was two-years-old, and Ulysses S. Grant was not yet born. Washington had been dead only nine years; John Adams, Jefferson, Madison, and many other patriots of that revolutionary generation were still alive and active.[5]

Young Lincoln became a reader at a very early age. The questions of when, where, and from whom he learned to read and write can be answered only from evidence derived from confusing and oftentimes conflicting recollections. He was, however, largely self-educated. His method of absorbing information was already apparent by the age of fourteen, according to Cousin John Hanks:

When Abe and I returned to the house from work he would go to the cupboard, snatch a piece of cornbread, sit down, take a book, cock his legs up high as his head, and read. We grubbed, plowed, and worked together barefooted in the field. Whenever he had a chance in the field at work, or at the house, he would stop and read.[6]

Lincoln's stepmother remembered that he "devoured everything in the bookline within his reach." He once told a friend that he "read through every book he had ever heard of in the country, for a circuit of fifty miles." If Lincoln came across anything while reading that took his fancy, he entered it in a copybook, where he stored everything worth preserving for future reference. Sometimes he read the volume over and over. Lincoln would bring a book to the field and while the horse was catching his breath, he would read at the end of each furrow. Lincoln's literary tastes were formed during this early period in his life. He believed he was extremely fortunate to be able to read the few available books owned by his neighbors. Lincoln also became a writer for his neighbors. Many of the settlers were illiterate and sought out Tom Lincoln's boy to write messages to their friends and family.[7]

Early on, Lincoln took to biographies of eminent men. His stepmother managed to buy a life of Henry Clay for him, which portrayed a man who had risen to political eminence from circumstances just as humble as his own. This book kindled Lincoln's ambition. Noah Brooks, Lincoln's close friend during the presidential years, later wrote, "From the day of his reading the biography of the great Kentuckian, Lincoln dated his undying admiration of Henry Clay."[8]

Subsequently, a young Lincoln read *The Life of Dr. Benjamin Franklin*, which gave him a good background for understanding the American Revolution. Franklin's love of America and the liberty and justice that it represented induced him to return to Philadelphia from England. Thus, Franklin played an important role in the Continental Congress, which induced his membership on the committee that drafted the Declaration of Independence. This was a new reading experience for young Lincoln. He found David Ramsay's *Life of Washington* and William Grimshaw's *History of the United States* among the Hoosier settlers and devoured them. Over the two biographies of Franklin and Washington, the boy "lingered with rapt delight." As Scripps related in his campaign biography:

He followed Washington and brave Ben. Franklin through their early trials and struggles as well as through their later triumphs; and even then, in the midst of his cramped surroundings, and in the face of the discouragements which beset him on every hand, his soul was lifted upwards, and noble aspirations which never afterwards forsook him, grew up within him, and great thoughts stirred his bosom—thoughts of emancipated nations, of the glorious principles which lie at the foundation of human freedom, and of honorable fame acquired by heroic endeavors to enforce and maintain them.[9]

Lincoln learned of another life of Washington, written by the Reverend Mason Locke Weems, which he borrowed when he was fourteen or fifteen from Josiah Crawford, "old Blue Nose," as Lincoln and others called him. This volume became one of his favorites and probably influenced him more than any other earlier book he read except the Bible. Weems gave Abraham Lincoln a hero—George Washington—to challenge his best. The book romanticized the American story and mythologized the founding fathers as immortal statesmen. Weems's description of the battle of Trenton thrilled the boy Lincoln. He certainly shared his generation's reverence for the American Revolution and subscribed to the romantic nationalism it fostered. Lincoln can be understood and appreciated only within the perception of early nineteenth-century Romantic America.[10]

Lincoln—boy though he was—had begun to think for himself when he searched for an explanation for the determination of the founding fathers, who had endured privation for a great promise for the world. Their example helped inspire the simple American ideal that if a boy is upright and industrious, he can aspire to any place in the gift of the nation. Everything he read confirmed the teachings of the founding fathers and furthered his passion to know and to be known. Lincoln's friends and neighbors in Indiana, and later in Illinois, recognized his determination to excel. His eagerness to learn interested and even involved those he called his friends.

While in Indiana, Lincoln borrowed another book much like Weems's *Life of Washington*, which would have a great impact on his life and political future. David Turnham of Gentryville loaned him *The Revised Laws of Indiana . . . To which Are prefixed the Declaration of Independence, the Constitution of the United States, the Constitution of the State of Indiana.* Already fired by the life of Washington, Lincoln now became acquainted with the Declaration of Independence, a document that his White House secretary, John Nicolay, called "his political chart and inspiration." Lincoln's stepmother remembered that newspapers had been in Indiana as early as 1824 and young Lincoln was a constant reader of them. One John Romine remembered lending Lincoln a paper that contained an editorial on Thomas Jefferson. When Lincoln returned it, Romine said that "It seemed he could repeat every word in that editorial and not only that but could recount all the news items as well as all about the advertisements." It is possible that this particular paper was published in July 1826, when newspapers were filled with articles and editorials occasioned by the fiftieth anniversary celebration of the signing of the Declaration of Independence and the double apotheosis, sudden deaths, of two of its signers— Thomas Jefferson and John Adams on 4 July 1826. Following the Declaration of Independence in the book Lincoln borrowed from Turnham was the Constitution of the United States and also the Ordinance of 1787, which contained that clause on which the future Lincoln based many an argument on the slavery question: "There shall be neither slavery, nor involuntary servitude in the said Territory." When Lincoln finished the book, he clearly understood the principles upon which the nation was founded.[11]

LINCOLN'S LEGISLATIVE AND CONGRESSIONAL YEARS

The Lincolns moved to Illinois in 1830, and in the spring of 1831, now twenty-two, Lincoln left his father's household. He settled in New Salem and hungered to better himself, hungered for both education and status. It cannot be doubted that Lincoln became a politician in New Salem. One of the first things he did was to vote in an election. The focal point of political discussion in Denton Ofut's store where he clerked was usually himself.

The old Federalist Party of Washington and Hamilton had died years before Lincoln had settled in New Salem. The Jeffersonian Republicans formed the only national political organization in the 1820s. With party lines divided, 1832 voters identified themselves as Jackson, Calhoun, or Clay men. The most popular national figure was President Andrew Jackson, who had appointed Lincoln postmaster of

New Salem. Jackson's chief rival was Clay of Kentucky. Like his father, young Lincoln was a Clay man. He "all but worshiped his name." He liked Clay's nationalism, his economic program, his goal of sectional interdependence, and his stand on colonization. Clay applauded the national programs of Alexander Hamilton, and Lincoln applauded both. Always respectful of tradition, Lincoln accepted the doctrine of the founding fathers and thus he adhered to Hamilton's ideas of utilizing banks as fiscal agencies of government.[12]

In New Salem Lincoln had a reputation as a reader. He became an ardent fan of such poets as Robert Burns and William Shakespeare. He might read a half-a-dozen books at a time from as many lenders. "In New Salem he devoted most of his time to the Scriptures, and books on science and to the acquisition of knowledge of men and things." These were the days when Lincoln was seen walking with a book in hand, reading, or meditating.[13]

Lincoln was bitten by the political bug. He was elected to the Illinois House of Representatives in 1834 and began to study law and read American history in earnest, paying specific attention to the Revolution, the Federalist era, and Hamilton's fiscal programs. These romantic histories encouraged Lincoln to view the founding fathers as apostles of liberty, who had begun an experiment in popular government to show Europe that people can govern themselves without kings and aristocracies. Lincoln believed that the Declaration of Independence contained the highest political truths in the history of all humankind—all men are created equal and are entitled to life, liberty, and the pursuit of happiness. He had acquired a very deep reverence for that document, which he called "the sheet anchor" of American republicanism and from which he insisted all political documents flowed. He maintained that the "central idea" was found in the union of liberty and equality in that sacred document. This was the "electric cord" that "links the hearts of patriotic and liberty-loving men together, that will link those patriotic hearts as long as the love of freedom exists in the minds of men throughout the world." Thus, Lincoln developed a reputation as an effective Whig "internal improvements" man and won reelection to the state legislature and received his license to practice law in 1836. The next year, 1837, he left New Salem and moved to the new state capital city of Springfield.[14]

One of the leading forces in the cultural activity of Springfield was the Young Men's Lyceum. On 27 January 1838, Lincoln delivered a lecture on "the Perpetuation of Our Political Institutions"—and Washington and the founding fathers were on his mind. He concluded his address:

They *were* the pillars of the temple of liberty; and now, that they have crumbled away, that temple must fall, unless we, their descendants, supply their places with other pillars, hewn from the solid quarry of sober reason. . . . Reason, cold, calculating, unimpassioned reason must furnish all the materials for our future support and defense. Let those [materials] be moulded into *general intelligence*, [sound] morality and, in particular, *a reverence for the constitution and laws*; and, that we improved to the last; that we remained free to the last, that we revered his name to the last, [tha]t, during his long sleep, we permitted no hostile foot to pass over to desecrate [his] resting place; shall be that which to learn the last trump shall awaken our Wash[ington]. Upon [these] let the proud fabric of freedom r[est, as the] rock of its basis, and as truly as has been said of the only greater institution, *"the gates of hell shall not prevail against it."*[15]

Lincoln took part in a debate between Democrats and Whigs in the Hall of Representatives at Springfield the week of Christmas 1839. He concluded the Whig argument on the Sub-Treasury, using Washington as part of his ammunition that the bank was constitutional. In fact, the first National Bank was established "chiefly by the same men who formed the constitution, at a time when that instrument was but two years old, receiving the sanction, as President, of the immortal Washington; that the second [bank] received the sanction, as President, of Mr. Madison, to whom common consent has rewarded the proud title of 'Father of the Constitution.' " Thus, Lincoln tried to show that because Washington and Madison signed the United States Bank bill, it was constitutional. He "labored hard to prove that Washington never [had] done a wrong thing in his life." Lincoln believed that "the last *ten* years under General Jackson and Mr. Van Buren, cost more money than the first *twenty-seven* did (including the heavy expenses of the late British war), under Washington, Adams, Jefferson, and Madison." Lincoln had his figures down:

Gen. Washington administered the Government *eight* years for *sixteen* million. Mr. Van Buren administered it *one* year (1838) *forty* million, so that Mr. Van Buren expended *twice and a half* as much in *one* year, as Gen. Washington did in *eight*, and being in the proportion of *twenty* to *one*—or, in other words, had Gen. Washington administered the Government *twenty* years, at the same average expense that he did for *eight*, he would have carried us through the whole *twenty*, for no more money than Mr. Van Buren has extended in getting us through the single *one* of 1838.[16]

In spite of his limited education, Lincoln developed a simple, direct, and at times even an eloquent style. He mastered argumentative analysis and became an effective persuader. In some of his earlier speeches, such as his address delivered before the Springfield Washington Temperance Society on 22 February 1848, he gave rein to lurid rhetoric, which he abandoned in his maturer years. The temperance revolution would be greater than "our political revolution of '76," he said. Although Lincoln did not connect dates or names with his temperance theme, he concluded:

This is the . . . birthday of Washington. . . . Washington is the mightiest name of earth, long since the mightiest in the cause of civil liberty; *still* mightier in moral reformation. . . . On that name no eulogy is expected. It cannot be. To add brightness to the sun or glory to the name Washington is alike impossible. Let none attempt it. In solemn splendor leaving it shining on.[17]

Although the lives of Washington that Lincoln read had left their mark, his references to Washington seem rather vague. The address was not well received, although Lincoln was pleased that it had been published and widely distributed throughout Springfield.

Among the founding fathers, it now became apparent that Jefferson offered more support for Lincoln's various positions, and he began to quote the author of the Declaration of Independence, his platform, his confession of faith, more frequently. Lincoln quoted Jefferson's letter to Benjamin Austin (6 April 1816) in support of a federal tariff for the promotion of domestic manufacturing. This was his first invocation of Jefferson's name in 1843.

As a congressman from Illinois, Lincoln delivered a speech on the floor of the House of Representatives on internal improvements in 1848 in which he cited that Jefferson's opinion "was against [that of] the present president [James K. Polk]." Then he added: "This opinion of Mr. Jefferson, in one branch at least, is, in the hands of Mr. Polk, like McFingal's gun: 'Bears wide, and kicks the owner over.' " Humor was his technique as well as a habit of mind. When Lincoln delivered his eulogy of Henry Clay in the Hall of Representatives in Springfield, he briefly mentioned Washington's name but quoted at some length Jefferson's warning of approaching danger in the Missouri crisis of 1819. Lincoln would evaluate Jefferson as "the author of the Declaration of Independence . . . a chief actor in the Revolution . . . who was, is, and perhaps will continue to be, the most distinguished politician of our history." More and more Lincoln grouped Washington with Jefferson and Madison as embodiments of the early republican spirit of opposition to the institution of slavery in the United States.[18]

LINCOLN AND SLAVERY:
THE LINCOLN-DOUGLAS CAMPAIGNS

Upon the passage of the Kansas-Nebraska Act in 1854, frayed party ties began to give way. As early as 22 February 1854 (Washington's birthday), a group of northern Democrats, Whigs, and Free-Soilers met at Ripon, Wisconsin, to organize a new party—an anti-Nebraska party—to resist the extension of slavery if the Kansas-Nebraska bill became law. A great fusion meeting at Jackson, Michigan, on 6 July adopted the name "Republican" in emulation of Thomas Jefferson's Democratic-Republican Party. This embryonic Republican Party looked to the principles of Jefferson for its ideals. More and more Lincoln let his mind dwell on Jefferson.

In his campaigning between 1854 and 1859, Lincoln inductively assembled his constructive case, using the founding fathers as authority to oppose the extension of slavery into the national territories. During this same time, he read, listened, rephrased, refocused, and strengthened his arguments—aimed at Stephen Arnold Douglas of Illinois and his fellow Democrats, whose interpretations of the founding fathers differed. Lincoln's knowledge gleaned from his earlier studies of American history, principally the era of the Revolution and the Federalists, stood him in good stead.

Lincoln began to reveal a great familiarity with Jefferson's views and his writings. As early as September 1854, Lincoln publicly declared that "Thomas Jefferson, being a Virginian, proposed the cession of this territory [the Northwest—Ohio, Indiana, Illinois, Michigan, Wisconsin] to the general government, and in carrying out the measure, had the clause especially inserted that slavery should never be introduced into it." Representing the founding fathers, Jefferson opposed slavery, he said. The founders of the nation had enacted the Northwest Ordinance of 1787, which banned slavery from the national territory, and then they prohibited the African Slave Trade in 1807, followed by their restriction of 1820, which forbade slavery north of Missouri as well as Maryland. Many of these founders owned slaves, Lincoln admitted, but they openly declared their hostility to the spread of slavery in principle while they temporarily tolerated the practice. Lincoln joined them in believing that the enslaving of one man by another was a moral wrong.[19]

Although Lincoln was not an avowed member of the new Republican Party, his eloquent speech at Peoria on 16 October 1854, expressed the platform of the new party. "Our republican robe is soiled, and trailed in the dust. Let us repurify it. . . . Let us re-adopt the Declaration of Independence, and with it, the practices, and policy, which harmonize with it. . . . If we do this, we shall not only have saved the Union; but we shall have so saved it, as to make, and to keep it forever worthy of saving." Although this "Republican" movement of 1854 in Illinois was to prove abortive, James M. McPherson in *Battle Cry of Freedom* writes:

Lincoln's affirmation of moral opposition to slavery, his belief that the national government had a right and duty to exclude it from the territories, and his conviction that this "cancer" must eventually be cut out, became hallmarks of the Republican party.[20]

Douglas would point out some holes in Lincoln's historical basis. The same supposedly antislavery fathers who excluded slavery from the Northwest Territory had permitted it to expand into the territories of the southwest. Nevertheless, the new Republicans of the 1850s were not about to repeat the same mistakes of the earlier Jeffersonian Republicans.

Republicans held their preliminary national convention in Pittsburgh, Pennsylvania, on Washington's birthday 1856. This move stimulated action in Illinois. On the same day, a group of antislavery editors met at Decatur, Illinois, and made plans for "a state convention of the Anti-Nebraska party of Illinois" at Bloomington on 29 May 1856. This action launched the Illinois state Republican party, and Lincoln was the one prominent leader who attended it. He was well ahead of many anti-Nebraska leaders in his promotion of the organization in Illinois. He sanctioned the attachment of his name to a "Call for [a] Republican Convention" of those who were "in favor of restoring the administration of the General Government to the Policy of Washington and Jefferson." This Springfield convention then appointed delegates to the Bloomington convention.

At the conclusion of the Illinois state Republican convention in Bloomington, Lincoln delivered what came to be known as his "Lost Speech," a trumpet call for a moral cause. In it Lincoln stressed that the "Union must be preserved in the purity of its principles as well as in the integrity of its territorial parts." Although he was somewhat slow to call himself a Republican because of its radical connotation, he played an important part just the same. During this 1856 campaign, he publicly demonstrated that the Republicans were walking "in the 'old paths,' " and "read the recorded sentiments of Washington, Jefferson, and dwelt at length upon the position of Henry Clay."[21]

The conflict over the Dred Scott decision in 1857 found Lincoln sharing Jefferson's views regarding the power of the Supreme Court. He criticized both the decision and the Court itself. Lincoln used Jefferson's views to confute the Democrats' claim to Jefferson as their party's founder. Lincoln believed that the Republican party was the truer to Jeffersonian principles.

On 16 June 1858, the Republican state convention met a second time in its history in Springfield, where it unanimously designated as its "first and only choice . . . for the United States Senate, as the successor of Stephen A. Douglas—Abraham Lincoln." That evening Lincoln responded with a speech he had carefully put together, anticipating his selection, which has been known ever since as the "House Divided" speech. At forty-nine, Lincoln stepped on the stage of national politics. "The nomination of a senatorial candidate by a state convention had no precedent in American politics," notes Lincoln scholar Don E. Ferhrenbacher. In that speech Lincoln's familiarity with Jefferson was demonstrated when he asked his audience to indulge the "tedious reading" of "a letter written by Mr. Jefferson in 1820, and now to be found in the seventh volume of his correspondence, at page 177." Lincoln stated that the power claimed for the Supreme Court by Douglas, Jefferson believed would "reduce us to the despotism of an oligarchy." "Now, I have said no more than this—at least I am sustained by Mr. Jefferson." Much of Lincoln's argument with Douglas concerned the meaning of Jefferson's legacy to their own age.[22] The historic contest between Lincoln and Douglas actually began in Chicago on 9 July 1858, when a great crowd welcomed Senator Douglas home from Washington. Lincoln was present at Douglas's invitation, despite the fact that Lincoln was the Republican candidate for Douglas's seat as United States senator from Illinois. After both candidates spoke in Chicago on successive evenings, a brisk running debate followed at Bloomington and Springfield, before any formal arrangements were made. Lincoln's supporters were afraid their candidate would lose face if he continued to follow Douglas around the state and conclude him every time. Thus, Lincoln invited Douglas to formalize a series of debates. Their first debate would take place at Ottawa on 21 August and the following debates would occur in Freeport, Jonesboro, Charleston, Galesburg, Quincy, and Alton, in that order. Lincoln agreed to Douglas's selection of locations. Before the first joint debate, Lincoln delivered "his sublime theme" for the contest at Lewistown, Illinois, just four days before they met at Ottawa. Lincoln focused on the meaning of the Declaration of Independence and pled, "Come back to the truths that are in the Declaration of Independence." He ended dramatically: "*But do not destroy that immortal emblem of Humanity—the Declaration of American Independence.*"[23]

In that first debate, Lincoln and Douglas both referred to the founding fathers for support, especially Thomas Jefferson. Douglas queried: "Why can [the nation] not exist divided into free and slave States? Washington, Jefferson, Franklin, Madison, Hamilton, Jay, and the great men of that day, made this Government divided into free States and slave States, and left each State perfectly free to do as it pleased on the subject of slavery. Why," he continued, "can it not exist on the same principles on which our fathers made it?" Lincoln's doctrine of uniformity among the institutions of the different states was a new doctrine, never dreamed of by Washington, Madison, or the framers of the American government, Douglas declared. "Mr. Lincoln and the Republican party set themselves up as wiser than these men who made this government, which has flourished for seventy years under the principle of popular sovereignty, recognizing the right of each State to do as it pleased." Then Douglas posited a warning:

I believe that this new doctrine preached by Mr. Lincoln and his party will dissolve the Union if it succeeds. They are to array all the Northern States in one body against the South, to excite a sectional war between the free States and the slave States, in order that the one or the other may be driven to the wall.[24]

In his response to Douglas's charges, Lincoln drew from the founders:

Now, I believe if we could arrest the spread, and place it [slavery] where Washington, and Jefferson, and Madison placed it, it *would be* in the course of ultimate extinction, and the public mind *would*, as for the eighty years past, believe that it was in the course of ultimate extinction. The crisis would be past and the institution might be left alone for a hundred years, if it should live so long, in the States, where it exists, yet it would be going out of existence in the way best for both the black and white races.

Douglas claimed he had put together the Kansas-Nebraska bill upon the "original principles." Lincoln declared amidst laughter and applause, "I am fighting it upon these 'original principles'—fighting it in the Jeffersonian, Washingtonian, and Madisonian fashion."[25]

Lincoln and Douglas clashed at Galesburg over what Douglas called Lincoln's "Chicago Doctrine"—declaring the Negro and white man are made equal by the Declaration of Independence and by Divine Providence. Douglas labeled it "a monstrous heresy." "The signers of the Declaration of Independence never dreamed of the negro when they were writing that document," Douglas challenged. "Let me remind him [Lincoln] that when Thomas Jefferson wrote that document he was the owner, and so continued until his death, of a large number of slaves." Lincoln boldly responded:

And I will remind Judge Douglas and this audience, that while Mr. Jefferson was the owner of slaves, as undoubtedly he was, in speaking upon this subject, he used the strong language that "he trembled for his country when he remembered that God was just"; and I will offer the highest premium in my power to Judge Douglas if he will show that He, in all his life, ever uttered a sentiment at all akin to that of Jefferson.[26]

Throughout the debates and the 1858 senatorial campaign, Lincoln pressed his case against Douglas and the democratic use of the founding fathers. Only the

Republican program, which was in full accord with the fathers, offered an alternative to legalizing slavery everywhere in the United States. The institution must be recognized as an evil and treated as an evil within the bounds of the nation's Constitution. Lincoln's disagreement with Douglas was broad and deep. "The Lincoln-Douglas campaign of 1858 proved to be a contest without a loser," writes Fehrenbacher. Lincoln emerged now as a national figure, despite his defeat and Douglas's reelection to the United States Senate formally in January 1859. Fehrenbacher declares: "The momentum gathered in their contest for a Senate seat carried both Lincoln and Douglas to the threshold of the White House, but only one could enter."[27]

More than just to confute and confuse his Democratic opponents, Lincoln believed Jefferson, as the author of the Declaration of Independence, was the source of all his basic political principles. Lincoln was invited to attend a festival in Boston to honor Jefferson on his birthday, 13 April. Declining the invitation because of his schedule, Lincoln wrote: "It is now no child's play to save the principles of Jefferson from total overthrow in this nation." "The principles of Jefferson are the definitions and axioms of free society," he believed. But they were being denied, evaded, with success. Jefferson's principles were called "glittering generalities"—"self-evident lies"—and only applicable to "superior races." "This is a world of compensations," he wrote, "and he who would *be* no slave, must consent to have no slave. Those who deny freedom to others, deserve it not for themselves; and, under a just God cannot long retain it." Lincoln's admiration for the person and his principle of equality gushed forth in his concluding paragraph.:

All honor to Jefferson—to the man who, in the concrete pressure of a struggle for national independence by a single people, had the coolness, forecast, and capacity to introduce into a mere revolutionary document, an abstract truth, applicable to all men and all times, and so embalm it there, that to-day, and in all coming days, it shall be a rebuke and a stumbling-block to the very harbingers of re-appearing tyranny and oppression.[28]

But Lincoln did not seem to be aware that most of Jefferson's antislavery principles were uttered in private, and Jefferson, who authored the Northwest Ordinance, also opposed the Missouri Compromise because it restricted the spread of slavery. Nevertheless, by identifying themselves with Jefferson, Lincoln and the Republicans intended to redefine the ideological grounds of the 1860 contest.

Lincoln gained new confidence from his senatorial contest with Douglas and assumed the role of a national leader. From August to December 1859, he delivered political speeches in Illinois, Iowa, Ohio, Indiana, Wisconsin, and Kansas. He had become a presidential candidate in the fall of 1859.

Beginning in the spring of 1859, Douglas turned to early American history to find precedents for popular sovereignty. He withdrew from the Library of Congress such works as Jonathan Elliot's *Debates*, Henry C. Carey's *Slave Trade*, George Bancroft's *History of the United States*, and several different histories of the colonies. The historian Bancroft aided Douglas's research efforts. Douglas purposed to write an article for *Harper's* magazine that would demonstrate first that popular sovereignty was firmly based on historical precedent—that the "fathers of the Revolution had recognized the inalienable right of dependent political communities to local self-government, and that the slavery question was considered by them to be a matter of domestic and internal concern." In addition, Douglas wanted to provide a constitutional justification for popular sovereignty. He aimed his article at his southern critics primarily, rather than at the Republicans.[29]

Republican leaders summoned Lincoln's aid in the Ohio political campaign in 1859. An extension of their joint debates, Lincoln made every speech a slashing rebuttal to Douglas's public addresses and his *Harper's* article. Once again, Lincoln marshaled Jefferson's help in attacking Douglas. Douglas "ought to remember that there was once in this country a man by the name of Thomas Jefferson supposed to be a Democrat—a man where principles and policy are not very prevalent amongst Democrats today, it is true," he said to a large crowd in Columbus. Then Lincoln charged: "But that man did not take exactly this view of the insignificance of the element of slavery which our friend Judge Douglas does." Lincoln reminded his audience that Jefferson at least trembled for his country when he remembered that God was just! To loud applause, Lincoln declared: "Choose ye between Jefferson and Douglas as to what is the true view of this element among us." Jefferson had expressly provided for the prohibition of slavery.[30]

At Cincinnati Douglas branded Lincoln as a warmongering radical. Following Douglas the next day, Lincoln aimed his remarks at Kentuckians across the Ohio River as if they were in his audience. "I think Slavery is wrong, morally, and politically." But he promised that Republicans would not harm them. "We mean to treat you as near as we possibly can, like Washington, Jefferson, and Madison treated you." He continued:

We mean to leave you alone, and in no way to interfere with your institution; to abide by all and every compromise of the Constitution, and in a word, coming back to the original proposition, to treat you, so far as degenerated men (if we have degenerated) may, according to the examples of those noble fathers—Washington, Jefferson, and Madison.[31]

On the way back to Springfield, Lincoln stopped at Indianapolis and reminded the Hoosiers that Douglas's maxims on slavery were affecting the principle of liberty itself. This was pernicious and dangerous. Good men of the Revolution never held Douglas's position that he did not care whether slavery was voted up or voted down. "It was not the expressed opinion of Mr. Jefferson." These were shrewd speeches which presented Republicans in a peaceful and liberty-loving light.

The Ohio addresses brought Lincoln praise from Republicans in and out of Ohio. Republicans carried the Ohio state elections in 1859, and Lincoln received part of the credit for the Republican victory. More invitations to speak in various areas poured in now. Lincoln was asked to speak in Wisconsin. After giving a political speech in Milwaukee, he delivered an address at Beloit the following day. Lincoln attempted to "prove the identity of the Republican principles with those of the Fathers of the Republic," it was reported. If he could find "twelve good sound democrats" in that county, Lincoln said he would put them on oath as a jury. Then he would bring his evidence in the form of depositions in a court and "wring from them the verdict that the Republicans hold to the same principles which Washington, Jefferson, Adams, Madison, and their compeers held." In Kansas, he did not cite Jefferson for support but referred to "the way adopted by Washington and his compeers." No one must be permitted to break up the government "administered by Washington and other good and great men who made it, and first administered it." The fathers did not intend to interfere with slavery where it existed but only wished to prevent its extension—the very policy of the Republican Party. Lincoln was now prepared to draw together the results of six years of study and testing.[32]

LINCOLN'S ELECTION AND THE SECESSION CRISIS

In the midst of campaigning for Republicans across the Midwest, Lincoln received an invitation to speak for a $200 fee at Henry Ward Beecher's famous Plymouth Church in Brooklyn. He agreed to speak in February provided the easterners "would take a political speech," if he could find the time "to get one up." When he arrived, he found the location had been moved to the Cooper Institute, in New York. Meanwhile, Lincoln searched for proof to substantiate some of the circumstantial evidence he had relied on previously. He poured over Elliot's six-volume *Debates in the Several State Conventions on the Adoption of the Federal Constitution*, works Douglas had used for his *Harper's* article in 1859. Lincoln owned his own copies. In addition, he considered the *Congressional Globe*, the *Annals of Congress*, and old newspaper files and clippings.

Lincoln carefully examined the public careers of the thirty-nine men who signed the Constitution of the United States and discovered that twenty-one, a clear majority, had allowed Congress to regulate slavery in the territories. The same Congress that voted to forbid slavery in the Northwest Territory had formulated the first ten amendments to the Constitution. Lincoln discovered the fathers' policy to be clear. "As those fathers marked it [slavery], so let it be again marked, as an evil not to be extended, but to be tolerated and protected only because of and so far as its actual presence among us makes that . . . a necessity." The Republican party simply clung "to the old and tried" policy of the fathers toward slavery.[33]

Once again, briefly referring to Jefferson, Lincoln drew repeatedly from the example of Washington. Washington had approved and had signed an act of Congress that prohibited slavery in the Northwest Territory. Washington had written Lafayette that he considered prohibiting slavery in the national territories to be "a wise measure" and expressed "his hope that we should at some time have a confederacy of free States." Washington would not accuse the Republican Party of sectionalism because it was the party that sustained his policy. There was no middle ground between right and wrong. Union men must not yield to Disunionists, reversing the divine rule of calling not sinners but the righteous to repentance, invoking Washington, but unsaying what Washington said, and undoing what Washington did. Lincoln's final words were an admonition: "*Let us have faith that right makes might, and in that faith, let us, to the end, dare to do our duty as we understand it.*"[34]

Elated over his New York reception, Lincoln proceeded to make a kind of "swing around the circle" through New England and spoke before a succession of enthusiastic crowds. He reminded his various audiences that the "old fathers" had said the same "irrepressible conflict" doctrine. "Jefferson said it; Washington said it." He returned home to Springfield weary, but he had gained both the respect of eastern Republicans and the firmer loyalty of the Illinois Republicans as well.[35]

Undoubtedly it was Lincoln's Cooper Institute address and his subsequent impressive New England tour that convinced many Illinoisans of his presidential stature. Lincoln was the only man upon whom Illinois Republicans could unite. And unite they did. They had anticipated nothing more than the vice presidential nomination at the next Republican national convention to be held in Chicago in May 1860. But Lincoln did not receive a single vote for the vice presidential slot; he was nominated on the third ballot for the president of the United States at the Wigwam convention. The delegates had made a hardheaded decision to select the more "available" Lincoln; they did not compromise themselves or their principles. In fact, Lincoln never tried to redefine America; rather, he had tried to reaffirm the original definition given the nation by the founding fathers.

During the summer and fall campaign in 1860, Lincoln remained at home in Springfield, keeping in touch with his managers and supporters. One of his supporters challenged a former governor of New York who supported Lincoln's presidential rival, John Bell, on the Constitutional Union ticket. Lincoln complimented the man on his speech but asked if he could point out an error. Correcting his supporter's single mistake, Lincoln noted: "John Adams was not elected over Jefferson by the H[ouse of] R[epresentatives]; but Jefferson was over Burr." The supporter wrote Lincoln that he had corrected the error of history in the pamphlet edition of his speech. Aware that the man was still somewhat embarrassed about his "great blunder," Lincoln soothed his feelings: "You must not lay stress on the blunder about Mr. Adams; for I made a mischievous one, in the first printed speech of mine, on the Slavery question—October 1854." Lincoln had declared that the prohibition of slavery in the Northwest Territory was made a condition in Virginia's deed of cession, which, in fact, was not the case. Lincoln understood factual errors committed in the heat of political campaigns.[36]

A much more serious campaign error occurred that gave Lincoln great concern, one that involved Thomas Jefferson himself. Lincoln received a newspaper clipping that undoubtedly was from the Chicago *Times and Herald*, a loyal Douglas organ. It quoted a speech Lincoln had made supposedly in 1844 in which he said that

the character of Jefferson was repulsive. Continually puling about liberty, equality, and the degrading curse of slavery, he brought his own children to the hammer [as slaves] and made money off his debaucheries. Even at his death he did not manumit his offspring, but left them soul and body to degradation and the cart whip.

Lincoln was furious: "I never said anything like it, at any time or place. I do not recognize it as anything I have ever seen before, emanating from any source." His friends would be "entirely safe in denouncing the thing as a forgery." Lincoln's Springfield paper, the *Illinois State Journal*, declared it to be "a bold and deliberate forgery."[37] It is possible that Lincoln himself had some part in the explanation that followed:

Throughout the whole of his political life, Mr. Lincoln has ever spoken of Mr. Jefferson in the most kindly and respectful manner, holding him up as one of the ablest statesmen of his own or any other age, and constantly referring to him as one of the greatest apostles of freedom and free labor. This is so well known that any attempt, by means of fraud or forgery, to create the contrary impression, can only react upon the desperate politicians who are parties to such disreputable tactics.[38]

Lincoln declared to another correspondent: "I never said anything derogatory of Mr. Jefferson." Evidently the anti-Jefferson charge was successfully squelched because it does not surface again during the remainder of the 1860 campaign. But Lincoln rarely quoted Jefferson after this time.[39]

Abraham Lincoln was legally and constitutionally elected the sixteenth president of the United States on 6 November 1860. George Washington had not been elected as a result of a "crucial" election. The presidential office was virtually tailored to fit Washington, and no other succeeding presidential choice was as necessary as Washington's was in 1789. His election had been a foregone conclusion. No other presidential aspirant received any electoral votes in 1789 or in 1792. But Lincoln's election was crucial. He won the presidential office by converting a mere 39 percent of the popular vote into 59 percent of the electoral vote. Modest changes in just a few strategic places undoubtedly would have produced a different result.[40]

President-elect Lincoln seemed to many friends and foes alike a bewildered man inadequate for the job of chief executive of a dividing nation. Crisis filled the air with the secession of South Carolina in December 1860, followed in January by Mississippi, Florida, Alabama, and Georgia. Louisiana and Texas joined them in February 1861. Two days after South Carolina seceded, Alexander H. Stephens of Georgia, Lincoln's close Whig friend since the 1840s, wrote the president-elect: "Personally, I am not your enemy—far from it; and however widely we may differ politically, yet I trust we both have an earnest desire to preserve and maintain the Union." Stephens told his old friend that he would have him do what he could to "save our common country." "A word fitly spoken by you now would be like 'apples of gold in pictures of silver,' " quoting Scripture. Lincoln assured Stephens that he fully appreciated the peril the country was in and the weight of responsibility upon him. If the people of the South were afraid that his Republican administration would directly or even indirectly interfere with their slaves, or with them, about their slaves, they need not be afraid. "The South would be in no more danger in this respect, than it was in the days of Washington," Lincoln assured him. "I suppose, however, this does not meet the case," he said. "You think slavery is *right* and ought to be extended; while we think it is *wrong* and ought to be restricted. That I suppose is the rub. It certainly is the only substantial difference between us."[41]

Southerners had been talking secession for many years, and most Northerners viewed such talk as a counter game of politics. If something was wanted, a threat was made if it did not happen; but it did not necessarily follow that the dire threat would be carried out. What Southern men like Jefferson Davis would later say about the secession movement sounded different in the secession winter of 1860–1861. Davis declared on the Senate floor: "Our Fathers fought the war of the Revolution to maintain the rights asserted in the Declaration of Independence." He even went so far as to assert: "From every quarter of it [this country] comes the wailing cry of patriotism pleading for the preservation of the great inheritance [the Union] we derived from our Fathers." President-elect Lincoln would not have disagreed with the words of this Mississippi senator. In fact, in an existing fragment possibly written in January 1861, Lincoln refers to the principle of "Liberty to all," which is expressed in "our" Declaration of Independence—a "happy" principle, a "fortunate" principle, which helped "our fathers" fight and endure, and resulted in our Union and the Constitution. In a matter of weeks, however, Lincoln and Davis citations of the intent of the fathers became radically different.[42]

The time for Lincoln's departure to assume the burdens of the presidential office in Washington drew near. In that first week of February 1861, he slipped quietly from Springfield for a farewell visit with his stepmother in Coles County, the woman who filled the vacant place left by his own dead mother and the one who had encouraged his education and defended his efforts as a young boy in Indiana.

The day of his departure for the nation's capital was cold and drizzly in Springfield. Lincoln climbed aboard the single passenger car of the presidential special, which would take him to Washington. With rain falling, Lincoln stood sadly for a moment looking at his friends and family gathered around. Mary and the two younger boys, Willie and Tad, would join him at the next stop in Indianapolis to celebrate his birthday together as a united family. And as a hush fell on the crowd, he told them that no one who had never been in his situation could possibly understand the feeling of sadness at this parting. He owed everything to "this place" and "the kindness of these people." But the heavy weight of responsibility was on his mind, as was the great Washington. "I now leave, not knowing when, or whether ever, I may return, with a task before me greater than that which rested on Washington." He needed divine support for the task ahead. "Without the assistance of that Divine Being who ever attended him, I cannot succeed. With that assistance I cannot fail." Trusting an omnipresent God to remain with them and yet go with him, he hoped all would yet be well. "To His care commending you, as I hope in your prayer you will commend me, I bid you an affectionate farewell."[43] Never again was Lincoln to make so many speeches in so few days as he did after he left Springfield in the rain.

On Lincoln's fifty-second birthday, he crossed southern Indiana near the grave of his own mother, Nancy Hanks Lincoln. In the afternoon, he set foot in the largest city in Ohio, Cincinnati. Although hoarse from speaking by now, he noted in the

large crowd who came to hear him that all political parties were represented. He
hoped that for centuries to come, under the free institutions of America, there
would be such goodwill for the constitutionally elected president of the United
States. To Kentuckians as Southerners just across the river, the site of his own birth,
he said: "We mean to treat you, as near as we possibly can, as Washington, Jefferson, and Madison treated you—according to the examples of these 'noble fathers.'
So that under the providence of God, who has never deserted us . . . we shall again
be brethren, forgetting all parties, ignoring all parties."[44]

When the Lincoln Special arrived at Trenton, New Jersey, Lincoln's thoughts returned to the Revolutionary war struggle, which he had studied so well. He recounted the impact on him of Weems's *Life of Washington* and its description of the
battle of Trenton. "I recollect thinking then, boy even though I was, that there
must have been something more than common that those men struggled for." He
was anxious that "this Union, the Constitution, and the liberties of the people shall
be perpetuated in accordance with the original idea for which that struggle was
made." "I shall be most happy indeed if I shall be an humble instrument in the
hands of the Almighty, and of this, his almost chosen people, for perpetuating the
object of that struggle." He suggested amid prolonged cheers that for the preservation of peace it might be necessary "to put the foot down firmly."[45]

As the Lincoln party drew closer to the nation's capital city, whispers of conspiracy and plots against his life became more and more articulate. It was settled, after
some careful investigation, that there was a plot to assassinate Lincoln as he passed
through Baltimore. The presidential party traveled from Trenton to Philadelphia,
where Lincoln had agreed to meet its citizens at Independence Hall, site of the
signing of the Declaration of Independence, and to raise a flag over that historic
building on Washington's birthday, thus joining together the fathers, Washington
and Jefferson. In addition, he had accepted an invitation to speak to the assembled
legislature of Pennsylvania at Harrisburg, the state capital, the following day. Despite the warnings and advice of well-meaning friends, Lincoln said: "Both of these
appointments I shall keep, if it costs me my life."[46]

On the morning of Washington's birthday, the president-elect officiated at the
scheduled flag raising at Independence Hall, with cheerfulness and dignity. For the
first time in his life, he stood in the very room where the Declaration was signed,
inspired by his own patriotic advocacy of the principle laid down in that document—all men are created equal. He regretted that he did not have more time "to
express something of my own feelings excited by the occasion—somewhat to harmonize and give shape to the feelings that had been really the feelings of my whole
life." He also addressed a crowd outside.[47]

Lincoln kept all of his scheduled appointments on Washington's birthday 1861.
He made two solid public speeches at Harrisburg, one of which was before the
state legislature. He shared his feelings of great honor to be at Independence Hall.
He hoped the success of the flag-raising ceremony was something of an omen of
what was to come. He was pleased with the sight of the assembled military force in
the city, which could be used in a "proper emergency." But while he acknowl-

edged the military force, he wanted no misunderstanding "that I do most sincerely hope that we shall have no use for them—that it will never become their duty to shed blood, and most especially never to shed fraternal blood." Lincoln made a solemn promise: "I promise that, in so far as I may have wisdom to direct, if so painful a result shall in any ways be brought about, it shall be through no fault of mine." Forced by his advisers to change his route and go by night to Baltimore, where a secret train to the capital awaited him, Lincoln pulled safely into Washington at six A.M. on Saturday, 23 February 1861. After nine days of weary activity, Abraham Lincoln was sworn in as the sixteenth president of the United States on 4 March 1861. "Thank God—we have a government," it was said.[48]

LINCOLN'S WHITE HOUSE YEARS, 1860–1865

During the Civil War, Lincoln still remembered Washington. Jefferson's legacy had become too ambiguous for Lincoln to use him effectively as a symbol through these years of war. As president, Lincoln rarely mentioned Jefferson, although he continued to hold the Declaration of Independence in high esteem. Library of Congress records reveal, however, that four volumes of Jefferson's writings were charged to the president in 1861.[49]

Lincoln wished to visit Mount Vernon, home of Washington, to pay his respects to the gravesite of the father of his country. He suggested that Mrs. Lincoln's sister, Mrs. Ninian Edwards of Springfield, make up a party of their home folk from Illinois to make the visit. So the following morning, president and Mrs. Lincoln joined a party that boarded a government steamer and sailed down the Potomac River, past the arsenal, and past Fort Washington. They arrived at Mount Vernon and spent a delightful hour and a half visiting Washington's tomb and wandering through the mansion and gardens. Lincoln enjoyed the visit immensely.[50]

The bombardment of Fort Sumter on 12 April 1861, began the civil war among Americans. The attack on the symbolic fortress was spectacular, momentous, almost anticlimactic. It was the visible symbol that war had commenced within an existing nation. It was an announcement to the nation, to all nations, that the American experiment in democracy was on trial. The day after the formal surrender of Federal forces at Sumter, Douglas had a meeting with the president, his old rival, who welcomed him cordially at the White House. They parted that evening with a warm feeling, united and friendly in the patriotic purpose to save the Union created by the founding fathers they both revered.

As the rebels attacked Federal troops at Fort Sumter, so citizens of Baltimore attacked Federal troops sent to defend the government in Washington, as well as to protect the lives and property in the city. Peace on any terms was beyond question now, Lincoln told a delegation from Baltimore at the White House. He would not break his oath "and surrender the government without a blow." "There is no Washington in that—no [Andrew] Jackson in that—no manhood nor honor in that," he declared. "I have no desire to invade the South; but I must have troops to defend the Capital." If force was needed to accomplish the task, it would be severe.[51]

Lincoln sent his message to Congress in special session the Fourth of July, 1861, the birthday of the nation. "Our adversaries have adopted some Declarations of Independence, in which, unlike the good old one, penned by Jefferson, they omit the words 'all men are created equal,' " he noted. Why? They had adopted a temporary national constitution for their new Confederacy, in the preamble of which, "unlike our good old one, signed by Washington," they omitted "We, the People," and substituted "We the deputies of the sovereign and independent states." What reasons did they have deliberately to press out of view, the rights of men and authority of the people? Many naval and army officers had remained true in the "People's Contest," Lincoln said. It was "the patriotic instinct of the plain people." "They understood, without an argument, . . . that destroying the government, which was made by Washington, means no good to them."[52]

Lincoln briefly mentioned Jefferson in his annual message to Congress, 3 December 1861. He mentioned the plan of sending black colonists to Africa, which would include the need to acquire additional territory. Sixty years of purchasing territory could no longer be questioned on constitutional grounds or grounds of precedent, for "Mr. Jefferson . . . , in the purchase of Louisiana, yielded his scruples on the plea of great expediency." "Mr. Jefferson . . . placed the importance of procuring Louisiana on political and commercial grounds [rather] than on providing room for population," Lincoln reasoned. "I have, therefore, in every case, thought it proper to keep the integrity of the Union prominent as the primary object of the contest on our part, leaving all questions which are not of vital military importance to the more deliberate action of the legislature." Lincoln's primary object was to save the Union.[53]

On 17 February 1862, Congressman Edward Haight of New York wrote Lincoln to suggest that the "Commander in Chief order that the Farewell Address of Washington be read on his birthday, as the head of Armies & Navies—and that the Loyal people of the *United States* in all their states, cities & hamlets—their churches, houses & hearts be requested to devote that day to Exaltation for victory and gratitude to the Almighty protector of the Republic." Lincoln issued the appropriate "Proclamation for Celebration of Washington's Birthday" on 19 February 1862:

It is recommended to the People of the United States that they assemble in their customary places of meeting for public solemnities on the twenty-second day of February instant, and celebrate the anniversary of the birth of the Father of His Country by causing to be read to them his immortal Farewell address.[54]

On that day, there was an elaborate celebration in the capital. Part of the scheduled ceremony was the presentation to Congress of captured Confederate flags, to be followed by the reading of Washington's Farewell Address. Representative John J. Crittenden of Kentucky, however, introduced a resolution opposing the acceptance of flags on the ground that they were flags of pirates and rebels and represented no recognized government. After heated debate, Crittenden's resolution was adopted seventy to sixty-one, to the vast disappointment of the crowd in the gallery, and the pursuant ceremony was disrupted by the commotion in the audience. Captain Nathan Darling, captain of the Capitol Police, arrested two people in the lobby of the gallery of the House of Representatives. Nearly a year later, Lincoln signed Darling's pardon (16 February 1863). But it was a sad Washington's birthday for Lincoln. Two days before the holiday, his son Willie had died. And the president's younger son, Tad, was still seriously ill upstairs in the White House. So Lincoln did not attend the Washington birthday celebration at the Capitol. The funeral for the boy was held two days later.[55]

In an order on 15 November 1862, for the observance of the Sabbath in the army, President Lincoln recalled that Washington's "first General Order" issued after the Declaration of Independence indicated "the spirit in which our institutions were founded and should ever be defended." Then Lincoln quoted Washington: "*The General hopes and trusts that every officer and man will endeavor to live and act as becomes a Christian soldier defending the dearest rights and liberties of his country.*" On still another occasion, Lincoln cited Washington's childless condition while urging free blacks to migrate to Africa. He told a black delegation:

In the American Revolutionary war sacrifices were made by men engaged in it; but they were cheered by the future. Gen. Washington himself endured greater physical hardships than if he had remained a British subject. Yet he was a happy man, because he was engaged in benefiting his race—something for the children of his neighbors, having none of his own.[56]

Their sacrifice in leaving America for Liberia would be like Washington's sacrifice in the Revolution. Blacks living in the District of Columbia received Lincoln's colonization proposal—with or without Washington's example—with open hostility.

Abraham Lincoln issued one of the most important state papers ever to emanate from an American president on 1 January 1863—the Emancipation Proclamation; its gist was that on that day all slaves held in a state or part of a state that was still in rebellion should be then "thenceforward and forever free." The Northern government was fighting for union and for human will as well. A new meaning was given to Daniel Webster's famous "Liberty and Union, now and forever, one and inseparable." In other words, the war was taking charge. In order to save the Federal Union, the North had to destroy the Confederate States of America, and to destroy the Confederacy it must destroy the institution of slavery.

The United States Christian Commission organized public meetings in Philadelphia, New York, Boston, and finally Washington "to check distrust and disloyalty and to restore confidence and support to the government." To give the Washington meeting the greatest weight, the House of Representatives was selected as the place, Washington's birthday was selected as the date, and Abraham Lincoln was selected chairman. Lincoln declined to preside but fully supported the meeting and its purpose: "To strengthen our reliance on the Supreme Being, for the final triumph of the right, can not but be well for us all." Then he said: "The birth-day of Washington, and the Christian Sabbath, coinciding this year [1863], and suggesting together, is most propitious for the meeting proposed."[57]

At the end of three days of battle on 1, 2, and 3 July 1863, "so rapidly fought that they might be called one great battle," General George Gordon Meade, commanding the Army of the Potomac, stopped Robert E. Lee's advance at Gettysburg, Pennsylvania. And Vicksburg surrendered to General Ulysses S. Grant "on the glorious old 4th," "cohorts of those who opposed that declamation that all men are created equal," "turned tail" and ran. Gettysburg ruined a Confederate offensive on Northern soil, but Vicksburg broke the Confederacy in two, gave the Union the Mississippi Valley, and inflicted a wound that ultimately proved to be mortal. When the Confederates lost at Gettysburg, they lost what they could not afford to lose—at all.[58]

On the evening of 7 July 1863, a large crowd gathered at the White House to celebrate Northern victories. Lincoln was glad to see them and thanked them for calling for him to appear. "I do most sincerely thank Almighty God for the occasion on which you have called," he said, followed by cheers. "How long ago is it? Eighty odd years—since on the Fourth of July for the first time in the history of the world a nation by its representatives, assembled and declared as a self-evident truth that 'all men are created equal.' That was the birthday of the United States of America." Since that time, Lincoln observed, the Fourth of July has had "several peculiar recognitions":

The two most distinguished men in the framing and support of the Declaration were Thomas Jefferson and John Adams—the one having penned it and the other sustained it the most forcibly in debate—the only two of the fifty-five who sustained [signed] it being elected President of the United States. Precisely fifty years after they put their hands to the paper it pleased Almighty God to take both from the stage of action. This was indeed an extraordinary and remarkable event in our history.[59]

Five years after their deaths on the fiftieth anniversary of that document, another president, James Monroe, died on 4 July. And now, Lincoln noted, on the past 4 July, "when we have a gigantic Rebellion, at the bottom of which is an effort to overthrow the principle that all men are created equal, we have the surrender of a most powerful position [Vicksburg] and army on that very day." What "a glorious theme," he observed, "the cause of the Union and liberties of the country."

In November Lincoln dedicated the first national cemetery at Gettysburg, where he reminded a vast audience that "Fourscore and seven years ago our fathers brought forth on this continent, a new nation, conceived in Liberty and dedicated to the proposition that all men are created equal." As early as 1840, Lincoln had referred to this struggle for freedom "more than three score years ago." It was the ambition of the founding fathers to present a practical demonstration of the truth of a proposition—the capacity of a people to govern themselves. But a civil war—a second American Revolution—had replaced the first.[60]

Lincoln journeyed to Philadelphia to visit the Sanitary Fair on 16 June 1864. There he delivered a principal speech, followed by General Lew Wallace, Edward Everett, and others. The former governor of Pennsylvania, James Pollock, presented Lincoln with a silver medal on behalf of the ladies of the fair. Lincoln accepted the gift as a token of their confidence in his efforts as president: "I do not need any further evidence of the loyalty and devotion of the women of America to the cause of the Union and the cause of Christian humility." A number of other presents were also presented to him.[61]

"The loyal ladies of Trenton" presented to Lincoln a very special gift. Many of them were descendants of those "Matrons and Maidens" who had scattered flowers in Washington's path when he passed through the triumph arch built in 1789. The arch marked the spot where, "by the blessing of Providence," General C. C. Cornwallis had been repulsed, an occasion that "reversed the gloomy fortunes of war for our National Independence." Lincoln approached near the character of and experienced "the trials and responsibilities of the venerated Father of our Country," most especially in his loyalty to free principles and the discharge of all the duties of his electoral position by 'a confiding people.' " They presented to Lincoln a staff or cane made of wood from the very arch under which Washington had passed at Trenton on his way to become the first president of the United States in New York City. Although Lincoln could not remember the name of the person who made the presentation of the "very pretty cane" at Philadelphia, he was sincerely grateful for it and its "hallowed associations."[62]

The war was now in its fourth year. Its problems, difficulties of government, and serious doubts about his reelection in November 1864, were taking their toll on the president's health. On one occasion, sitting at his desk in his second-floor office at the Executive Mansion, he remarked whimsically, but wearily, "I wish George Washington or some of those old patriots were here in my place so that I could have a little rest."[63]

Secretary of State William H. Seward, whom Lincoln called "Governor," had early grasped Lincoln's capabilities. Seward could see what others could not. After observing the man who blocked his own chance to be president, Seward wrote his wife, "He is the best of us." Four years later, Seward cast his ballot for president on the Union ticket. He responded to a large crowd gathered in front of his Washington residence on Lafayette Square:

Henceforth all men will come to see him as you and I have seen him: a true, loyal, patient, patriotic, and benevolent man. . . . Abraham Lincoln will take his place alongside Washington, Franklin, Adams, Jefferson, and Jackson, among the benefactors of the country and of the human race.[64]

The day of the election came at last, and Lincoln received an overwhelming majority of votes. Every state that voted in the 1864 election, except for three, gave majorities to Republican or Union candidates; two states were former slave states,

Kentucky and Delaware. Among Northern states, only New Jersey gave its vote to General George B. McClellan, the Democratic candidate for president. West Virginia, Tennessee, Arkansas, and Louisiana supported Lincoln. At last, the time had come for the fulfillment of Lincoln's Cooper Institute speech more than four years before. The Republican Party had ceased to be sectional by obtaining Southern state support. "I am thankful to God for this approval of the people," Lincoln said on the evening of his election. "I give thanks to the Almighty for this evidence of the people's resolution to stand by free government, and the rights of humanity." Lincoln's election demonstrated that "a people's government can sustain a national election in the midst of a great civil war." His election destroyed the last hope of the rebellion.[65]

Lincoln took time out from his very busy schedule to write an old man a thank-you note for his vote. John Phillips was a Democrat of the Jeffersonian school, who had voted for George Washington for president. With his son, Colonel Edward Phillips, who was 79 years old, he rode two miles to Sturbridge, Massachusetts, town hall. When offered two votes, to take his choice, McClellan or Lincoln, he said, "I vote for Abraham Lincoln." John Phillips was 105 years old, the oldest citizen in his town, and, most likely, the oldest man in all Massachusetts. Lincoln expressed his gratitude "for the compliment paid me by the suffrage of a citizen so venerable." On behalf of the country, and himself, Lincoln thanked him. Phillips replied to Lincoln's note (16 January 1865):

I feel that I have no desire to live but to see the conclusion of this wicked rebellion, and the power of God displayed in the conversion of the nation. I believe by the help of God you will accomplish the first—and also be the means of establishing universal freedom and restoring peace to the Union.[66]

Three months later, Lincoln would be dead.

LINCOLN'S DEATH AND FUNERAL

Abraham Lincoln was assassinated at Ford's Theatre on the evening of 14 April 1865, sitting with his wife and two friends in a box festooned with American flags and a prominent gilded engraving of George Washington on the front of the box over the stage. Lincoln died the next morning at 7:22. Red-white-and-blue decorations, celebrating General Lee's surrender of the Army of Northern Virginia, were now suddenly replaced with black cloth and crepe. Gloom pervaded—everywhere. "Our hearts stand still as we take our pen to speak of the awful tragedy of last night," wrote a reporter for the *Washington National Intelligencer*. "He who yesterday was our good, gentle, wise, upright, affectionate President is no more!" "*The Assassins have murdered the peace!*" The New York *Herald* declared that for the first time in the history of "this democratic republican government, the tragic scenes of the Roman Empire and the French Revolution were enacted in America almost within sight of the last resting place of the Father of the Country."[67]

Plans were made for the longest state funeral in the history of the United States, the longest in distance and time. Although distraught, unwell, and bedridden upstairs in the White House, the president's widow had to make some vital decisions. She said no at least three times but had to give in as many. Mrs. Lincoln said no to enshrining her husband's remains in New York City. She said no to his interment in Washington (the Congressional Cemetery was an additional recommendation). She said no to his remains being deposited in the vault under the Capitol building (originally designed for George Washington, whose wife, Martha, insisted that he be interred at Mount Vernon).[68]

Mrs. Lincoln did agree to a funeral procession after the White House obsequies. And she yielded to his lying in state at the Capitol rotunda—en route home. The rotunda was heavily draped; all the paintings depicting American history themes, and all the statuary were completely shrouded. All except Houdon's white plaster statue of George Washington, which was simply hung with a black sash in the military fashion. Streamers of black cloth extended from the frieze up to the cupola— imparting an air of a sepulcher. After the lying in state, the first lieutenant general since Washington, Ulysses S. Grant, followed the hearse to the railroad station for the departure of the Lincoln funeral train.

After a nearly 1,700-mile journey—where the coffin was open in major cities where Lincoln had spoken on his journey to become president—Abraham Lincoln came to rest, together with his son Willie, in Oakridge Cemetery, Springfield, Illinois.

After Lincoln's death, it was recalled that there had also been an earlier plot to assassinate General Washington in 1776, and one of the privates in his bodyguard had been hanged as a result. After Lincoln's death, comparisons were increasingly made between these two Americans. Washington was rated as the greatest American who ever lived, in both North and South, during the 1860s.

In their eulogies of Lincoln, Northern preachers naturally drew comparisons between the first president and the sixteenth. Lincoln was called "the second Father of his Country." If the first niche in the pantheon of the illustrious belonged to Washington, the second now belonged to Lincoln. Since the days of Washington, there had been no purer statesman, or wiser, nobler Christian man at the head of the government than the martyred president. Many preachers called Washington the first Saviour of his Country, Lincoln was the second and Washington's equal. Washington must now divide his glory with Lincoln. The pastor of St. Paul's Lutheran Church in Washington, D.C., J. G. Butler, declared on 16 April, the day after Lincoln died: "In all future this name [Lincoln] will stand beside that of Washington. If he was the father of his country, under God, Abraham Lincoln was its saviour."[69] There were those who proclaimed Lincoln even greater than Washington because the nation that Lincoln saved was greater than the nation Washington had founded.

CONCLUSION

In the twentieth century, Lincoln's fame has eclipsed that of Washington and the other founding fathers. In polls taken in 1948, 1962, 1968, and 1982, sampled opinion was gleaned from American historians on the quality of American presidents. In agreement with the many who had eulogized and mourned the death of Lincoln in 1865, Lincoln now rated first and Washington second. Lincoln joined Washington as a second national deity. The joining of the two leaders was expressed poetically at the time of Lincoln's apotheosis:

> Heroes and Saints with fadeless stars have crowned him—And
> Washington's clear arms are clasped around him.[70]

What Abraham Lincoln clearly accomplished was not only the preservation of the Union, first formed by the founding fathers, from the most dangerous threat in the nation's history—but the reestablishment of the United States of America on its founding principles, in both theory and practice. Lincoln continued the work begun by the nation's founders. He preserved what they had established. He realized one of their greatest dreams, the emancipation of slaves. For this reason, among many, Abraham Lincoln should be recognized not only as a noble and great successor to the founding fathers of the nation but as one of them. It would appear that Abraham Lincoln has become "first in war, first in peace, and first in the hearts of his countrymen."

NOTES

1. John Locke Scripps, *Life of Abraham Lincoln*, ed. Roy P. Basler and Lloyd A. Dunlap (Bloomington: Indiana University Press, 1961), 13. I wish to acknowledge my deep appreciation to Keith Pacholl, my finest graduate assistant and my friend, whose research skills and editing made this chapter possible.

2. Ibid.

3. "Address to the New Jersey Senate at Trenton, New Jersey, February 21, 1861," in *The Collected Works of Abraham Lincoln*, ed. Roy P. Basler, 9 vols. (New Brunswick, N.J.: Rutgers University Press in association with the Abraham Lincoln Association, 1953–55), 4: 236 hereafter cited as *CWAL*.

4. Ida M. Tarbell, *The Life of Abraham Lincoln* (New York: Lincoln Memorial Association, 1900), 1: 35.

5. Albert J. Beveridge, *Abraham Lincoln: 1809–1858* (Boston: Houghton Mifflin, 1928), 1: 2.

6. J. G. Holland, *The Life of Abraham Lincoln* (Springfield, Mass.: Gundon Bull, 1866); William H. Herndon and Jesse W. Werts, *Herndon's Life of Lincoln* (New York: DaCapo Press, 1983), 39.

7. Noah Brooks, *Abraham Lincoln and the Downfall of American Slavery* (New York: G. P. Putnam's Sons, 1894), 23–24.

8. Holland, *Life*, 31; Brooks, *Abraham Lincoln*, 24.

9. Holland, *Life*, 31; Louis A. Warren, *Lincoln's Youth: Indiana Years, Seven to Twenty-One, 1816–1830* (New York: Appleton-Century-Crofts, 1959), 90–91; Roy P. Basler, ed., *Abraham Lincoln: His Speeches and Writings* (Cleveland: World Publishing, 1946), 12; Scripps, *Life*, 35–36.

10. Brooks, *Abraham Lincoln*, 24; "Address to the New Jersey Senate," in *CWAL*, 4: 236; Robert W. Johannsen, *The Frontier, the Union, and Stephen A. Douglas.* (Urbana: University of Illinois Press, 1989), 250–251.

11. Johannsen, *Frontier*, 166–167; Warren, *Lincoln's Youth*, 168–169.

12. Stephen B. Oates, *With Malice toward None: The Life of Abraham Lincoln* (New York: Mentor Books, 1978), 20–21; Benjamin P. Thomas, *Abraham Lincoln: A Biography* (New York: Alfred A. Knopf, 1952), 80.

13. Kunigunde Duncan and D. F. Nichols, *Mentor Graham: The Man Who Taught Lincoln.* (Chicago: University of Illinois Press, 1944), 135.

14. Johannsen, *Frontier*, 250–251; "Speech at Chicago, Illinois, July 10, 1858," in *CWAL*, 2: 500.

15. "Address before the Young Men's Lyceum of Springfield, Illinois, January 27, 1838," in *CWAL*, 1: 115.

16. "Campaign Circular from the Whig Committee, March 4, 1843," in *CWAL*, 1: 312; "Speech on the Sub-Treasury, December [26], 1839," in *CWAL*, 1: 172–173; "Speeches in Virginia, Illinois, February 22, 1844," in *CWAL*, 1: 333.

17. "Temperance Address, February 22, 1842," in *CWAL*, 1: 279.

18. James G. Randall, *Lincoln the President* (New York: Dodd, Mead, 1952), 1: 23–24, 67; "Campaign Circular for the Whig Committee, March 4, 1843," in *CWAL*, 1: 310; "Speech in United States House of Representatives on Internal Improvements, June 20, 1848," in *CWAL*, 1: 485, 487; "Speech in the United States House of Representatives on the Presidential Question, July 27, 1848," in *CWAL*, 1: 502; "Eulogy on Henry Clay, July 6, 1852," in *CWAL*, 2: 127; "Speech at Springfield, Illinois, October 4, 1854," in *CWAL*, 2: 249.

19. "Speech at Bloomington, Illinois, September 12, 1854," in *CWAL*, 2: 232–233.

20. "Speech at Peoria, Illinois, October 16, 1854," in *CWAL*, 2: 276; Don E. Fehrenbacher, *Prelude to Greatness: Lincoln in the 1850's* (Stanford, Calif.: Stanford University Press, 1962), 35; James M. McPherson, *Battle Cry of Freedom: The Civil War Era* (New York: Ballantine Books, 1988), 127.

21. Fehrenbacher, *Prelude to Greatness*, 44–47; "Speech at Vandelia, September 23. 1856," in *CWAL*, 2: 378.

22. "Speech at Springfield, Illinois, July 17, 1858," in *CWAL*, 2: 378.

23. "Lewistown Speech, August 17, 1858," in *CWAL*, 2: 544–547.

24. "First Debate with Stephen A. Douglas at Ottawa, Illinois, August 21, 1858," in *CWAL*, 3: 8, 12.

25. Ibid., 18–19.

26. "Fifth Debate with Stephen A. Douglas at Galesburg, Illinois, October 7, 1858," in *CWAL*, 3: 216, 220.

27. Fehrenbacher, *Prelude to Greatness*, 120.

28. "To Henry L. Pierce and Others, April 6, 1859," in *CWAL*, 3: 374–376.

29. Robert W. Johannsen, *Stephen A. Douglas* (New York: Oxford University Press, 1973), 707–708.

30. "Speech at Columbus, Ohio, September 16, 1859," in *CWAL*, 3: 410, 414.

31. "Speech at Cincinnati, Ohio, September 17, 1859," in *CWAL*, 3: 453; "Speech at Indianapolis, Indiana, September 19, 1859," *CWAL*, 3: 469; Oates, *With Malice toward None*, 165.

32. "Speech at Beloit, Wisconsin, October 1, 1859," in *CWAL*, 3: 484; "Speech at Leavenworth, Kansas, December 3, 1859," in *CWAL*, 3: 498; "Second Speech at Leavenworth, Kansas, December 5, 1859," in *CWAL* 3: 502.

33. "Address at the Cooper Institute, New York City, February 27, 1860," in *CWAL*, 3: 522–550.

34. Ibid., 3: 527, 536–537, 541.

35. "Speech at Manchester, New Hampshire, March 1, 1860," in *CWAL*, 3: 551; "Speech at Hartford, Connecticut, March 5, 1860," in *CWAL*, 4: 6–7, 11.

36. "Lincoln to James O. Putnam, 29 July 1860," *CWAL*, 4: 89; Lincoln to James O. Putnam, 18 September 1860," *CWAL*, 4: 115.

37. Lincoln to Anson G. Chester, 5 September 1860, *CWAL*, 4: 111.

38. Ibid., 112.

39. Lincoln to James H. Reed, 1 October 1860, *CWAL*, 4: 124–125.

40. Don E. Fehrenbacher, *Lincoln in Text and Context: Collected Essays* (Stanford, Calif.: Stanford University Press, 1987), 67.

41. Lincoln to Alexander H. Stephens, 22 December 1860, *CWAL*, 4: 160–161.

42. U.S. Congress, *Congressional Globe*, 36th Cong., 2d sess., 1860–1861, 306; "Fragment on the Constitution and Union," in *CWAL*, 4: 168–169.

43. Thomas, *Abraham Lincoln*, 238–239; "Farewell Address at Springfield, Illinois, February 11, 1861," in *CWAL*, 4: 190–191.

44. "Speech at Cincinnati, Ohio, February 12, 1861," in *CWAL*, 4: 199.

45. "Address to the New Jersey Senate at Trenton, New Jersey, February 21, 1861," in *CWAL*, 4: 235–236.

46. Brooks, *Abraham Lincoln*, 230–231.

47. "Address to the Pennsylvania General Assembly at Harrisburg, February 22, 1861," in *CWAL*, 4: 244.

48. Ibid., 245.

49. Lauriston Ballard, "Lincoln as a Jeffersonian," *More Books* 23 (1948), 289.

50. Thomas, *Abraham Lincoln*, 477–478.

51. "Reply to the Baltimore Committee, April 22, 1861," in *CWAL*, 4: 341–342.

52. "Message to Congress in Special Session, July 4, 1861," in *CWAL*, 4: 438–439.

53. "Annual Message to Congress, December 3, 1861," in *CWAL*, 5: 48–49.

54. "Proclamation for the Celebration of Washington's Birthday, February 19, 1862," in *CWAL*, 5: 136–137.

55. Lincoln to Edwin Bates, 16 February 1863, in *CWAL*, 6: 106–107.

56. "Order for Sabbath Observation, November 15, 1862," in *CWAL*, 4: 497–498; "Address on Colonization and Deportation of Negroes, August 14, 1862," in *CWAL*, 4: 373.

57. Lincoln to Alexander Reed, 22 February 1863, in *CWAL*, 6: 114–115.

58. Lincoln to Frederick F. Low, 8 July 1863,*CWAL*, 6: 321; Lincoln to E. Delafield Smith, 8 July 1863, *CWAL*, 6: 321.

59. "Response to a Serenade, July 7, 1863," in *CWAL*, 6: 319–320.

60. Henry J. Raymond, *History of the Administration of President Lincoln* (New York: J. C. Derby & N. C. Miller, 1864), 381–382; Holland, *Life*, 422–423.

61. "Speech Accepting a Medal Presented by Ladies of the Fair, June 16, 1864," in *CWAL*, 7: 396–397; Lincoln to William O. Snider, 25 July 1864, *CWAL*, 7: 458.

62. "To the Loyal Ladies of Trenton, New Jersey, July 25, 1864," in *CWAL*, 7: 458.

63. Ruth P. Randall, *Lincoln's Sons* (Boston: Little, Brown, 1955), 184.

64. Victor Searcher, *The Farewell to Lincoln* (New York: Arlington Press, 1965), 183.

65. Holland, *Life*, 489–490.

66. Lincoln to John Phillips, 21 November 1864, in *CWAL*, 8: 118.

67. Searcher, *Farewell*, 34–35.

68. Ibid., 57, 85–86.

69. J. G. Butler, *The Martyr President* (Washington, D.C.: McGill & Witheron, Printers and Stereotypers, 1865), 9.

70. Barry Schwartz, *George Washington: The Making of an American Symbol* (New York: Free Press, 1987), 196.

3 Abraham Lincoln and the Declaration of Independence: The Meaning of Equality

Joseph R. Fornieri

The agony of the Civil War compelled Americans to redeem the sacred principles upon which their nation was founded. By establishing a government through "reflection and choice" rather than by "accident and force,"[1] they conceived of their experiment as "a light unto all nations," "a city upon a hill," a second Israel.[2] How could a country suffused with divine purpose devour itself in bloody fratricide? The enchanting murmur of glory soon gave way to the shrieking horror of mounting carnage, swirling chaos, and thriving pestilence. Pandemonium convulsed the land and devoured any hope of a sudden triumph. Some interpreted the paroxysm as divine retribution for the canker of slavery; the sins of the "almost chosen people"[3] must be expiated through the penance of blood, fire, and steel.[4] Above all else, however, the Civil War was a struggle over the nation's soul; for it would resolve the paradoxical meaning of the American experiment: the antipathy between a nation's dedication to liberty and its acceptance of slavery.[5] Tragically, North and South fought to define incompatible visions of the American dream.

A profound breakdown of first principles stirred Abraham Lincoln to elucidate the substance of the American creed. At Gettysburg, he poetically distilled the essence of a preeminent expression of America's birthright. Notwithstanding its monumental impact, however, the Gettysburg Address relies upon the Declaration of Independence as its inspirational source. According to Lincoln, the latter conveys the "the central idea" of the nation—that is, "the proposition that all men are created equal." In what follows, I shall explicate Lincoln's interpretation of the Declaration and the meaning of equality therein; subsequently, I shall evaluate the arguments of conservative revisionists who have objected so poignantly to his vision of the American political order. By interpreting the Declaration as a "standard maxim for free society," did Lincoln apply consistently or transform radically the nation's first principles?

THE DECLARATION AS A FOUNDING DOCUMENT

The resounding "four score and seven years ago" of the Gettysburg Address places the country's birth at 1776, the year of independence. This historical detail is noteworthy; for Lincoln argued that a tacit Union among the colonies antedated the Constitution of 1787:

[I]n legal contemplation, the Union is perpetual, confirmed by the history of the Union itself. The Union is much older than the Constitution. It was formed in fact, by the Articles of Association in 1774. It was matured and continued by the Declaration of Independence in 1776. It was further matured and the faith of all the then thirteen States expressly plighted and engaged that it should be perpetual, by the Articles of Confederation in 1778. And finally, in 1787, one of the declared objects for ordaining and establishing the Constitution, was "to form a more perfect union."[6]

Unlike the despotisms of Europe that were established upon the accidents of birth, the United States justified its founding upon a creed of civil and religious liberty. This creed was enshrined by the Declaration of Independence, "the foundation of the American experiment."[7] By defining the spirit of collective American identity, the Declaration consummated the nation's free birth; and it reminded succeeding generations of the obligation to preserve and extend the founding's legacy of freedom. In a word, Lincoln views the Declaration as a moral covenant for the nation.[8] Its anniversary on the Fourth of July has commemorated the country's nativity for more than two hundred years.

The Declaration signifies the form or essence of the American nation; it proclaims the end to which the Union is dedicated.[9] Lincoln interprets the principles of the Declaration to be morally prior to the Constitution. The former undergird the Constitution's framework. For example: (1) the Declaration's commitment to uphold liberty was reaffirmed in the Constitution's preamble; (2) the Declaration's principle of equality was reaffirmed by the Constitution's explicit prohibitions against titles of nobility and religious tests; (3) the Declaration's principle of consent was reaffirmed by the Constitution's proclamation of "We the people" and by its explicit pledge to ensure the states a republican form of government. In sum, the two founding documents complement each other and are therefore contiguous. According to Lincoln, the Declaration provides the spirit and guiding principles that animate the Constitution; likewise, the Constitution provides the specific institutions whereby the aims of the Declaration can be realized prudently.[10]

Indeed, Lincoln celebrates the Declaration as the inspirational source of American leadership. It is quintessential to his political opinions:

[All] the political sentiments I entertain have been drawn . . . from the sentiments which originated and were given to the world in the Declaration of Independence. . . . I have inquired of myself, what great principle or idea it was that kept this Confederacy so long together. It was not the mere matter of separation of the colonies from the mother land; but something in the Declaration giving liberty, not alone to the people of this country, but *hope to the world for all future time*. It was that which gave promise that in due time the weights should be lifted from the shoulders of all men, and that all should have an equal chance. This is the sentiment embodied in that Declaration of Independence.[11] [italics added]

The Declaration functions as the nation's moral compass; its guiding needle has been meticulously calibrated so that navigators may plot the ship of state's destination.

The principles of the Declaration are necessary truths, which are universal, unchanging, and absolute—that is, *not relative* to human whim or caprice.[12] Lincoln's acknowledgment of an objective truth is fundamental to his interpretation of the Declaration as a founding document.[13] As general aspirations, the moral imperatives of the Declaration are independent of time and place. In the abstract, they apply to free governments everywhere and at all times:

I have never manifested any impatience with the necessities that spring from the actual presence of black people amongst us, and the actual existence of slavery amongst us where it does already exist; but I have insisted that, in legislating for new countries, where it does not exist, there is no just rule other than that of moral and abstract right.[14]

The principles of the Declaration are not only universal but also self-evident. Reiterating the teachings of Aristotle and Thomas Aquinas, Harry V. Jaffa explains: "A self-evident truth is not one which everyone necessarily admits to be true; it is one the evidence for which is contained in the terms of the proposition, and which is admitted to be true to everyone who already grasps the meaning of the terms."[15] Applying Euclidean terminology, Lincoln characterizes the self-evident truths of the Declaration as axiomatic: "The principles of Jefferson are the definitions and axioms of free society."[16] Order requires a consensus on such principles; their validity must be accepted as a condition of political reflection. That is to say, the axioms of the Declaration must serve as the starting point of civil discourse, just as the law of contradiction serves as the starting point for speculative discourse.

Axioms and definitions are indemonstrable: they are grasped intuitively, not discursively. The negation of an axiom precludes any further inquiry into the subject matter and is therefore logically impossible. In order to discern Lincoln's view of self-evident truth, it is instructive to consider the impossibility of rejecting the first principles of speculative reasoning; for one who rejects the law of contradiction undermines the very rationality upon which his or her rejection is predicated. By analogy, Lincoln exposes Stephen Douglas's moral indifference to slavery as a negation of practical reason: "When he [Douglas] says he 'cares not whether slavery is voted down or voted up,'—that it is a sacred right of self-government—he is in my judgment penetrating the human soul and eradicating the light of reason and the love of liberty in the American people."[17] Thus, Lincoln appeals to reason as a guide to political life: the "light of reason" intuits self-evident truths that are consonant with the pursuit of liberty and human happiness. Unlike the "value-free" orientation of many present-day social scientists, he acknowledges the existence of an ordered cosmos and the human mind's access to an immutable law of nature that is ordained by the supreme legislator and providential creator of the universe: the God of Israel. In a word, Lincoln's view of political order is ultimately theocentric.[18]

Fidelity to the Declaration binds members of the political community to a common good. Its aspirations forge a community chain between generations and among ethnicities. In the stirring language of religious metaphor, Lincoln explains:

We have besides these men—descended by blood from our ancestors—among us perhaps half our people who are not descendants at all of these men, they are men who have come from Europe—German, Irish, French and Scandinavian—men that have come from Europe themselves, or whose ancestors have come hither and settled here, finding themselves equals in all things. If they look back through this history to trace their connection with those days by blood, they find they have none, they cannot carry themselves back into that glorious epoch and make themselves feel that they are parts of us, but when they look through that old Declaration of Independence they find that those old men say that "we hold these truths to be self-evident that all men are created equal," and then they feel that that moral sentiment taught in that day evidences their relation to those men, that it is the *father of all moral principle* in them, and that they have a right to claim it as though they were blood of blood, and flesh of flesh of the men who wrote that Declaration, and, so they are. That is the electric cord in that Declaration that links the hearts of patriotic men together, that will link those patriotic hearts as long as the love of freedom exists in the minds of men throughout the world.[19] [italics added]

He celebrates Independence Day as a time of moral and political renewal, a time of rededication to the nation's origins. The religious metaphors of blood and flesh symbolize participation in a shared union, a collective identity that transcends the vicissitudes of individual self-interest. Lincoln envisions the Declaration as an "*electric cord*," a durable conduit between generations and among peoples. As stated, he views the document as a moral covenant that binds citizens to a higher order.

The foregoing metaphors evoke Christianity's extension of the new covenant to the Gentiles. By the superabundant grace of the incarnation, God's covenant is made accessible to all peoples of the earth. Participation in the mystical body of Christ transforms disparate individuals into one body that is united by spirit. Adherence to this new covenant binds members of the Christian community to a higher order despite their ethnic particularities as Jews, Greeks, or Romans.

Analogously, the Declaration binds members of the American regime to a common good of public life. The document provides a shared aspiration among citizens, one that transcends their subjective whims, caprices, and desires. Devotion to the nation's creed transforms individuals into one body that is united in *public spirit*. Indeed, the country's motto, *E Pluribus Unum*, conveys this transformative relationship between the whole and its parts. To be sure, Lincoln argues that individual citizens (*Pluribus*) are made one (*Unum*) through their shared commitment to the Declaration.

The Civil War evinced that fidelity to a moral covenant does not occur spontaneously. On the contrary, such constancy requires strenuous habituation and arduous public sacrifice. Conceivably, a nation can abandon its birthright. In the Lyceum Address, Lincoln espouses a "political religion," which will elicit reverence for the laws.[20] He celebrates patriotism insofar as the nation's particular laws conform to the spirit of the Declaration. At the same time, however, he emphatically denies that positive law—that is, the commands of a sovereign, are the ultimate measure of political order.[21] For Lincoln as well as for the Stoic tradition and its medieval and modern derivatives, law and morality coincide. Human positive law must uphold the general precepts of the natural law, which have been promulgated by the Declaration. Thus, unlike Hobbes, Lincoln does not derive law (*lex*) from the priority of a prepolitical right (*jus*), which is grounded exclusively upon the self-preservational urges of an autonomous self. Rather, like the Stoics and their later counterparts—Blackstone, for example, whom Lincoln had read[22]—he grounds law upon a theocentric basis. Positive law is derived ultimately from the obligations of an all-embracing, eternal, moral order.[23]

By virtue of its moral imperatives, the Declaration constitutes a bulwark against despotism: "The assertion that 'all men are created equal' was of no practical use in effecting our separation from Great Britain; and it was placed in the Declaration, not for that, but for future use. Its authors meant it to be, thank God, it's now proving itself, a stumbling block to those who in after times might seek to turn a free people back into the hateful paths of despotism."[24] As will be demonstrated, this "national charter of freedom," this "magna charta [*sic*] of human liberty,"[25] places negative and positive injunctions upon the activity of government.

Arguing that ideas have consequences, Lincoln defends the practical relevance of adhering to the Declaration's normative guidance: "I submit that the proposition that the thing which determines whether a man is free or a slave, is rather concrete than abstract. I think you would conclude that it was, if your liberty depended upon it."[26] Nonetheless, the aspirations of the Declaration *do not* constitute a blueprint for a utopia! Although its principles are universally applicable in the abstract, their actualization must involve the prudential discernment of circumstances. For Lincoln, the concrete application of rights to groups of individuals must be weighed against the public interest and the constraints of political order. Contrary to the demands of radical abolitionists, he denied that human positive law should enforce grandiose projects of revolutionary transformation. Although law has a normative function in guiding the country toward its aspirations, it can neither reconstitute people's inner dispositions nor transfigure society. Law must not attempt to purge away all of society's vices; it must tolerate some as necessary evils. Because the institution of slavery was inextricably woven into the material of Southern society, it had to be removed gradually. Providing the South was willing to compromise, slavery had to be removed without tearing apart the entire social fabric of Southern life, including those noble elements that were worth preserving.

Lincoln explains how the principles of the Declaration are to be extended: The [Declaration's signers] did not mean to assert the obvious untruth, that all were enjoying equality, nor yet, that they were about to confer it immediately upon them. In fact they had no power to confer such a boon. They meant simply to declare the right so that its enforcement of it might follow as fast as circumstances should permit. They meant to set up *a standard maxim for free society*, which should be familiar to all, and revered by all; constantly looked to, constantly labored for, and even spreading and deepening its influence, and augmenting the happiness of people everywhere.[27] [italics added]

Unlike those of both North and South who viewed slavery as being either a moral or a legal question exclusively, Lincoln prudently reconciled his moral obligation to the Declaration with his legal obligation to the Constitution:

Now, I confess myself as belonging to that class in the country who contemplate slavery as a moral, social and political evil, having due regard for its actual existence amongst us and the difficulties of getting rid of it in any satisfactory way, and to all the constitutional obligations which have been thrown about it; but nevertheless, desire a policy that looks to the prevention of it as a wrong, and looks hopefully to the time when as a wrong it may come to an end.[28]

To be sure, Lincoln is neither a utopian, agnostic, nor an idealist. Seeking to harmonize moral and legal obligation, he opposed the extension of slavery; and at the same time, he supported a strict interpretation of the fugitive slave law.[29] Moreover, prior to the exigencies of the Civil War, he argued that the Constitution prohibited executive interference with slavery where it already existed.[30] Throughout his struggle to apply the principles of the Declaration, Lincoln consistently endorsed the prudential counsel of Henry Clay: The proposition that all men are created equal "is true as an abstract principle . . . but . . . we cannot practically apply it in all cases."[31] To ignore practical limits for the sake of upholding a metaphysical abstraction would undermine the very political order that the Declaration seeks to guide. Those who fail to appreciate how one's commitment to abstract principles can be reconciled with the prudential application of those principles will inevitably interpret Lincoln to be either a idealist or a hypocrite.

Because politics is the art of the possible, statesmen must do what they can to promote the nation's moral imperatives. Indeed, for Lincoln, it is the preeminent task of American statesmanship to ensure that public sentiment is consonant with the Declaration: "Our government rests in public opinion. Whoever can change public opinion can change the government, practically just so much."[32] The Dred Scott decision and the Kansas-Nebraska Act degraded public opinion by transforming the discussion of slavery from that of a necessary evil into that of a positive good.[33] According to Lincoln, this blatant disregard of moral imperative violated national fidelity, debauched civic virtue, and summoned the ghastly spectre of despotism to haunt the land.

Despite its appeal to generations of Americans, who have uncritically accepted it as a national dogma, Lincoln's interpretation of the Declaration raises the following quandary about the American political tradition: How could the principles of 1776 have guided the Constitution if the latter sanctioned slavery?[34] Moreover, how could the Declaration have guided the Constitution, if the explicit language of the latter does not mention the term *equality*? One may object to Lincoln's interpretation of the Declaration as a moral covenant on the following grounds: (1) he was simply wrong in interpreting the Declaration to prohibit the extension of slavery; (2) he was correct; however, the Constitution *de jure* nullified the Declaration's broad affirmation of human equality.

Lincoln dismisses each of the foregoing alternatives as an inadequate explanation of the American political order. On the contrary, he interprets the logic of the Declaration to oppose slavery in principle despite the fact that the institution was sanctioned by the Constitution. The Declaration contained both positive injunctions and negative prohibitions against slavery, which obligated succeeding generations. Negatively, it prohibited the nation from identifying slavery as morally correct. Positively, it obligated the nation to abolish slavery eventually. Contrary to what the champions of popular sovereignty demanded, Lincoln refused to acknowledge slavery as anything other than a moral evil. He consistently opposed those who identified it as either (1) a matter of moral right or (2) a matter of moral indifference. The pernicious institution could be tolerated only insofar as it was a necessary evil. In a word, Lincoln characterizes slavery as an anomaly within the American political tradition:

It may be argued that there are certain conditions that make necessities and impose them upon us, and to the extent that a necessity is imposed upon a man he must submit to it. I think that was the condition in which we found ourselves when we established this government. We had slaves among us, we could not get our Constitution unless we permitted them to remain in slavery, we could not secure the good we did secure if we grasped for more; and having by necessity submitted to that much, it does not destroy the principle that is the charter of our liberties. Let that charter remain as our standard.[35]

By refusing to identify slavery as a moral right, the fathers of the nation intended to place it on a path to ultimate extinction. Both the letter and the spirit of the Declaration necessitated its abolition at some point. Indeed, according to Lincoln, the fathers anticipated succeeding generations to complete their work, not to forsake their design by promoting the institution as a "sacred right of self-government."

In the following passage, Lincoln expounds the fathers' view of the anomalous slavery question:

I particularly object to the New position which the avowed principle of this Nebraska law gives to slavery in the body politic. I object to it because it assumes that there can be Moral Right in the enslaving of one man by another. . . . I object to it because the fathers of the republic eschewed and rejected it. The argument of "Necessity" was the only argument they ever admitted in favor of slavery. . . . They found the institution existing among us, which they could not help; and they cast blame upon the British King for having permitted its introduction. Before the constitution, they prohibited its introduction in the north-western Territory—the only country we owned, then free from it. At the framing and adoption of the constitution, they forbore to so much as mention the word "slave" or "slavery" in the whole instrument. In the provision for the recovery of fugitives, the slave is spoken as a "Person Held To Service Or Labor." In that prohibiting the abolition of the African slave trade for twenty years, the trade is spoken of as "The migration or importation of such persons as any of the States now Existing, shall think proper to admit." . . . Thus, the thing is hid away, in the constitution, just as an afflicted man hides away a wen or a cancer, which he dares not cut out at once, lest he bleed to death; with the promise, nevertheless, that the cutting begin at the end of a given time.[36]

To summarize, Lincoln interprets American history as the unfolding of implications within the Declaration. The document is foundational in the following ways: (1) it commemorates the birth of the nation; (2) it defines the creed of collective American identity; (3) it represents a moral covenant; (4) it guides the nation's political institutions; (5) it constitutes a bulwark against despotism. Lincoln envisions a historical progression that is based upon the country's fidelity to the universal precepts within the Declaration. However, this progression arises from a moral obligation rather than from a dialectical necessity. Faithfulness to the national creed can be abandoned. According to Lincoln, the extension of slavery into the territories and its consequent identification as a *positive good* constituted such an abandonment. Indeed, the substance of Lincoln's political thought consists in his prudential discernment of the incompatibility between slavery and a nation that claimed to be founded upon the self-evident truth of human equality. In 1858, he prophetically warned his countrymen: "Let no one be deceived. The spirit of seventy-six and the spirit of Nebraska, are utter antagonisms; and the former is being rapidly displaced by the latter."[37]

THE MEANING OF EQUALITY IN THE DECLARATION

Among the principles of the Declaration, Lincoln assigns priority to the self-evident truth of human equality: "Public opinion, on any subject, always has a 'central idea,' from which all its minor thoughts radiate. That 'central idea' in our political public opinion, at the beginning was, and until recently has continued to be, 'the equality of all men.' "[38] Equality is the common thread in the moral fibre of the Declaration. For Lincoln, it is "the father of all moral principle."

He interprets equality to be the very essence of free government. The following syllogism demonstrates the relationship between the two: (1) The definition of a free government is one that operates upon the principle of consent of the governed. Lincoln states: "No man is good enough to govern another man, without the other's consent. I say this is the leading principle—the sheet anchor of American republicanism."[39] (2) Consent of the governed is derived from the proposition of human equality. (3) Therefore, free government—one that involves consent—is derived necessarily from the proposition of human equality.

Before demonstrating how consent of the governed is derived from equality, the latter term requires further elaboration. Mortimer Adler provides a concise definition: "Two things are equal when one is neither more nor less than the other in an identified respect. When they are unequal, their inequality consists in one being more, the other less—one superior, the other inferior—in some respect."[40] Based upon this definition, experience *seems* to suggests that human beings are inherently unequal: they differ in intellectual, artistic, physical, moral, and spiritual capacities. For example, it is manifestly true that certain individuals are either stronger, taller, or more intelligent than others. If so, in what sense can it be said that all men are created equal?

Lincoln understands the self-evident truth of equality in the light of man's relationship to the subhuman and the superhuman. Slavery is wrong because it degrades Negros "[f]rom the rank of a man to that of a brute."[41] Lincoln's interpretation of equality presupposes a hierarchical chain of being in which man is the in-between participant. Human life occupies the realm in between time and eternity, finitude and infinity, mortality and immortality, ignorance and certitude. The term *equality* may be expressed negatively in the following way: since man is neither a beast nor a god, he may not govern other human beings as if they were brutes. Correlatively, he may not govern other human beings from the privileged standpoint of Divine omnipotence and omniscience. To state the obvious: because human beings are neither more than human nor less than human, they are equally human and therefore must be treated accordingly. As the in-between being, man possesses a unique rational and spiritual dignity that distinguishes him from the arationality of a beast and the perfect rationality of a god. Jaffa eloquently describes the Declaration's assertion of equality:

In affirming that all men are created equal, [the men who founded our system of government], expressed their conviction that human freedom depends upon the recognition of an order that man himself does not create. Man is not free to disregard the hierarchy of souls in nature. The equality of man flows from and corresponds to the inequality of the human and the superhuman. For man is part of the order of nature, and his dignity derives from the whole of which he is a part . . . all our liberties rest upon the objective fact of the human soul from sub-human souls, and the highest virtue of this difference is the human capacity to confront the mystery of existence. This is what we mean when we say that the Declaration of Independence affirms the principle of the dignity of man.[42]

In defending the common humanity of the Negro, Lincoln conceives of human equality in view of the aforementioned hierarchy of being. Man's dignity is derived from his likeness to God. According to Lincoln, the Declaration is a fitting tribute to the justice of the Creator to his creatures; for its assertion of equality celebrates the Judeo-Christian understanding of man having been created *imago Dei*:

This was [the authors of the Declaration's] majestic interpretation of the economy of the universe. This was their lofty, and wise, and noble understanding of the justice of the Creator to his creatures. Yes, gentlemen, to all His creatures, to the whole family of man. In their enlightened belief, nothing stamped with the Divine image and likeness was sent into the world to be trodden on, and degraded, and imbruted by its fellows.[43]

To emphasize a point that has often been ignored or overlooked in present-day political discourse, Lincoln's interpretation of equality relies upon a biblical view of man, society, and sin. He exposes the psychological motives behind slavery: greed and pride. To submit another human being to the lash on account of his or her skin color is to degrade the inherent goodness of God's creation; to judge another from the standpoint of divine omnipotence and omniscience is to act as if one were God. Consonant with the Christian understanding of man's fallen nature, Lincoln characterizes slavery as a manifestation of the *libido dominandi* and human *amor sui*:

Slavery is founded in the selfishness of man's nature—opposition to it is [in?] his love of justice. These principles are an eternal antagonism; and when brought into collision so fiercely, as slavery extension brings them, shocks and throes, and convulsions must ceaselessly follow. Repeal the Missouri Compromise—repeal all compromises—repeal the declaration of independence [sic]—repeal all past history, you still can not repeal human nature. It still will be the abundance of man's heart, that slavery extension is wrong; and out of the abundance of his heart, his mouth will speak.[44]

If the Negro is a human being, it follows that his inherent dignity as a rational being who is created in God's image must be acknowledged. Lincoln blames the "popular sovereigns . . . [for] blowing out the moral lights around us; teaching that the negro is no longer a man but a brute; that the Declaration has nothing to do with him; that he ranks with the crocodile and the reptile; that man, with body and soul, is a matter of dollars and cents."[45] He poetically depicts the Declaration as a moral light that illuminates the truth of human equality. The treatment of human beings as property divests individuals of their "God-given rights to enjoy the fruits of their own labor."[46] In the words of Martin Luther King, racial discrimination divests human beings of their spiritual dignity by relegating them to the status of things.

Although Lincoln argues for the equality of all men, he does not believe that human beings are equal in all respects. As we have seen, human beings are equal in the possession of a common rational and spiritual dignity. Specifically, Lincoln interprets the Declaration's affirmation of equality to mean the equality of opportunity. To be sure, his view is eminently reconcilable with the principle of merit. In fact, equality of opportunity and merit are related. The former is the condition of the latter: genuine merit can only be ascertained on the condition that a competing individual is neither subhuman nor superhuman. In assessing the talents of a human being, one would not apply the same standard that one would to an animal or to God. That is to say, negatively speaking, the rewards or penalties of society ought not to be distributed on the basis of a claim that certain people are either more or less than human. Lincoln distinguishes between equality of opportunity and equality of condition in the following manner:

I think the authors of [the Declaration] intended to include all men, but they did not intend to declare all men equal in all respects. They did not mean to say all were equal in color, size, intellect, moral developments, or social capacity. They defined with tolerable distinctness, in what respects they did consider all men created equal—equal in "certain inalienable rights, among which are life, liberty, and the pursuit of happiness."[47]

Politically speaking, equality of opportunity has a positive and a negative aspect: positively, it means that government must promote, at the very least, a fit habitation for human life so that people may actualize their potential talents and productively compete for status, wealth, and honor within society; negatively, it means that government must not impose penalties or confer rewards that discriminate on the basis of race, creed, or color. A truly just nation cannot take away its citizens' hope for personal improvement: "Free labor has the inspiration of hope; pure slavery has no hope. The power of hope upon human exertion, and happiness, is wonderful."[48] Thus, Lincoln rejects the purely academic assertion that the slave laborers of the South fared better than the industrial laborers of the North. In response to such sophistry, he describes equality of opportunity as the substance of the American dream:

On the side of the Union, it is a struggle for maintaining in the world, that form, and substance of government, whose leading object is, to elevate the condition of men—to lift artificial weights from their shoulders—to clear paths of laudable pursuit for all—to afford all, an unfettered start, and a fair chance in the race of life. Yielding to partial, and temporary departures, from necessity, this is the leading object of the government for whose existence we contend.[49]

If government cannot actively promote the full social and political equality of the Negro, at the very least, it must not enslave him. Lincoln evokes a biblical analogy in order to convey this important point:

The Savior, I suppose, did not expect that any human creature could be perfect as the father in heaven; but he said, "As your father in heaven is perfect, be ye also perfect." He set that up as a standard, and he who did most towards reaching that standard, attained the highest degree of moral perfection. So I say in relation to the principle that all men are created equal, let it be as nearly reached as we can. If we cannot give freedom to every living creature, let us do nothing that will impose slavery on any other creature.[50]

As demonstrated, the principles of the Declaration place positive injunctions upon and negative prohibitions against the activity of government. The revolutionary document constitutes a bulwark against tyranny:

"Certainly the negro [sic] is not our equal in color—perhaps not in many other respects; still, in the right to put into his mouth the bread that his own hands have earned, he is the equal of every other man. . . . In pointing out that more has been given [to] you, you cannot be justified in taking away the little which has been given [to] him. All I ask is that if you do not like him, let him alone. If God gave him little . . . that little let him enjoy."[51]

Thus, at the very least, the Declaration's assertion of equality entitles citizens to enjoy the fruits of their own labor.

Most important, Lincoln views equality as a principle of justice and reciprocity: "This is a world of compensations; and he who would be no slave, must consent to have no slave. Those who deny freedom to others, deserve it not for themselves; and, under a just God, can not long retain it."[52] As a principle of justice, equality has two senses: (1) equality before the law and (2) equality of rights, privileges, and immunities. According to Lincoln, it is a matter of simple distributive justice to guarantee all citizens equality before the law and equality of rights.[53] If we may define justice as rendering one his or her due, then equality as a principle of distributive justice may be defined as rendering members of society their fair due as human beings. That is to say, the privileges and immunities of society must be distributed equally amongst citizens irrespective of their race, creed, or color. By treating Negros as beasts of burden, society has failed to render them their fair due as human beings and has therefore acted unjustly; for slavery "repress[es] all tendencies in the human heart to justice and mercy."[54] Discerning the manifest injustice of slavery, Lincoln states: "Equal justice to the south, it is said, requires us to consent to the extending of slavery to new countries. That is to say, inasmuch as you do not object to my taking my hog to Nebraska, therefore I must not object to you taking your slave. Now I admit this is perfectly logical, *if there is no difference between hogs and negros [sic]*" [italics added].[55] Thus, Lincoln's view of equality as distributive justice is predicated upon the fair distribution of privileges and immunities and rewards and penalties to members of society.

We are now prepared to explain how consent of the governed is derived from the proposition of human equality. As demonstrated, free government and equality are correlative. Lincoln states: "As I would not be a slave, so I would not be a master. This expresses my idea of democracy. Whatever differs from this, to the extent of the difference is no democracy."[56] Because humans possess an equal dignity as a rational and spiritual being, they must not govern others of the same species as they would either an animal—that is, despotically. Unlike an animal, a human being must consent to be governed. Because slavery treats other human beings as if they were subhuman, that is, as if they were things or beasts, it is tantamount to governance without consent and is therefore unjust: "The master not only governs the slave without his consent; but he governs him by a set of rules altogether different from himself."[57]

In order to demonstrate the correspondence between equality and free government, Lincoln rhetorically asks the following question: By what principle may one justly enslave another human being? He presents a logical dilemma for those who would deny equal dignity to others:

If A. can prove, however conclusively, that he may, of right, enslave B.—why may not B. snatch the same argument, and prove equally, that he may enslave A.?—You say A. is white, and B. is black. It is color, then; the lighter, having the right to enslave the darker? Take care. By this rule, you are to be slave to the first man you meet, with a fairer skin than your own.

You do not mean color exactly?—You mean the whites are intellectually the superiors of the blacks, and, therefore have the right to enslave them? Take care again. By this rule, you are to be slave to the first man you meet, with an intellect superior to your own. But, say you, it is a question of interest; and, if you can make it your interest, you have the right to enslave another. Very well. And if he can make it his interest, he has the right to enslave you.[58]

To be sure, any standard that is used to justify slavery can be turned around to justify one's own enslavement. Accordingly, the only fair principle of governance is to recognize the equal dignity of all men and its correlative, consent of the governed. Lincoln's argument may be summarized in the following way: (1) those who deny the equality of others on the basis of a certain principle may by the same standard justify their own servitude; (2) no rational person would consent to his own servitude; (3) therefore, one cannot fairly endorse the slavery of others.

The viability of free government depends upon the recognition of each citizen's humanity. If human dignity is derived from man's participation in an eminent reality, then, ultimately, the defense of human equality relies upon a transcendent foundation. Lincoln's concrete struggle with the moral question of slavery led him to the conclusion that moral discourse cannot be conducted in a political vacuum. The vindication of human dignity depends upon the ultimate nature of reality: politics and ethics are grounded in metaphysics. That is to say, if the universe is chaotic, if intelligent life is an accident, if all human experience is subjective, if man differs from an animal by degree and not in kind, then it follows that there can be no absolute and fixed basis to oppose slavery. Lincoln recognizes the need to pursue political questions to their ultimate core: "Whenever this question [of slavery] shall be settled, it must be settled on some philosophical basis. No policy that does not rest upon some philosophical public opinion can be permanently maintained."[59]

His speech in New Haven, Connecticut, profoundly integrates the political, moral, and theological issues associated with slavery:

To us [Northerners] it appears natural to think that slaves are human beings; men, not property; that some of the things, at least, stated about men in the Declaration of Independence apply to them as well as to us. I say, we think, most of us, that this Charter of Freedom applies to the slave as well as to ourselves, that the class of arguments put forward to batter down that idea, are also calculated to break down the very idea of free government, even for white men, and to undermine the foundations of free society. We think Slavery a great moral wrong, and while we do not claim the right to touch it where it exists, we wish to treat it as a wrong in the Territories, where our votes will reach it. We think that a respect for ourselves, a regard for future generations and for the God that made us, require that we put down this wrong where our votes will properly reach it. We think that species of labor an injury to free white men—in short, we think Slavery a great moral, social and political evil, tolerable only because, and so far as its actual existence makes it necessary to tolerate it, and that beyond that, it ought to be treated as a wrong.[60]

If the equality of human dignity is not respected as a condition of government, the coercive instruments of the state may justify the arbitrary and capricious subjugation of others on the basis of their accidental qualities. Thus, slavery is incompatible with free government. Correlatively, the defense of free government enjoins a moral obligation to oppose slavery. Indeed, the defense of equality is fundamental to (1) Lincoln's critique of slavery and (2) his vindication of free government. He states:

My faith in the proposition that each man should do precisely as he pleases with all which is exclusively his own, lies at the foundation of the sense of justice there is in me. I extend the principles to communities of men, as well as to individuals. . . . The doctrine of self-government is a right absolutely and eternally right—but it has no just application here attempted. Or perhaps I should rather say that whether it has such just application depends on whether a negro is not or is a man. If he is not a man, why in that case, he who is a man may, as a matter of self-government, do just as he pleases with him. But if the negro is a man, is it not to that extent, a total destruction of self-government, to say that he too shall not govern himself? When the white man governs himself, and also governs another man, that is more than self-government—that is despotism.[61]

In justifying the revolution, the colonists accused King George III of being a despot because he governed without consent. Because America claimed to be founded upon the principle of equality, and its derivative, consent of the governed, it may not consistently endorse slavery as a positive good. To do so, would undermine the very principles upon which the nation was founded. It would constitute the apex of hypocrisy.

The denial of equality to one group of people promotes a master-slave relationship among the citizenry. Such a relationship corrodes the integrity of self-government. Lincoln predicts that the moral habit of servitude and mastery will intensify like a cancer until it ravages the entire body politic:

You will find that all the arguments in favor of kingcraft were of this class; they always bestrode the necks of the people, not that they wanted to do it, but because the people were better off for being ridden. That is their argument, and this argument . . . is the same old serpent that says you work and I eat. You toil and I will enjoy the fruits of it. Turn it in whatever way you will—whether it comes from the mouth of one race as a reason for enslaving the men of another race, it is all the same old serpent, and I hold if that course of argumentation is made for the purpose of convincing the public mind that we should not care about this, it should be granted, it does not stop with the negro.[62]

In the foregoing passage, he prophetically warns that the deterioration of public sentiment will spread: slavery will "not stop with the negro." The habit of servitude will engulf the nation until government finally degenerates into "the will of the stronger," a condition whereby moral pretense is perverted completely:

Our progress in degeneracy appears to me to be pretty rapid. As a nation, we began declaring that "all men are created Equal." We now practically read it "all men are created equal except negroes." When the Know-Nothings get control, it will read "all men are created equal except negroes, and foreigners, and catholics." When it comes to this I should prefer emigrating to some country where they make no pretense of loving liberty—to Russia, for instance, where despotism can be taken pure, and without the base alloy of hypocracy [*sic*].[63]

THE CONSERVATIVE REVISIONIST
CRITIQUE OF LINCOLN

I have demonstrated that Lincoln interprets equality to be the universal principle at the heart of the Declaration of Independence and that he understands the Declaration to be the moral touchstone of the American experiment. Conservative critics such as Wilmoore Kendall and M. E. Bradford have rejected both these assertions. That is, they deny the universal import of the word *equality*, and they reject further Lincoln's treatment of the Declaration as a founding document. According to Bradford, "Equality as a moral imperative, pursued as an end in itself—Equality, with the capital 'E'—is the antonym of every legitimate conservative principle.[64] These authors have assessed Lincoln's foundational use of the Declaration not as an elucidation of the country's aspirations but as a radical transformation of its commitments. The profound issues raised by the conservative critique are extremely helpful in clarifying Lincoln's interpretation of equality. Kendall advances a fundamental question about the nation's heritage: "Is the American tradition the tradition of the textbooks, which indeed situates the 'all men are created equal' clause at the center of our political experience, or is it the tradition of American life as it is actually lived and thus a tradition of inequality."[65]

According to the revisionists, Lincoln's alleged reconstitution of the American founding subverted the fathers' vision of political order; and it subsequently promoted the development of the imperial presidency. Kendall argues that the praise of Lincoln encourages an "endless series of Abraham Lincolns, each persuaded that he is superior in wisdom and virtue to the Fathers, each prepared to insist that those who oppose this or that application of the equality standard are denying the possibility of self-government, each ultimately willing to plunge America into Civil War rather than concede his point."[66] Thus, if the revisionist argument is true, Lincoln betrayed the letter and the spirit of the founding: he imposed a radical doctrine of equality that was contrary to the fathers' intention and thereby transmuted the ethos of American life. By accepting Lincoln's interpretation of the Declaration, is one necessarily committed to a doctrine of permissive egalitarianism? Can equality and conservatism be reconciled in the American political tradition?

Kendall emphatically denies the status of the Declaration as a founding document. The document merely performed a narrow function in justifying the colonies' separation from Great Britain. He says: "The Declaration of Independence did not, as Lincoln proclaimed, establish our independence as a nation. Rather what it did was to establish a baker's dozen of new sovereignties."[67] Although it asserts that "all men are created equal," the Declaration was intended to guarantee the equality of peoples as collective entities, not the equality of individuals. I must stress that Kendall and Bradford deny that the Declaration promotes individual liberty. Rather, they understand the document's assertion of equality to mean the equality of Americans as a people compared to the equality of the British or the French as a people.

Furthermore, Kendall repudiates Lincoln for interpreting equality as the nation's supreme political principle. In making equality a political obligation, Lincoln illegitimately endowed the Declaration with a constitutional status. Kendall argues:

In Lincoln's view the Declaration enjoys what we best term a constitutional status. He so much as informs us that the "new nation" of the United States of America was established with the signing of the Declaration and that it is to this document we must look if we are to understand our origins and thus the meaning of our political experience as a people, organized for action in history and capable of defining its appointed role in history. . . . [It] is to this document that he refers for the identification of our supreme commitment. And the very notion that we are honor-bound to preserve and advance that commitment surely means that the document does enjoy constitutional status—for this, above all else, is precisely the raison d'etre for documents of this nature. Yet the facts in more than one way do not bear out Lincoln's view of the Declaration. The "four score and seven years" of Lincoln's speech does put us back to the Declaration. . . . Conceivably, he could have selected any number of dates prior to the Declaration—he might for example, have selected the year of the Mayflower Compact.[68]

Garry Wills's best-seller, *Lincoln at Gettysburg: The Words That Remade America*, offers a current variation of Kendall's interpretation. Wills's subtle ambiguity concerning his own approval or disapproval of Lincoln's words at Gettysburg can be misleading to the less than careful reader. Nevertheless, in a prior work, *Inventing America: Jefferson's Declaration of Independence*, Wills explicitly reveals his distaste for Lincoln's interpretation of the Declaration: "[Lincoln's] assertions are inoffensive to most Americans—which explains why things like the House Un-American Activities Committee were inoffensive for so long. . . . When the Declaration is read in Lincoln's romantic glass, darkly, its content becomes entirely a victim of guess and bias."[69]

Let no one be deceived! Garry Wills blames Lincoln for reconstituting the American political tradition.[70] He agrees with Kendall's assertion that Lincoln transformed the nation's commitments: "Kendall rightly says Lincoln undertook a new founding of the nation, to correct things felt to be imperfect in the founders' own achievement."[71] The parallels between the two authors are unmistakable. For example, Kendall maintains,

Equality, we are told, is therefore one of the basic principles of the American political tradition and we are, in consequence, committed as a nation to equality . . . *Equality just disappears from our political vocabulary*, disappears as the ink dries on the Declaration of Independence and is not heard of again, to all intents and purposes, until Abraham Lincoln reminds his contemporaries of the language of the Declaration and begins to insist that America has failed to live up to one of its deepest commitments.[72] [italics added]

According to Wills,

> But Lincoln was a revolutionary in another sense, as well as the one Wilmoore Kendall denounced him for—he not only put the Declaration in a new light as a matter of founding law, but put its central proposition, equality, in a newly favored position as a principle of the Constitution (which as the Chicago Times noticed, never uses the word). What had been a mere theory of lawyers like James Wilson, Joseph Story, and Daniel Webster—that the nation preceded the states, in time and importance—now became a lived reality of the American tradition.[73]

According to Wills, the president's rhetorical feat at Gettysburg was tantamount to a coup d'état; the poetic spell he cast at Gettysburg "remade America." Wills explains that

> The crowd [at Gettysburg] departed with a new thing in its ideological baggage, that new constitution Lincoln substituted for the old one they brought there with them. They walked from those curving graves on the hillside, under a changed sky, into a different America. Lincoln had revolutionized the Revolution, giving people a new past to live that would change their future indefinitely. Some people, looking on from a distance, saw that a giant (if benign) swindle had been performed.[74]

The conservative revisionists are in fundamental agreement that Lincoln transformed the ethos of the nation in the following ways: (1) he subverted the Constitution by interpreting the Declaration as a moral covenant; (2) he identified equality as the central idea of the nation; (3) he "internalized" the Declaration's assertion of equality by applying it to individuals.

LINCOLN'S VINDICATION:
THE FATHERS' VIEW OF THE DECLARATION

Is Lincoln's interpretation of the Declaration and the meaning of equality therein consonant with that of the founding fathers? Must we convict Lincoln of betraying the letter and spirit of the founding? Did Lincoln transform the ethos of American life by ascribing a constitutional status to the Declaration? Contrary to the assertions of the revisionists, it must be recalled that Lincoln understood his own position to be "eminently conservative"—that is, concordant with the overall spirit of the founding fathers.

> This chief and real purpose of the Republican party is eminently conservative. It proposes nothing save and except to restore this government to its original tone in regard to this element of slavery, and there to maintain it, looking for no further change, in reference to it, than that which the original framers of the government themselves expected and looked forward to.[75]

It now remains to consider whether or not Lincoln's self-proclaimed conservatism was either true, disingenuous, or delusory.[76] While a detailed comparison between Lincoln and the founding fathers is beyond the scope of this chapter (see chapter 2 in this volume), the writings of Thomas Jefferson and James Madison accord with Lincoln's interpretation of the Declaration. This is not to say that Lincoln's interpretation was the only self-understanding of the founding generation; it is to say that his interpretation is concordantly derived from important antecedent sources of that generation.

Without equivocation, Jefferson's interpretation of the Declaration coincides with Lincoln's view of the document as a bulwark against despotism. The latter explains that "the flames kindled on the 4th of July, 1776, have spread over too much of the globe to be extinguished by the feeble engines of despotism, they will consume these engines and all who work them."[77]

Furthermore, in assessing the universal import of the Declaration's moral imperatives, Jefferson proclaims:

May it be to the world, what I believe it will be (to some parts sooner, to others later, but finally to all), the signal arousing men to burst the chains under which monkish ignorance and superstition had persuaded them to bind themselves, and to assume the blessings and security of self-government. That form which we have substituted, restores the free right to the unbounded exercise of reason and freedom of opinion . . . the mass of mankind has not been born with saddles on their backs, nor a favored few booted and spurred, ready to ride them legitimately, by the grace of God. These are the grounds of hope for others. For ourselves, let the annual return of this day forever refresh our recollections of these rights, and an undiminished devotion to them.[78]

In the foregoing passage, Jefferson interprets equality to mean the equality of opportunity: "the mass of mankind have not been born with saddles on their back." Indeed, the Virginian's theory of liberal education and his distinction between a natural and a pseudo-aristocracy depends upon equality of opportunity as a necessary condition of societal advancement and progress.

Consequently, Jefferson's view of equality is consonant with that of Lincoln; and it is discordant with Bradford's assertion that equality of opportunity is indistinguishable from equality of condition. According to Bradford,

[It] is nothing less than sophistry to distinguish between equality of opportunity (equal starts in the "race of life") and equality of condition (equal results). For only those who are equal can take equal advantage of a given circumstance. And there is no man equal to any other, except perhaps in the special and politically untranslatable, understanding of the Deity, not intellectually or physically or economically or even morally. Not equal! Such is, of course, the genuinely self-evident proposition."[79]

By failing to distinguish between equality of rights and equality of ability, conditions, or character, Bradford imposes a false dilemma. To be sure, Jefferson and Lincoln agree with Bradford that "only those who are equal can take equal advantage of a given circumstance." Unlike Bradford, however, Jefferson and Lincoln define equality in terms of human essence, not in terms of accidental qualities. As demonstrated, equality before the law and equality as the just distribution of privileges and immunities within society apply universally to all people on account of their humanity—that is, on account of their unique essence as a rational being and spiritual being. In a word, Jefferson and Lincoln interpret equality in reference to rights that exist irrespective of human accidental qualities such as talent, ability, and circumstance. In response to Bradford's assertion, one must simply refuse the terms of the argument on the grounds that it constitutes an inaccurate characterization of both Lincoln's and Jefferson's position.

Furthermore, like Lincoln, Jefferson views the Declaration as a moral covenant. The Virginian's description of the nation's essence parallels Lincoln's conception of political religion: "the sacred attachments of our fellow citizens to the event of which the paper of July 4th, 1776, was but the Declaration, *the genuine effusion of the soul of our country* at that time. Small things may, perhaps, like relics of saints, help to nourish our devotion to this holy bond of Union, and keep it longer alive and warm in our affections" [italics added].[80]

In sum, the parallels between Lincoln and Jefferson are not coincidental; the former explicitly acknowledged the latter's influence:

All honor to Jefferson—to the man who, in the concrete pressure of a struggle for national independence by a single people, had the coolness, forecast and capacity to introduce into a merely revolutionary document, an abstract truth, applicable to all men and all times, and so to embalm it there, that to day, and in all coming days, it shall be a rebuke and a stumbling block to the very harbingers of reappearing tyranny and oppression.[81]

A further difficulty with Kendall's analysis of Lincoln in *The Basic Symbols of the American Political Tradition* may be stated thus: In critiquing the latter's view of equality he fails to give prominence to the concrete role that the issue of slavery played in the formulation of Lincoln's interpretation of the American political order. Kendall abstracts from Lincoln's political thought by tearing it out of its experiential context. Lincoln's view of equality does not occur in a theoretical vacuum; rather, it is formulated in response to the concrete disorder of slavery and its consequent identification as a moral right.

James Madison, one of the chief architects of the Constitution, also views the Declaration as a foundational document. In a letter to Thomas Jefferson that considers the first principles of the nation, Madison says, "And on the distinctive principles of the Government of our own State, and of that of the United States, the best guides are to be found in—1. The Declaration of Independence, as the fundamental act of Union of these States."[82] Furthermore, in *Federalist Paper* no. 39 Madison states: "It is evident that no other form [of government] would be reconcilable with the genius of the people of America; with the fundamental principles of the Revolution; or with that honorable determination which animates every votary of freedom, to rest all our political experiments on the capacity of mankind for self-government."

Madison's discussions of "the genius of the people of America" and "the fundamental principles of the revolution" are inconceivable as anything other than references to the principles enshrined by the Declaration. Jefferson describes the Declaration in a similar manner: the revolutionary document "was intended as an expression of the American mind."[83] Thus, Madison explains that the principles of the Declaration have guided the framework of the Constitution. Like Lincoln, both Madison and Jefferson interpret the Declaration as a "foundation of the American experiment." In defining the collective identity and aspirations of the American people, the Declaration is the very soul of the nation.

In *Federalist Paper* no. 43, Madison explicitly interprets the Declaration as possessing a constitutional status. "The transcendent law of nature and of nature's God . . . declares that the safety and happiness of society are the objects at which all political institutions aim and to which all such institutions must be sacrificed." Furthermore:

In a confederacy founded on republican principles, and composed of republican members, the superintending government ought clearly to possess authority to defend the system against aristocratic or monarchic innovations. . . . Whenever the States may choose to substitute other republican forms, they have a right to do so and to claim the federal guaranty for the latter. The only restriction imposed on them is that they shall not change republican for anti-republican Constitutions; a restriction which, it is presumed, will hardly be considered a grievance.

According to Madison, the possibilities of 1787 were constrained by the principles of 1776. The precepts of the Declaration prohibited the framers from instituting a monarchy or an aristocracy: in the words of Madison, this prohibition was "hardly . . . considered a grievance." The restriction is acceptable to the American people because it is consonant with the principles enshrined by the Declaration. Thus, the revisionists commit a non sequitur in arguing that the Constitution's silence about equality necessarily denies the Declaration's status as a guide to free government. Contrary to these assertions, the Constitution's explicit prohibition against titles of nobility and religious tests can only be understood in light of equality as a political principle. To be sure, the spirit of the revolution guided the framers at the convention. As stated, the Constitution can be seen as providing the concrete framework and safeguards whereby the principles of the Declaration can be actualized.

Did Lincoln transform the nation's ethos by interpreting equality as the supreme political principle? Jefferson's understanding of equality as the basis of free government vindicates Lincoln's interpretation. According to Jefferson, "The first principle of republicanism is, that the *lex major partis* is the fundamental law of every society of individuals of equal rights."[84] Jefferson's statement not only identifies equality as the "central idea" of the nation, it also expresses an individual conception of equality. Furthermore, the historical record contradicts Kendall's assertion that equality "disappears" from the regime's "political vocabulary." The language of equality is mentioned in seven of the original state constitutions! The preambles and bills of rights to these documents indicate that they were established upon the principles of equality. In each case, equality was identified as an axiom of self-government. In his response to Kendall, Jaffa provides a concise list of states that erected their governmental foundations upon the principle of individual and collective equality:

Virginia stated "That all men are by nature equally free and independent"; Pennsylvania, "That all men are born equally free and independent"; Vermont, "That all men are born equally free and independent"; Massachusetts, that "All men are born free and equal"; New Hampshire, that "All men are born equally free and independent"; Delaware, "That all government of right originates from the people [and is founded in compact only]". . . . Maryland, . . . "that all government of right originates from the people [and] is founded in compact only."[85]

CONCLUSION: THE ASSESSMENT OF LEADERSHIP

In this chapter I have attempted to assess Lincoln's interpretation of the Declaration and the meaning of equality therein. Furthermore, I have attempted to prove that his view was consonant with that of Jefferson and Madison, two of the most prominent founding fathers of the nation. Lincoln's clarification of first principles emphasizes that the Constitution must be informed by a higher source of political order. Without such a grounding, the Constitution would lack moral legitimacy; it would represent a willful assertion of power. To be sure, the framers acknowledged the moral legitimacy of the Constitution and the extent to which it relied upon the principles of the Declaration. However, their work was both incomplete and anomalous; it would have to undergo a "fiery trial" of experience. Perhaps the disorder wrought by the Civil War impelled Lincoln to discern more clearly than the fathers the extent to which political order must depend upon a higher, moral order?

Indeed, Lincoln's view of equality is comprehensible in so far as there is a kinship between the human and the divine. Human dignity is derived from what is highest in man, his rational and spiritual nature. Those who reduce human experience to random clumps of matter, who proclaim that man differs from an animal by degree, who fail to distinguish between human rights and animal rights, undermine the distinctive spiritual quality that confers dignity upon human beings. In doing so, they are inadvertently paving a road to a new slavery of the appetites, a servitude that may easily degenerate into sociopolitical tyranny. Lincoln's view of equality necessarily rejects today's permissive egalitarianism. Those who fail to distinguish between what is sacred and what is profane in human life must heed his prophetic warning. True liberty as distinguished from license consists in the submission to moral duty:

On the question of liberty, as a principle, we are not what we have been. When we were the political slaves of King George, and wanted to be free, we called the maxim that "all men are created equal" a self-evident truth; but now when we have grown fat, and have lost all dread of being slaves ourselves, we have become so greedy to be masters that we call the same maxim "a self-evident lie." The Fourth of July has not quite dwindled away; it is still a great day—for burning firecrackers!!![86]

Finally, although the conservative revisionists alert us to the dangers of political idealism, they fail to acknowledge the prominent role of equality within the American political tradition. While their diagnosis of today's permissive egalitarianism is correct, their derivation of Lincoln as its source is incorrect. Consequently, their appraisal of Lincoln's leadership is excessively pessimistic. On the other side of the political spectrum, liberal progressives who criticize Lincoln's defense of equality as a sham because he failed to promote complete social and political equality amongst the races are likewise incorrect in their assessment of his leadership. Their refusal to acknowledge the manner whereby circumstances limit decision making renders their expectations of political leadership naively idealistic. In sum, neither the conservative revisionist nor the liberal progressive interpretation of Lincoln's leadership is adequate. By harmonizing the normative precepts of the Declaration within the concrete framework of the Constitution, Lincoln embodies the prudential statesman par excellence. His magnanimous example must continue to serve as a virtuous paragon of American leadership.

NOTES

1. Alexander Hamilton, James Madison, and John Jay, *The Federalist Papers*, ed. Clinton Rossiter (New York: Mentor Books, 1961), no. 1, p. 33.

2. In *A Modell of Christian Charity*, John Winthrop describes the New World: "[W]ee shall finde that the God of Israell is among vs, when tenn of vs shall be able to resist a thousand of our enemies, when hee shall make vs a prayse and glory, that men shall say of succeeding plantacions: the lord make it like that of New England; for wee must Consider that wee shall be as a Citty vpon a Hill, the Eies of all people are vppon vs; soe that if wee shall deale falsely with our god in this worke wee haue vndertaken and soe cause him to withdrawe his present help from vs, wee shall be made a story and a by-word through the world [*sic*]." Quoted from Michael B. Levy, ed., *Political Thought in America: An Anthology* (Belmont, Calif.: Dorsey Press, 1988), 12.

3. Abraham Lincoln, *The Collected Works of Abraham Lincoln*, ed. Roy P. Basler, 9 vols. (New Brunswick, N.J.: Rutgers University Press in association with the Abraham Lincoln Association, 1953–55), 4: 236 (hereafter cited as *CWAL*).

4. Less than a month after he had learned of Virginia's secession from the Union, Robert E. Lee stated: "I forsee that the country will have to pass through a terrible ordeal, a necessary expiation perhaps for our national sins." For background, see the following concise account of the Civil War: James M. McPherson, *Battle Cry of Freedom: The Civil War Era* (New York: Ballantine Books, 1988), 281.

5. Harry V. Jaffa, *Equality and Liberty* (New York: Oxford University Press, 1965), 138. As Jaffa explains: "The Civil War cannot be understood except as an attempt to resolve in action dilemmas imposed upon American Politics by doctrines that gave birth to the nation."

6. *CWAL*, 4: 253.

7. Stephen B. Oates, *With Malice toward None: The Life of Abraham Lincoln* (New York: Mentor Books, 1978), 32.

8. John P. Diggins, *The Lost Soul of American Politics* (Chicago: University of Chicago Press, 1984), 296–333.

9. Harry V. Jaffa, *Crisis of the House Divided* (Chicago: University of Chicago Press, 1982), 330–346.

10. For a specific analysis of the relationship between the Declaration and the Constitution see George Anastaplo, *The Constitution: A Commentary* (Baltimore: Johns Hopkins University Press, 1989).

11. *CWAL*, 4: 240.

12. See Hadley Arkes, *First Things* (Princeton: Princeton University Press, 1986).

13. Jaffa, *Crisis*, 308–329.

14. Ibid., 222.

15. Jaffa, *Equality and Liberty*, 177.

16. *CWAL*, 3: 375.

17. Ibid., 3: 29.

18. "Abraham Lincoln's Theological Outlook," in *Essays on Lincoln's Faith and Politics*, by Hans J. Morgenthau and David Hein (Lantham, Md.: University Press of America, 1983), 103–205. Although an analysis of the theological ground of Lincoln's political philosophy is beyond the scope of my inquiry, it is important to mention that despite certain areas of agreement, I disagree with Harry V. Jaffa's view of Lincoln's civil theology. Contrary to Jaffa, I believe that Lincoln's private and public piety was not disingenuous. Moreover, I disagree with Jaffa's interpretation of Lincoln's "political religion" as being a rhetorical expedient in its entirety—that is, I disagree with the wholesale reduction of Lincoln's civil theology to utilitarian considerations. Indeed, Lincoln's civil theology fuses biblical and enlightenment symbolisms. However, he views these two sources as philosophically compatible. Moreover, his theological grounding of the Declaration in natural law cannot be reduced to Spinoza's *religio catholica*. Rather, it resembles that of the Stoic tradition beginning with Cicero, continuing with the medieval philosophers, and adapted by modern thinkers such as Blackstone, whom Lincoln had read and admired. See the following works by Cicero: *De republica* 3. 23. 33: "sed et omnes gentes et omni tempore una lex et sempiterna et immutabilis continebit, unusque erit communis quasi magister et imperator omnium deus, ille legis huius inventor, disceptator, lator." Also see Cicero: *De legibus* 2. 4. 8–10; *De legibus* 2. 7. 15–16. In tracing the influence of the Stoic tradition upon Lincoln's theological grounding of law, it may be helpful to compare the foregoing passages of Cicero to William Blackstone, *Commentaries on the Laws of England*, intro. Stanley N. Katz (Chicago: University of Chicago Press, 1979), vol. 1: "Of the Rights of Persons," 38–45. For Jaffa's interpretation of Lincoln's "political religion" see Jaffa, *Crisis of the House Divided*, 238–239; 245; 249; 251–252; 265; 418–419, especially notes 16 and 21 to chapter 10.

19. *CWAL*, 2: 499–500.

20. Ibid., 1: 112.

21. Jaffa, *Crisis*, 317–318.

22. *CWAL*, 3: 344; 4: 121. For a discussion of Blackstone's influence upon the American political order see Russell Kirk, *America's British Culture* (New Brunswick, N.J.: Transaction Publishers, 1993).

23. For an accessible presentation of the continuity within the natural law tradition from the Stoics to the medieval philosophers and finally to modern thinkers, see Peter J. Stanlis, *Edmund Burke and the Natural Law* (Lafayette, La.: Huntington House, 1986).

24. *CWAL*, 2: 406.

25. Ibid., 3: 78, 80.

26. Ibid., 2: 518. Also see Jaffa's elaboration of this point: Jaffa, *Crisis*, 375–376.

27. *CWAL*, 2: 406.

28. Ibid., 3: 266.

29. Ibid.

30. Ibid., 3: 92, 222, 254–257, 334. For an account of the historical circumstances that influenced Lincoln's decision to emancipate see McPherson, *Battle Cry*, chap. 16, 490–510.

31. *CWAL*, 3: 303.

32. Ibid., 2: 385.

33. Jaffa, *Crisis*, 347–362.

34. For elaboration of this point see George Anastaplo, "Slavery and the Constitution: Explorations," *Texas Tech Law Review* 20 (1989), 677–785.

35. *CWAL*, 2: 501.

36. Ibid., 274.

37. Ibid., 275.

38. Ibid., 385.

39. Ibid., 266.

40. Mortimer J. Adler, *Six Great Ideas* (New York: Collier Books, 1981), 155.

41. *CWAL*, 3: 424

42. Harry V. Jaffa, *The Conditions of Freedom* (Baltimore: Johns Hopkins University Press, 1975), 177–178.

43. *CWAL*, 2: 544–547.

44. Ibid., 2: 271.

45. Ibid., 3: 425.

46. Ibid., 3: 81.

47. Ibid., 3: 88.

48. Ibid., 3: 328.

49. Ibid., 3: 188.

50. Ibid., 3: 147.

51. Quoted from Harry V. Jaffa, *How to Think about the American Revolution* (Durham, N.C.: Carolina Academic Press, 1978), 33–34.

52. Abraham Lincoln, *Speeches and Writings 1832–1858* (New York: Viking Press, Library of America, 1989), 116.

53. Jaffa. *Crisis*.

54. *CWAL*, 3: 80

55. Ibid., 2: 264.

56. Ibid., 2: 532.

57. Quoted from Jaffa, *How to Think*, 43.

58. *CWAL*, 2: 222–223.

59. Ibid., 4: 17.

60. Ibid., 4: 16.

61. Ibid., 2: 265–266.

62. Ibid., 2: 500.

63. Ibid., 2: 323.

64. Quoted from Jaffa, *How to Think*, 141.

65. Wilmoore Kendall and George Carey, *The Basic Symbols of the American Political Tradition* (Baton Rouge: Louisiana State University Press, 1970), 14–15.

66. Quoted from Jaffa, *How to Think*, 33.

67. Kendall and Carey, *Basic Symbols*, 90.

68. Ibid., 89.

69. Garry Wills, *Inventing America: Jefferson's Declaration of Independence* (Garden City, N.Y.: Doubleday, 1978), xxii–xxiii.

70. See Jaffa's refutation of Wills's thesis: Harry V. Jaffa, "Inventing the Gettysburg Address," *Intercollegiate Review* 28 (fall 1992): 51–56.

71. Garry Wills, *Lincoln at Gettysburg, The Words That Remade America* (New York: Simon & Schuster, 1992), 39.

72. Kendall and Carey, *Basic Symbols*, 14.

73. Wills, *Lincoln*, 145.

74. Ibid., 38.

75. *CWAL*, 3: 404.

76. For an assessment of Lincoln's conservatism see Russell Kirk, *The Roots of American Order* (Washington, D.C., Regnery Gateway, 1992), 449–457.

77. Adrienne Koch and Willian Peden, eds. *The Life and Selected Writings of Thomas Jefferson* (New York: Modern Library, 1944), 703.

78. Ibid., 729.

79. Quoted from Jaffa, *How to Think*, 146.

80. Koch and Peden, *Jefferson*, 722.

81. Lincoln, *Speeches and Writings*, 216.

82. Marvin Meyers, ed., *The Mind of the Founder: Sources of the Political Thought of James Madison* (Hanover, N.H.: University Press of New England, 1973), 350.

83. Koch and Peden, *Jefferson*, 719.

84. Ibid., 681.

85. Quoted from Jaffa, *How to Think*, 37.

86. Ibid., 101.

4 Lincoln's Poetry and Prose

James A. Stevenson

Although many observers have noted Abraham Lincoln's penchant for reading and memorizing poetry,[1] virtually none of them have studied or analyzed the role that Lincoln's own poetry played in the development of his writing skills. In fact, it is largely owing to the reading and writing of poetry that Lincoln acquired the competence to write his mature prose with the rhythm, alliteration, imagery, economy of words, and flexibility of structure that so distinguish it. After the 1840s, Lincoln's best prose passages not only contained a frequent use of imagery and metaphor, but they were guided by a sense of vernacular sound and rhythm as well as meaning and logic. Although this aesthetic accomplishment peaked during the years of his presidency, it had its origins in his poetic efforts of the mid-1840s.

When, in 1838, Lincoln used his rhetorical pen to compose "The Perpetuation of Our Political Institutions," he was in many respects a very unpolished writer. According to the scholars Herbert Edwards and John Hankins, Lincoln's writing, in this early period, occasionally slips into the "rhetorical vices of his time" and, instead of eloquence, comes "perilously close to the florid pomposity of his age."[2] Certainly, "The Perpetuation of Our Political Institutions" contains a number of stylistic flaws. While, on the whole, it is a lucid and logical law-and-order argument from definition (i.e., the unchanging human nature of ambition), its lapses are significant. Some of the unevenness in Lincoln's grammatical style can be detected in this passage of his tortured prose and poor punctuation:

As the patriots of seventy-six did to the support of the Declaration of Independence, so to the support of the Constitution and Laws, [sic] let every American pledge his life, his property, and his sacred honor;—let every man remember that to violate the law, [sic] is to trample on the blood of his father, [sic] and to tear the character [charter?] of his own, [sic] and his children's liberty. Let reverence for the laws, [sic] be breathed by every American mother, [*sic*] to the lisping babe, [*sic*] that prattles on her lap—let it be taught in schools, in seminaries, and in colleges;—let it be written in Primmers, spelling books, and in Almanacs;—let it be preached from the pulpit, proclaimed in legislative halls, and enforced in courts of justice. And, in short, let it become the *political religion*[3] of the nation; and let the old and the young, the rich and the poor, the grave and the gay, of all sexes and tongues, and colors and conditions, sacrifice unceasingly upon its altars.[4]

While nineteenth-century writers and speakers frequently inserted commas for pauses at arbitrary locations within a sentence, Lincoln's early writing practices exhibit uncommon, if not confusing, punctuation usage. Yet, although the preceding passage contains seven unnecessary commas and many superfluous words, it also reveals Lincoln's early propensity for using anaphora and for creating rhythm. Unfortunately, this latter forensic skill is achieved mainly by placing commas around restrictive phrases or by supplanting periods with dashes or by letting commas, dashes, and semicolons combine to create caesuras as well as to jumble thoughts.

There were, of course, many glimmers of Lincoln's future literary promise in his 1838 speech. His gift for metaphor and for creating balanced antitheses in parallel structures (visible at the end of the previous quotation) is apparent in several passages of the speech. But more important, the vivid lines and rhythmic patterns in the oration serve to highlight his impulse to express a poetic outlook. For example, in one metaphorical passage, he describes his feelings for the passing of the founding fathers in a grim, artistic contemplation of death:

They *were* a forest of giant oaks; but the all-resistless hurricane has swept over them, and left only, here and there, a lonely trunk, despoiled of its verdure, shorn of its foliage; unshading and unshaded, to murmur in a few more gentle breezes, and to combat with its mutilated limbs, a few more ruder storms, then to sink, and be no more.[5]

As an expression of Lincoln's morose personality, this passage forecasts the emotive suggestion that streaks much of the moving writing of his later years. Still, as of 1838, Lincoln's writing lacks the mechanical and stylistic precision that lends eloquence to his mature compositions. And in arriving at that powerful expression of thought and emotion, Lincoln's poetics play the crucial role of perfecting and disciplining his prose.

Underlying that development were the painful incidents that riddled his youth and young manhood. In their wake Lincoln adopted the somber and poetic outlook of one who has experienced life in "'all its tragic intensity.'"[6] His youth and frontier experience had taught him that life was unpredictable and transitory, a lesson that fed his sense of fatalism and helped inspire his not infrequent dark moods. This doleful outlook, when combined with his unusually keen mind, provided the poetic impulse behind Lincoln's literary ambition to describe his deepest emotions in a form that skillful poets might appreciate.

Guided by that desire, he composed some poetry in 1846 about an emotional visit to his boyhood home in Indiana in 1844. In the light of these poems, it is clear that Lincoln had studied the mechanics of poetic techniques with enough diligence to express his own thoughts in carefully crafted metric lines. The poems were written in the same stanza pattern and similar iambic rhythm that are found in Henry W. Longfellow's "The Wreck of the Hesperus." They demonstrate that Lincoln had absorbed, in addition to a Shakespearean poetic influence, some of the conventional poetic imagery and the mechanical practices of early nineteenth-century English and American Romantic poets. Yet, if Lincoln's verses were not stylistically unique, they were proof of the unusually high value that he placed on the mechanics of poetic expression. In total, this literary concern produced three lengthy poems.

Given the lines that he wrote in 1846, it is possible that Lincoln intended to compose a four-canto poem. If so, however, he failed to complete one of the cantos. Still, counting the thirteen untitled stanzas that he wrote about Matthew Gentry as a separate canto, Lincoln wrote two more cantos entitled "My Childhood-Home I See Again" and "The Bear Hunt."[7] He originally sent "My Childhood-Home I See Again" and twelve stanzas on Gentry, plus two additional stanzas (of a new canto?) to Andrew Johnston at the end of February, 1846.[8] He mailed a revised Gentry canto of thirteen stanzas to Johnston on 6 September 1846. And, his final, finished canto of "The Bear Hunt" has been dated 6 September 1846.[9] When Lincoln's September canto on Gentry is compared with the February one, it is evident that Lincoln's only major change was to remove the final two stanzas from the February version and add a different final stanza.

No matter how mediocre portions of Lincoln's poetry may be, his writing is highly crafted and intriguing. All three cantos are written in quatrain stanzas of alternating tetrameter (four-foot) and trimeter (three-foot) iambic lines. The rhyme scheme of the stanzas follows an alternate rhyming pattern (ABAB, CDCD, EFEF, GHGH, etc.) throughout each canto. By carrying this pattern of rhyme and meter through the twenty-two stanzas of "The Bear Hunt" and the ten stanzas of "My Childhood-Home I See Again" as well as the thirteen stanzas of the Gentry canto (separately counted), Lincoln demonstrates an impressive ability to produce a mechanical rhyme and rhythmic regularity. When he blends this ability with his melancholic reflections on memory, his poetry approaches the art of some fine poems (e.g., Gray, "Elegy Written in a Country Church Yard"). Using the iambic scansion of alternating tetrameter and trimeter lines (indicated in the first few stanzas), Lincoln's best verses from "My Childhood-Home I See Again" read as follows:

Iambic Scansion	*Rhyme Pattern*
My chíld/hood-hóme/ I sée/ agáin	A
And glád/den with/ the víew;	B
And stíll/ as mém'/ries crówd/ my bráin,	A
There's sád/ness ín/ it tóo.	B
O mém/ory!/ thou míd-/way world	C
'Twixt Earth/ and Pá/radíse,	D

Where things/ decayed,/ and loved/ ones lost   C
  In dream/y sha/dows rise.   D

And freed/ from all/ that gross/ or vile,   E
  Seem hal/lowed, pure,/ and bright,   F
Like scenes/ in some/ enchan/ted isle,   E
  All bathed/ in li/quid light.   F

As dis/tant moun/tains please/ the eye,   G
  When twi/light cha/ses day—   H
As bu/gle tones,/ that, pass/ing by,   G
  In dis/tance die/ away—   H

As leav/ing some/ grand wa/ter-/fall   I
  We ling'/ring, list/ it's roar,   J
So mem/ory/ will hal/low all   I
  We've known,/ but know/ no more.   J

While these stanzas capture the ethereal quality of thought, life, and death, Lincoln's next two stanzas are mechanically flawless but poetically mundane.

Now twenty years have passed away,
  Since here I bid farewell
To woods, and fields, and scenes of play
  And school-mates loved so well.

Where many were, how few remain
  Of old familiar things!
But seeing these to mind again
  The lost and absent brings.

As transitions to Lincoln's most deeply felt emotions, these unexceptional stanzas forecast a sadder mental journey.

In taking that journey, Lincoln exposes his morose personality in these more moving lines:

The friends I left that parting day—
  How changed, as time has sped!
Young childhood grown, strong manhood grey,
  And half of all are dead.

I hear the lone survivors tell
  How nought from death could save,
Till every sound appears a knell,
  And every spot a grave.

> I range the fields with pensive tread,
>   And pace the hollow rooms;
> And feel (companions of the dead)
>   I'm living in the tombs.[10]

Although filled with the misery of loss, these poignant passages are devoid of excessive sentimentality. They carry a mood of sincere sorrow, and they use colloquial diction to do it. By expressing such heartfelt feelings in simple English words, Lincoln is adopting a style that will become an integral part of his prose-poetry of later years.

As further evidence of this facet of his writing, Lincoln's canto on a boyhood acquaintance named Matthew Gentry is stark and terrifying. In recalling the trauma of seeing the "bright" nineteen-year-old fall into a sudden and unexpected madness, Lincoln exhibits a poet's capacity to empathize with another human being. He had, after all, witnessed Matthew's effort to maim himself as well as the youth's maniacal attacks on his own mother and father. Brooding over these events, Lincoln was led, in near morbid fascination, occasionally to stand near the Gentry farm and listen to Matthew's insane weeping and swearing.[11] It is by projecting his own fear of madness onto the insanity that arbitrarily befell Matthew that Lincoln imbues his poetry with an unmistakable dimension of personal anxiety and despair. Certainly, Lincoln's verses make clear that he prefers death to madness. And, in that sense, his opening stanza about Matthew conveys an interesting insight into Lincoln's psyche.

> But here's an object more of dread
>   Than ought the grave contains—
> A human form with reason fled,
>   While wretched life remains.

While the introspection implicit in these lines is blunted by Lincoln's use of the words "Poor Matthew" in his following line, he also inserts an element of pathos into the next stanza by observing that "Poor Matthew" once had been "bright" and economically fortunate.

> Poor Matthew! Once of genius bright,
>   A fortune-favored child—
> Now locked for aye, in mental night,
>   A haggard mad-man wild.

From "mad-man wild," Lincoln uses his next four stanzas unambiguously to describe the course of Matthew's madness as starting with violence and ending in mindless quiescence. While present-day critics might complain that Lincoln's iambic and metric regularity of ta TUM, ta TUM, ta TUM is inappropriate for the frenzied condition that his words describe, this criticism may be offset by his gift for choosing appropriate diction. By using words such as "howling," "shrieked," "sinews," "fiendish," "maniac," "pangs," and "burning eye-balls," he vividly describes Matthew's mental breakdown.

Poor Matthew! I have ne'er forgot,
  When first, with maddened will,
Yourself you maimed, your father fought,
  And mother strove to kill;

When terror spread, and neighbours ran,
  Your dange'rous strength to bind;
And soon, a howling crazy man
  Your limbs were fast confined.

How then you strove and shrieked aloud,
  Your bones and sinews bared;
And fiendish on the gazing crowd,
  With burning eye-balls glared—

And begged, and swore, and wept and prayed
  With maniac laugh[ter?] joined—
How fearful were those signs displayed
  By pangs that killed thy mind!

It is noteworthy that Roy P. Basler and his associate editors of Lincoln's collected works are wrong to question whether Lincoln inadvertently omitted the syllable [ter?] from "laugh" in the line "With maniac laugh[ter?] joined—." Had Lincoln included that additional syllable, it would have upset the precision of his alternating tetrameter and trimeter iambic lines. Lincoln's February version of that line did read "With maniac laughter joined," but he must have noticed that mechanical flaw in his iambic trimeter pattern, and he eliminated it from the poem's September version. As a poetic fetish, such precise, mechanical considerations may be deplorable, but as a necessary step toward greater poetic skill and confidence, this attention to detail indicates Lincoln's devotion to mastering the poetic technique of mechanical, rhythmic regularity. Once confident of that mastery, Lincoln will free himself to express his fundamental poetic nature in the ultimate free verse of prose.

Meanwhile, after the highly alliterative ("strove and shrieked," "bones and sinews bared," and "burning eye-balls") and parallel structures ("strove and shrieked," "bones and sinews," "And begged, and swore, and wept and prayed") in these latter two stanzas, Lincoln provides a transition stanza for a return to his more introspective verses. This next stanza breaks the tension created by the previous verses and moves us away from the violent, descriptive language of the previous four stanzas:

And when at length, tho' drear and long,
  Time soothed thy fiercer woes,
How plaintively thy mournful song
  Upon the still night rose.

By breaking from the almost gothic diction of his previous stanzas, this stanza introduces five more stanzas in which Lincoln achieves an almost Wordsworthian quality of personal reflection and nature-associated diction. Filling his verses with alliterative "d" and "s" sounds, he writes:

> I've heard it aft, as if I dreamed,
>   Far distant, sweet, and lone—
> The funeral dirge, it ever seemed
>   Of reason dead and gone.

> To drink it's [sic] strains, I've stole away,
>   All stealthily and still,
> Ere yet the rising God of day
>   Had streaked the Eastern hill.

> Air held his breath; trees, with the spell,
>   Seemed sorrowing angels round,
> Whose swelling tears in dew-drops fell
>   Upon the listening ground.

> But this is past; and nought remains
>   That raised thee o'er the brute.
> Thy piercing shrieks, and soothing strains,
>   Are like, forever mute.

> Now fare thee well—more thou the *cause*,
>   Than *subject* now of woe.
> All mental pangs, by time's kind laws,
>   Hast lost the power to know.

Having concluded that a catatonic Matthew is finally free of feeling pain, Lincoln writes a concluding stanza that not only reminds readers of the more dreary passages in *Hamlet* or *Macbeth* but of Shakespeare's persistent grappling with the finite limits of man's religious perception.

> O death! Thou awe-inspiring prince,
>   That keepst the world in fear;
> Why dost thou tear more blest ones hence,
>   And leave him ling'ring here?[12]

In ending his ruminations on Matthew's fate with such a troubling and unanswerable question, Lincoln merges his psychological outlook and his philosophical perspective in a moment of personal melancholia and poetic rhyme.

Although Lincoln does not use "The Bear Hunt" to raise philosophical observations, he does express an intensely personal distaste for the blood lust connected with trophy hunting (that is, for the animal's hide). While his humorless mood is established as early as the second stanza, his total disgust with the hunt and with the hunters' behavior is not apparent until the last seven stanzas. Then, too, until the final ironic stanza, the entire canto is a detailed, but largely unexceptional, piece of work. It has, like the other two cantos that Lincoln wrote, virtually no flaws in the pattern of its mechanical and rhyme regularity.

Thus, continuing his canto pattern of iambic meter, Lincoln traces the events of the bear hunt through the course of various mishaps and a brutal killing of the hapless bear.

> A wild-bear chace, didst never see?
>   Then hast thou lived in vain.
> Thy richest bump of glorious glee,
>   Lies desert in thy brain.

Although the final line of this first stanza contains intriguing imagery, such imagery is abandoned as Lincoln turns to less imaginative language to describe the menace that bears once presented to frontier people:

> When first my father settled here,
>   'Twas then the frontier line:
> The panther's scream, filled night with fear
> And bears preyed on the swine.

Moving, now, into his third stanza, Lincoln uses ordinary words to describe the bear's alarm and his flight for safety. With little alliteration and few parallel structures, Lincoln writes in economical, descriptive verses:

> But wo for Bruin's short lived fun,
>   When rose the squealing cry;
> Now man and horse, with dog and gun,
>   For vengeance, at him fly.

> A sound of danger strikes his ear;
>   He gives the breeze a snuff:
> Away he bounds, with little fear,
>   And seeks the tangled *rough*.

> On press his foes, and reach the ground,
>   Where's left his half munched meal;
> The dogs, in circles, scent around,
>   And find his fresh made trail.

> With instant cry, away they dash,
>   And men as fast pursue;

> O'er logs they leap, through water splash,
>   And shout the brisk halloo.
>
> Now to elude the eager pack,
>   Bear shuns the open ground;
> Th[r]ough matted vines, he shapes his track
>   And runs it, round and round.

With the bear, at this point, seeking to elude his eager pursuers, Lincoln turns his attention to the thrill and joy of the chase. As he introduces the merry band of hunters, he identifies one of the hunting dogs as a "short-legged fice." With its rhyming similarity to lice, this is a subtle foreshadowing that Lincoln does not approve of the hunt. He writes,

> The tall fleet cur, with deep-mouthed voice,
>   Now speeds him, as the wind;
> While half-grown pup, and short-legged fice,
>   Are yelping far behind.
>
> And fresh recruits are dropping in
>   To join the merry *corps*:
> With yelp and yell,—a mingled din—
>   The woods are in a roar.
>
> And round, and round the chace now goes,
>   The world's alive with fun;
> Nick Carter's horse, his rider throws,
>   And more, Hill drops his gun.

Amid these final mishaps, the poem reaches its turning point. And, in the next five stanzas, Lincoln strives to create sympathy for the trapped and exhausted bear. After the measured rhythm of his first few lines, Lincoln uses punctuation to produce the frequent pauses and hectic phrases that seem to match the panic of the bear's final, desperate struggle for survival:

> Now sorely pressed, bear glances back,
>   And lolls his tired tongue;
> When as, to force him from his track,
>   An ambush on him sprung.
>
> Across the glade he sweeps for flight,
>   And fully is in view.
> The dogs, new-fired, by the sight,
>   Their cry, and speed, renew.

The foremost ones, now reach his rear,
  He turns, they dash away;
And circling now, the wrathful bear,
  They have him full at bay.

At top of speed, the horse-men come,
  All screaming in a row.
"Whoop! Take him Tiger. Seize him Drum."
  Bang,—bang—the rifles go.

And furious now, the dogs he tears,
  And crushes in his ire.
Wheels right and left, and upward rears,
  With eyes of burning fire.

At this point, Lincoln definitely twists the poem away from the promise of a joyful adventure, which had been suggested by the poem's first fifteen stanzas. He does so by writing a gruesome description of the bear's death:

But leaden death is at his heart,
  Vain all the strength he plies.
And, spouting blood from every part,
  He reels, and sinks, and dies.

Once the bear has been killed, Lincoln registers his disgust with the whole "sporting" process. He brings the excitement of the chase and its climactic kill to the ugly conclusion of hunters and dogs squabbling over the rightful winner of the bullet-riddled hide of the bear:

And now a dinsome clamor rose,
  'Bout who should have his skin;
Who first draws blood, each hunter knows,
  This prize must always win.

But who did this, and how to trace
  What's true from what's a lie,
Like lawyers in a murder case
  They stoutly *argufy*.

With the men now arguing like lawyers, or perhaps like dogs ("dinsome"), Lincoln adds a hint of irony in allowing "fice" to slip in and to claim the hide by tearing into the bear's carcass with "grinning teeth":

Aforesaid fice, of blustering mood,
  Behind, and quite forgot,

> Just now emerging from the wood,
>   Arrives upon the spot.
>
> With grinning teeth, and up-turned hair—
>   Brim full of spunk and wrath,
> He growls, and seizes on dead bear,
>   And shakes for life and death.
>
> And swells as if his skin would tear,
>   And growls and shakes again;
> And swears, as plain as dog can swear,
>   That he has won the skin.

In his final contemptuous verses, Lincoln adds the crowning ironic touch by identifying "not a few" men with such a "conceited" dog:

> Conceited whelp! we laugh at thee—
>   Nor mind, that not a few
> Of pompous, two-legged dogs there be,
>   Conceited quite as you.[13]

Artistically lacking in deliberate ambiguity, psychological complexity, unusual imagery, metaphorical figures, and unique ideas, "The Bear Hunt," nevertheless, is a skillful work. With such unusual diction as "munched," "halloo," "fice," "new-fired," "leaden death," "dinsome," and "argufy," Lincoln rigorously maintains an iambic meter and alternating rhyming pattern throughout the poem. And, this, while unspectacular as poetry, is a significant achievement. It directly contributes to Lincoln's facility to write more-disciplined and rhythmic prose. It also contributes, by building his literary skills and confidence, to a greater flexibility in producing poetry with internally varied metric patterns.

Hence, more than a decade after writing his 1846 cantos, Lincoln creates some mechanically less restrictive verses in Winchester, Illinois. After addressing these 1858 verses to Rosa and Linnie Haggard, Lincoln uses his preferred four-line stanza, but he abandons the rigid pattern of the alternating iambic tetrameter and iambic trimeter lines that distinguished his earlier poems. His 1858 verses reflect his growing ability to produce poetic musicality through the variation of stress and meter. Thus, the verses which Lincoln wrote in Rosa Haggard's autograph album ("To Rosa Haggard" and "To Linnie Haggard") have a dominant trochee metric form, but the last three lines of the second stanza are written in iambic tetrameter. From them, we may deduce that Lincoln no longer feels the need to maintain a precise pattern of metric feet from line to line. His mixed stress patterns as well as his fondness for antithetical pairings are plainly visible in this example of his carpe diem poetry:

> Yóu are/ yoúng, and/ Í am/ ólder;
>   Yóu are/ hopéful./ Í am/ nót—

Énjoy/ life, ere/ it grow/ cólder—
   Plúck the/ roses/ ere they/ rot.

Teách your/ béau to/ héed the/ láy—
   That sún/shine sóon/is lóst/ in sháde—
That *now's*/ as goód/ as an/y dáy—
   To take/ thee, Ró/sa, ere/ she fáde.[14]

While the morose and contemplative Lincoln is fully evident in these lines, they reveal a less somber Lincoln as well. He clearly expresses some humor by punning on the implied contrast between a fading rose and a fading "Rosa." More important, his metaphor on aging and death, in the lines "Enjoy life, ere it grow colder" and "That sunshine soon is lost in shade," is the mark of a talented writer.

Certainly, there is no doubt that Lincoln's 1858 poems reflect aspects of his profoundly sad disposition. In his poem to Linnie, Lincoln seems unable to voice a hopefulness without expressing his awareness of pain. He states his outlook with the rhythmic variability that, once again, demonstrates his greater comfort and familiarity with the purely mechanical aspect of poetry. Using a dominant trochee pattern throughout the poem, Lincoln writes four lines of varying lengths in metric feet:

A sweet/ plaintive/ song did/ I hear,
   And I/ fancied/ that she/ was the/ singer—
May e/motions/ as pure, / as that/ song set/ a-stir
   Be the/ worst that/ the fu/ture shall/ bring her.[15]

It is evident that, in these few simple verses, Lincoln has completely merged his poetic sensitivity with rhythmic form.

This accomplishment is worth noting because it portends an artistic competence that, when freed of the most rigid constraints of predictable versification, will characterize the best of his future writing. In only one example from his later presidency, Lincoln wrote a famous letter of condolence (21 November 1864) to a mother, Lydia Bixby, who had been identified as having lost five sons in battle.[16] Through the use of mainly iambic scansion and stress on only a few of the syllables that ought to have no more than secondary stress, the beautiful sensitivity of the letter may be better illustrated in the form of free verse. In that form, it clearly shows Lincoln's concern for both emotional eloquence and the mechanical aspects of stress and rhythmic expression. With only the more poignant lines of the letter accented, it reads:

Dear Madam,—
I have been shown in the files of the War Department
A statement of the Adjutant-General of Massachusetts,

That you are the mother of five sons
Who have died gloriously on the field of battle.
I féel/ how wéak/ and frúit/less múst/ be añ/y wórds/ of míne
Which shóuld/ attémpt/ to bé/guile yóu/ from the/ gríef
Of a/ loss so/ ovér/whelmíng.
But I cannot refrain from tendering to you
The consolation that may be found
In the thanks of the Republic they died to save.
I práy/ that oúr/ Heáven/lý Fá/ther may/ ássuage
The añ/guish of/ yóur be/reávement,
And leáve/ you on/lý the
Chérished/ mémo/rý of/ the lóved/ and lóst,
And the/ solémn/ príde that/ múst be/ yóurs,
To have/ laíd so/ cóstly
A sác/rificé/ upón/ the aĺ/ter of/ fréedom.[17]

Simply put, President Lincoln demonstrates a matchless ability to compose, with rhythm and meaning, a prose that has the grace of poetry.

This exquisite prose, however, was made possible, in part, by the slavish apprenticeship to orthodox poetic conventions that Lincoln imposed on his first serious poetic efforts. In writing his 1846 poems, he, no doubt, learned the rhythmic virtue of monosyllabic words. In effect, "My Childhood-Home I See Again," the canto on Matthew Gentry, and "The Bear Hunt" are the precursors of the sophisticated poetic imagery, metaphor, rhythm, and rhyme sounds that are the hallmarks of Lincoln's mature prose. Similarly, Lincoln's study of poetry may have helped him to purge his more awkward prose of its overly ornamental style. After the 1830s, at any rate, he abandoned the elaborate literary models of his day and rendered his prose precise, vernacular, rhythmic, melodic, and elegant. Such an achievement, according to Jacques Barzun, and, more recently, Garry Wills, helped to establish a new model for American writers.[18] That model broke with the "dealers in literary plush"[19] and has led American literature from Lincoln to Mark Twain to Hemingway to the present. In the end, Lincoln used his early efforts at poetic expression to help build the writing techniques that, in meaning and style, have placed him among the literary great and have come to epitomize the best of the American way.

NOTES

1. Francis B. Carpenter, *Six Months at the White House with Abraham Lincoln* (New York: Hurd & Houghton, 1867), 50–51, 59–63, 115, 331; William H. Herndon, *Herndon's Lincoln: The True Story of a Great Life*, 3 vols. (Springfield, Ill.: Herndon's Lincoln Publishing, 1889), 1: 320; Martin L. Houser, *Lincoln's Education and Other Essays* (New York: Bookman, 1957), 137; David Mearns, "Mr. Lincoln and the Books He Read," in *Three Presidents and Their Books*, by David Mearns, Arthur E. Bestor, and Jonathan Daniel (Urbana: University

of Illinois Press, 1955), 72, 82–83; Louis A. Warren, *Lincoln's Youth: Indiana Years, Seven to Twenty-One, 1816–1830* (New York: Appleton-Century-Crofts, 1959), 211.

2. Herbert Joseph Edwards and John Erskine Hankins, *Lincoln the Writer: The Development of His Literary Style* (Orono: University of Maine Press, 1962), 37.

3. Lincoln's emphasis. Unless indicated as added emphasis, all emphases will be those of the quoted author.

4. Abraham Lincoln, *The Collected Works of Abraham Lincoln*, ed. Roy P. Basler, 9 vols. (New Brunswick, N.J.: Rutgers University Press in association with the Abraham Lincoln Association, 1953–55), 1: 112 (hereafter cited as *CWAL*).

5. Ibid., 1: 115.

6. Edwards and Hankins: *Lincoln*, 88–89.

7. *CWAL*, 1: 367, 367–370, 384–389.

8. Ibid., 1: 367–370.

9. Ibid., 1: 384, 386.

10. Ibid., 1: 367–368.

11. Stephen B. Oates, *With Malice toward None: The Life of Abraham Lincoln* (New York: New American Library, 1977), 13.

12. *CWAL*, 1: 385–386. The resemblance between the diction, tone, and/or outlook of Lincoln's final stanza and these Shakespearean verses is unmistakable. Compare the following lines from Shakespeare's plays to Lincoln's last stanza on Matthew Gentry.

> Imperious Caesar, dead and turn'd to clay, Might
> stop a hole to keep the wind away. O that that
> earth which kept the world in
>   awe
> Should patch a wall t'expel the [winter's] flaw!
>   (*Hamlet* 5.1.213–216)

>   Out, out brief candle!
> Life's but a walking shadow, a poor player,
> That struts and frets his hour upon the stage,
> And then is heard no more. It is a tale
> Told by an idiot, full of sound and fury,
> Signifying nothing.
>   (*Macbeth* 5.5.23–28)

13. *CWAL*, 1: 386–389.

14. Ibid., 3: 203.

15. Ibid., 3: 204.

16. Although such leading Lincoln authorities as Roy Basler, F. Lauriston Bullard, and Mark Neely, Jr., have accepted the letter to Bixby as written by Lincoln himself, some individuals maintain that it was authored by John Hay. And, while those in this latter school of thinking may offer ingenious suppositions and arguments to support their contentions, they cannot point to a single instance where John Hay claimed, in writing, to have authored the letter to Bixby. Indeed, according to Neely, "John Hay himself in 1904 said in a letter to New Hampshire politician William E. Chandler that the 'letter of Mr. Lincoln to Mrs. Bixby is genuine.' " In a short but thorough textual examination of the Bixby letter, Joe Nickell concluded that the "cumulative evidence clearly restores the pen to the great President's hand and reveals the Bixby letter as his own." See Mark E. Neely, Jr., *The Abraham Lincoln Ency-*

clopedia (New York: Da Capo Press, 1982), 29; Joe Nickell, "Lincoln's Bixby Letter: A Study in Authenticity," *Lincoln Herald* 91 (winter 1989): 139.

17. *CWAL*, 8: 116–117.

18. Jacques Barzun, "Lincoln the Literary Genius," *Saturday Evening Post*, 14 February 1959, 30+; Garry Wills, *Lincoln at Gettysburg: The Words That Remade America* (New York: Simon & Schuster, 1992), 148–175.

19. Barzun, "Lincoln," 64.

Part II

Style and Quality of Leadership: Lincoln as Civil War Leader

5 "I Shall Never Recall a Word"

David E. Long

It has become chic in the politically correct era of the late twentieth century to assess the merits and morality of historical personages by a standard that is relevant only to our own era. Historians afflicted with this analytical myopia are often judgmental of those figures who have traditionally been regarded as benevolent or important to the struggle against injustice. Judged by their measuring stick, Abraham Lincoln was a racist who had little relevance in the effort to extinguish slavery in the United States. He was merely a tool whose issuance of the Emancipation Proclamation was mandated by the circumstances and exigencies of the Civil War. He simply expedited the slaves' freeing themselves. By this judgment, the single most important act ever performed by an American president is relegated to the trash heap of history by people incapable of appreciating the burden that weighed upon Lincoln.

From the moment he first considered emancipating the slaves, Abraham Lincoln struggled with the awareness that he could be wrong and the knowledge that if he was, the consequences of his mistake would be the crushed hope and pain of millions to whom a promise had been made. If the promise of freedom had been defaulted upon, by a government either incapable of, or unwilling to exert, the force to make that dream come true, then the suffering of those who relied on that promise by running away or assisting Federal troops would be incalculable.

The presidency of Abraham Lincoln has been scrutinized, analyzed, and criticized under the microscope of historical inquiry by every generation of historians since the Civil War. Opinions and interpretation regarding his occupancy of the White House have sometimes possessed the ethical quality and professional scholarship of a loose cannon. Abraham Lincoln did not enjoy the luxury of having his mistakes rendered harmless. If he had acted recklessly or prematurely in encouraging slaves deep inside enemy territory to act in their own behalf in reliance on his promise of freedom, then his failure to deliver would have constituted a moral breach of contract of tremendous proportion. It would not be his back that would bear the sting of the lash; it would not be his neck that would stretch the noose that ended the spark of life. Those who would pay with their own bodies and lives would be those who had believed him, who had trusted his honor when he penned the words "forever free."

So the nineteenth-century prophets of correctness, like their twentieth-century heirs, could judge him "a first rate, second rate man"; they risked nothing in doing so, certainly not the lives of those most vulnerable to the wrath created by their rhetoric. To only a few in each generation falls the awful responsibility of having to make decisions that will affect the lives and well-being of large numbers of people. For such leaders virtually every utterance takes on a significance immeasurably greater than the same words if spoken by any of their contemporaries. Lincoln realized that as the political chief and symbol of strength of his nation at the hour of its greatest peril, it was incumbent upon him *not* to act precipitously. When he spoke publicly, he crafted the words he used like a neurosurgeon performing a delicate operation. And the masterful phrases he constructed in defense of emancipation became the scalpel that excised the cancer of slavery while saving the life of the patient.

THE EMANCIPATION PROCLAMATION

Abraham Lincoln's Emancipation Proclamation was an act of staggering importance. If it had resulted in the loss of Missouri and Kentucky to the Confederacy, thus the loss of the war by the federal government, then Lincoln would have been consigned long ago to history's hall of shame, and the powerful Western Hemisphere democracy that evolved to play such an important role in the twentieth century might not have survived the nineteenth century. If it had resulted in the large-scale desertion of Union troops from Illinois, Indiana, and Ohio, then the government would have been hard-pressed to continue the war effort and might well have had to sue for peace. Coming when it did, the Emancipation Proclamation descended like a figurative moral blockade, halting the probable intervention of the western European powers, an intervention that would have improved the prospects of Confederate independence immeasurably.

Lincoln's legal justification for the proclamation was based upon the war power, an authority not expressly stated in the Constitution. According to tradition and the laws of civilized nations, in time of war military commanders are vested with certain extraordinary powers that they do not enjoy during times of peace. The principle holds that whatever weakens the ability of the enemy to wage war effectively, thereby increases reciprocally the capability of the government to defeat that enemy. Since all legitimately constituted governments have the natural right to defend their continued existence, the exercise of some powers that would not be legal in time of peace become legal by virtue of the threat to the continuation of the government. Lincoln's adoption of "military necessity" as a justification for the proclamation resulted in support from many who otherwise would have been very reticent to endorse such a revolutionary undertaking. Thus the president could continue to insist that his primary purpose always had been and continued to be to restore the Union. He merely attached a rider to the conditions of victory that would automatically result in the destruction of slavery, which many felt had to be the focal point of the government's war efforts. That is consensus building of impressive proportion.

But in the 1990s, some would judge him tardy, reluctant to act, vacillating, dragged down the path of emancipation against his will and resisting the progress at every opportunity. Having been forced down the path by his more progressive contemporaries, some argue, he would have returned at the first chance if somebody had just offered him sufficient reason to do so. Among those who have questioned his commitment to the freedom of the slaves, there have been some highly respected Lincoln historians who have suggested that if certain things had happened in 1864 or 1865, Lincoln would have withdrawn emancipation as a condition for the peaceful return of the seceded states. To reach that conclusion, one must ferret through the bountiful evidence to the contrary, in order to locate a couple of instances in which Lincoln's words, enhanced by a very strained and creative interpretation, might permit the interpreter to make such a finding.

Could Lincoln have retracted the Emancipation Proclamation after 1 January 1863? Absolutely. After all, it was nothing more than an executive proclamation mandated by the military necessity created by the war. He could simply issue a new proclamation decreeing that since military necessity no longer compelled it, the Emancipation Proclamation was now rescinded. Or he could claim that upon subsequent consideration he had concluded that his action in issuing the proclamation had been an unconstitutional usurpation of power and thereby retroactively ordered that it was null and void. Since he clearly could have done it, the germane question becomes, Would he have done it? In considering the evidence as to whether Abraham Lincoln would have reduced the scope of the Emancipation Proclamation in any way, we must look to the period following the effective date of the proclamation, and only to that period. We must also consider what the effect would have been if he had done so and whether Lincoln was cognizant of that effect. I would suggest that nobody in 1863 was any more sensitive to the historical and political implications of the Emancipation Proclamation than was Abraham Lincoln.[1] The period when Lincoln would have been most likely to withdraw the proclamation, and the only period during which there is any evidence to suggest that he gave it serious consideration, was during the summer and fall months preceding the 1864 presidential election. It is that difficult period in Lincoln's presidency which will be the focus of this chapter.

During the year and a half prior to that election season, Lincoln's actions had demonstrated a determination to expand, not retract, the parameters of his proclamation. He had added to his requirements for reestablishing state governments in

Louisiana and other states that had come under Union control, the condition that the new governments abolish slavery.[2] The Emancipation Proclamation had not been universally applicable in these states because parts of them had not been in rebellion against the United States on 1 January 1863. One well-known Lincoln historian wrote that "He probably would not have insisted upon emancipation as an absolutely necessary step in all the rebel states, if peace without complete emancipation could have been had in the summer or fall of 1864."[3] What this statement literally means is that if all the rebels had suddenly stacked their arms and stopped resisting federal authority, then Lincoln would have considered stopping the prosecution of the war against them. Of course he would have, and that is exactly what happened on 9 April 1865. The suggestion that Lincoln might have demanded universal emancipation in the rebel states before agreeing to peace implies that if Robert E. Lee had attempted to surrender unconditionally to Ulysses S. Grant during the summer or fall of 1864, Lincoln would have ordered Grant to reject the offer and continue waging war. That is an absurd idea, and the speculation as to whether he would have accepted peace without universal emancipation in the Confederate states begs the question.

The pertinent question is, Would Lincoln have restored these states to normal relations with the federal government while they still sanctioned slavery within their borders? Would he have withdrawn Federal troops, lifted martial law, and foresworn the possibility of prosecution for treason, thereby simply restoring the status quo ante bellum? The answer to this question is no. The evidence is both clear and abundant.

There was a great deal of pressure put on Lincoln to renounce emancipation during the summer months prior to the 1864 election.[4] As usual, military events in the East were going poorly for the Union. In a campaign that had brought him no closer to Richmond than George B. McClellan had come two years earlier, Grant had employed tactics that had resulted in unprecedented casualties. Within the Confederacy a number of leaders had begun to realize that their armies could not achieve military victory over a Federal army that was determined to continue relentlessly prosecuting the war. The existence of a substantial and growing peace movement in the North, however, might be manipulated by a rebel government desperate to find an alternative to military victory. The knowledge that Lincoln had to stand for reelection that November meant he would be particularly vulnerable to any public perception that peace was attainable on reasonable terms. The rebel government dispatched so-called peace commissioners to Canada, and though they possessed no binding authority, they represented themselves otherwise.[5] Lincoln realized this, but the mercurial Horace Greeley did not and he initiated a public and potentially embarrassing (for the president) correspondence with Lincoln urging him to respond to this Confederate peace initiative. This action resulted in an exasperated Lincoln issuing a statement that he knew Greeley would eventually publish. On 9 July the president wrote a letter to the *Tribune* editor that would subsequently be used against him repeatedly in the upcoming campaign.

Washington, D.C.
July 9, 1864

Hon. Horace Greeley

Dear Sir

Your letter of the 7th, with enclosures, received. If you can find, any person anywhere professing to have any proposition of Jefferson Davis in writing, for peace, embracing the restoration of the Union and abandonment of slavery, whatever else it embraces, say to him he may come to me with you, and if he really brings such proposition, he shall, at the least, have safe conduct, with the paper (and without publicity, if he choose) to the point where you shall have met him. The same, if there be two or more persons.

Yours truly
A. Lincoln[6]

The man who signed his name to the Emancipation Proclamation at noon on 1 January 1863, would not have rescinded that order unless the life of the nation had required it. It almost did. That is not to say that Lincoln did not have occasion to second-guess the wisdom of his action. However, when the question was whether he would undo anything he had done in freeing those slaves in the areas in rebellion, whether he would have returned to slavery any person who had been freed on that first day of 1863, the answer was no. So long as he commanded armies capable of continuing the war, peace would not be had without the Emancipation Proclamation taking effect in those areas over which it claimed jurisdiction. The best evidence we have of that was provided during what was the most important campaign of the war. It was not a campaign waged on a battlefield but the one carried on to win the hearts and minds of the more than 4 million voters who would cast ballots in the 1864 presidential election.

THE DAUNTING PROSPECT OF THE ELECTION OF 1864

In the fourth year of the war, Abraham Lincoln faced a daunting prospect that no popularly elected national leader had ever faced in history. He would have to survive a national plebiscite held while the nation he led was engaged in a huge civil war. Of the previous presidents, only James Madison in 1812 had ever run for reelection while the country was at war. On that occasion, war against Great Britain had been declared only a few months before the election was to occur, the jingoism that always characterizes the nation when it goes to war was at its peak, and no significant military events had yet occurred when the people voted. None of those circumstances were present to assist Lincoln in 1864.

On the contrary, at the time of the election the war had been raging for three and a half years; the first term had been rife with controversy caused by thousands of military arrests of civilians, the issuance of hundreds of millions of dollars in paper currency, a number of stunning military reverses suffered by the army, and serious setbacks in the midterm elections of 1862. In addition, more than half a million young American soldiers were in their graves, and the president had by executive decree undertaken to extinguish an institution that had been guaranteed by the Constitution since the nation's birth and that represented several billion dollars in investment capital and assets.

As president, Lincoln enjoyed quite less than the enthusiastic support of his own political party, and a number of important Radical Republicans were eager to oust him in favor of a stronger candidate. His relations with Congress reached an all-time low during the summer of 1864, when several congressional Republicans issued a manifesto calling his pocket veto of the Wade-Davis bill the most "studied outrage on the legislative authority of the people" that had ever been perpetrated.

THE *MISCEGENATION* HOAX

In New York in the fall of 1863 the editor of the leading newspaper of the Democrats, along with a young reporter for the *New York World*, concocted a scheme specifically designed to influence the election. It was a blatant attempt to stir up the racism of the Northern voting public and at the same time embarrass the Republican Party. David Goodman Croly and George Wakeman had seen the fury of the largely Irish mob that had for several days in July 1863 controlled the streets of New York City, lynching or beating free blacks, burning a black orphanage, and terrorizing the population generally. Now in an overtly racist hoax, they drafted a seventy-two-page pamphlet entitled *Miscegenation: The Theory of the Blending of the Races, Applied to the American White Man and Negro*. No author was listed, suggesting that because the topic was so volatile and controversial the creator wished to remain anonymous. The pamphlet introduced to the American vocabulary the word *miscegenation*, a term that created enough of a sensation in 1864 that it would become a permanent fixture in the English language, at least as it is spoken on this side of the Atlantic. Noting that the word is formed from the Latin *miscere*, meaning "to mix," and *genus*, meaning "race," the tract suggested that the sexual union of whites and blacks would produce the most desirable reproductive result, offspring that would combine the best qualities of both races in a new "copper-colored" man. It claimed that in some of the "lower" orders of whites, particularly the Irish, this union would benefit the white primarily, the "more brutal race and lower in civilization than the negro." By contrast, the pamphlet claimed the black was "mild, spiritual, fond of melody and song, warm in his attachments, fervid in his passions, but inoffensive and kind."[7]

The two assertions that would most likely have produced a violent and emotional response in the typical nineteenth-century white American male was that his sister or daughter could or should mate with a black man and that he himself was intellectually and culturally inferior to Americans of African descent. Croly, who was born in Ireland, and Wakeman were very aware of this likelihood and purposely sought language they knew would inspire the strongest response. But they did not intend to produce great literature; they sought to produce something that would convince antislavery activists that its creator was a well-intentioned, even if naive, kindred spirit in the cause. At that they succeeded.

In December 1863 they sent advance copies of the pamphlet to leading abolitionists and Republicans along with a cover letter inviting the readers to respond in
writing to a New York post office box. These copies were sent to almost every
well-known antislavery figure from Wendell Phillips and William Lloyd Garrison
to Charles Sumner and William Seward. When they responded, their words would
be published conspicuously in the Democratic press, thereby embarrassing Republicans and alienating them from many potential voters. Although no leading figure
of the Republican Party made the mistake of responding, several prominent abolitionists did, including Lucretia Mott, Sarah and Angelina Grimke, and Parker Pillsbury.

What *Miscegenation* did accomplish was to inspire an enormous and venomous
editorial campaign among most of the important newspapers from New England
to Philadelphia. During the spring months all of the eastern seaboard press waged
a frenzied campaign of accusation and counter-accusation based on whether a
newspaper had endorsed or condemned the tract. This campaign was inspired in
part by a speech given on the floor of the House of Representatives by Samuel
"Sunset" Cox of Ohio, the Democratic candidate for Speaker in the Thirty-eighth
Congress. Cox's speech was delivered on 17 February during the debate regarding
the Freedman's Bureau bill. He cited the letters of Mott, Pillsbury, and others, in
response to the anonymous author. He claimed that those letters were unqualified
endorsements of the ideas presented by *Miscegenation* and that it would be only a
matter of time before the Republican Party would join the bandwagon.[8] When the
Democratic press published Cox's speech across the country, the Republican press
responded and the battle was on. It continued without diminishing in intensity
until June, when other events began to make Democratic prospects of gaining the
White House look much brighter.

Though the subject of miscegenation would command less news print during
the summer and fall months, the frenzy of racist rhetoric that it inspired continued
up to election day. Stories of abolitionist schoolmistresses from New England al-
legedly giving birth to mulatto babies on the sea islands off the Carolinas were featured prominently. The slightest rumor of a black Federal soldier abusing a
Southern woman or acting insubordinately toward a white officer was given head-
line coverage by the Democratic press. Invariably the articles blamed such atrocities
on Lincoln and his "Abolitionist Party." The Democrats saw Lincoln and the ante-
bellum antislavery zealots as fellow travelers, though probably few genuine abolitionists would have agreed with the characterization.

There is evidence to suggest that the *Miscegenation* hoax was not merely the idi-
otic scheme of a couple of pranksters at the *New York World*; it may very well have
involved a conspiracy that extended to the highest leadership of the national
Democratic Party. When "Sunset" Cox delivered his tirade against *Miscegenation*
and its Republican advocates, he was aware of who had responded to the tract,
though their letters had been sent to an anonymous post office box. That post office box had been rented by Croly and Wakeman, and knowledge of the contents
of correspondence addressed to that box had to originate from them. After the

Civil War, Cox revealed in his *Memoirs and Speeches* that the tract *Miscegenation* "was written by two young men connected with the New York press. So congenial were its sentiments with those of the leading Abolitionists, and so ingeniously was its irony disguised, that it was not only endorsed by the fanatical leaders all over the land, but no one in Congress thought of questioning the genuineness and serious-ness of the document."[9] Cox was one of the leading Democrats in the House of Representatives and during 1863 had frequently corresponded with Manton Mar-ble, one of the most powerful Democratic power brokers in the country and the owner and editor of the *New York World*.[10] Marble had purposely built the *World* up to be the leading journalistic organ of the Democrats in the country, and it syndi-cated many of its stories about the war, which were picked up by Democratic newspapers across the United States.

In November 1863, Cox had declined an invitation to attend the dedication cer-emony at Gettysburg in order to meet with Marble in New York. The purpose of that meeting was to discuss Cox's request that Marble support him for the speaker-ship in the upcoming Congress. Their meeting would have taken place at the time Croly and Wakeman were finishing their composition of *Miscegenation*. It is very likely that Marble either introduced Cox to Croly and Wakeman or discussed their scheme with him in the expectation that the congressman would be the vehicle for exposing the anticipated respondents on the floor of Congress. In that way the *World* would be protected from exposure, while a controversial speech on the floor of the House of Representatives would certainly be picked up by the press. Re-publican embarrassment could be exploited without implicating the *World*. That Cox knew the true source and inspiration for the publication of the tract is admit-ted in his *Memoirs and Speeches* published the year after the war ended, though he did not at that time reveal who the two young men were. There is no indication of a connection between Cox and Croly or Wakeman, except for their common as-sociation with Manton Marble. As managing editor vested with the day-to-day op-eration of the newspaper, Croly was in virtual daily communication with the owner/editor, and it is difficult to imagine that the employee would have involved the *World* in a scheme as potentially damaging (if it became known before the elec-tion) as the *Miscegenation* hoax, without apprising Marble and gaining his approval. And if Marble knew about the scheme and supported or acquiesced in it, then it was a conspiracy that reached the highest level of leadership in the national Demo-cratic Party.

DEMOCRATIC OPPOSITION

No Democratic energy was left unexpended in the quest to characterize Lincoln and his racial policies as the cause of the continuation of the war. Though much of this effort appears ridiculous to observers in 1994, in 1864 it had a tremendous im-pact. The combination of war weariness, the absence of military successes during those long summer months, and the growing feeling that the rebels could not be defeated militarily, gave rise to a very substantial peace movement in the Northern states. Relentless Democratic hammering at the theme that the president had usurped his constitutional authority by converting the war into a personal vendetta against slavery and slaveholders began seriously to undermine the resolve of the people to continue the struggle.

By August, Lincoln had sunk to the depths of despair. Many prominent Republicans had come to the conclusion that he would be defeated in November and that their only hope was to hold another convention and nominate a different candidate. General Benjamin Butler, the taste of political office ever in his mouth, was being seriously considered for the position. One of Butler's admirers, following a two-hour conversation with the prominent New York politico, Thurlow Weed, wrote to the general that Weed felt Lincoln could be persuaded to withdraw. Also around this time Weed told Lincoln candidly "that his reelection was an impossibility." Several days later, writing to William Seward from a meeting of Republican state chairmen, he said of Lincoln's imminent defeat, "Nobody here doubts it; nor do I see anybody from other States who authorizes the slightest hope of success." Also, "The people are wild for peace. They are told that the President will only listen to terms of Peace on condition Slavery be 'abandoned.' " Leonard Swett, longtime friend and political ally of the president, had tested the waters of public opinion and was in apparent agreement with Weed's assessment.[11] And then Lincoln received a letter from his campaign manager, Henry Raymond, which demonstrated just how dismal the picture was.

I feel compelled to drop you a line concerning the political condition of the country as it strikes me. I am in active correspondence with your staunchest friends in every state and from them all I hear but one report. The Tide is setting strongly against us. Hon. E. B. Washburne writes that "were an election to be held now in Illinois we should be beaten." Mr. Cameron writes that Pennsylvania is against us. Gov. Morton writes that nothing but the most strenuous efforts can carry Indiana. This State [New York], according to the best information I can get, would go 50,000 against us to-morrow. And so of the rest.[12]

Raymond went on to point out why Lincoln would be defeated. "Two special causes are assigned for this great reaction in public sentiment—the want of military successes, and the impression in some minds, the fear and suspicion in others, that we are not to have peace *in any event* under this administration until Slavery is abandoned. In some way or other the suspicion is widely diffused that we *can* have peace with Union if we would."[13]

THE PEACE COMMISSION

Raymond proposed a political stratagem that might help to stanch and perhaps even reverse the loss of popular support. He suggested that Lincoln appoint a special commission "to make [a] distinct proffer of peace to Davis, as the head of the rebel armies, on the sole condition of acknowledging the supremacy of the Constitution, all other questions to be settled in a convention of the states." Raymond

was suggesting that Lincoln withdraw his oft-uttered second condition for peace
. . . the abolition of slavery. But there he pointed out that it would not really be
abandoning slavery, for "if it should be rejected, (as it would be), it would plant
seeds of disaffection in the South, dispel all the delusions about peace that prevail in
the North," and thus would "unite the North as nothing since the firing on Fort
Sumter" had done. "Even your radical friends could not fail to applaud it when
they should see the practical strength it would bring to the common cause."[14]

It is difficult to imagine what Abraham Lincoln was going through at this stage
in his life. He had led the nation for three and a half years through its most trying
ordeal and had successfully brought it to the brink of victory over a massive internal
rebellion. While doing so he had also struck a death blow at slavery, that terrible
blemish on American democracy. Yet having led the nation to the point that that
glorious victory was within reach, he was about to be turned out of office by the
people, because the greater triumph of freedom and democracy no longer burned
as a vision held in common by a war-weary population. The sacrifice of more than
half a million lives, and the incomprehensible misery and suffering by many thousands of others, among whom were the slaves who had believed his promise of
emancipation, were in jeopardy of becoming the ugly byproduct of a meaningless
and destructive civil war. Moreover, not only was he going to be defeated while
victory was so near; he was going to lose to George B. McClellan, the man who
had repeatedly displayed contempt and ingratitude in relations with his commander in chief. One of the reasons he would lose was the presence in the race of a
third-party candidate, John Charles Fremont, the other general officer who had
been openly contemptuous and disrespectful in his conduct toward the president.
Fremont had been the nominee of the Republicans in 1856. In 1864 he was nominated by a group of radical abolitionists, dominated by Germans from Missouri
who regarded Lincoln and his administration as too conservative regarding slavery.
Any votes this candidate received in November would be votes that would have
gone to Lincoln in a two-man race.

For the first time in his political life, Abraham Lincoln sought election not because of a driving ambition to scale the ladder of political success. At the September 1862 Cabinet meeting at which he read his preliminary Emancipation
Proclamation, he had said:

I know very well that many others might . . . do better than I can; and if I was satisfied that
the public confidence was more fully possessed by anyone of them than by me, and knew of
any constitutional way in which he could be put in my place, he should have it. I would
gladly yield it to him. But though I believe that I have not so much of the confidence of the
people as I had some time since, I do not know that . . . any other person has more; and . . .
there is no way in which I can have any other man put where I am. I am here. I must do the
best I can and bear the responsibility of taking the course which I feel I ought to take.[15]

On that occasion, just as in 1864, there were questions of such importance that
personal gain and achievement paled into irrelevance. The future of the United

States as the geographical entity which he had been elected to serve in 1860, hung in the balance. The future of millions of people born into slavery and then given the hope of freedom, hung in the balance. The significance and meaning of hundreds of thousands of lives lost in the service of their country hung in the balance. In light of those stakes, even a man as possessed of integrity and character as Abraham Lincoln had to be tempted to resort to some political chicanery. And he was. The president gave very serious consideration to Raymond's proposed peace commission.

On 23 August, the day after Lincoln received Raymond's dispatch, he attended a Cabinet meeting and passed around the famous blind memorandum, sight unseen, requesting each of the secretaries to sign on the outside of the sealed document. Inside was a memorandum that he had composed that morning.

This morning, as for some days past, it seems exceedingly probable that this Administration will not be re-elected. Then it will be my duty to so co-operate with the President elect, as to save the Union between the election and the inauguration; as he will have secured his election on such ground that he cannot possibly save it afterwards.[16]

Clearly Lincoln accepted the likelihood of his defeat in November. He also knew that he was right in not recanting on his two conditions for peace, restoration of the Union and abandonment of slavery. Yet lesser men than he had been right and stood on principle only to lose election or be turned out of office. Was he truly doing what was best for his nation and his people in refusing to participate in a political ploy that might still save all of those noble goals? On 17 August in a letter to a War Democrat who had expressed concern that Lincoln had broadened the goals of the war to include the destruction of slavery, the president had said:

On this point, nearly a year ago, in a letter to Mr. Conkling, made public at once, I wrote as follows: "But negroes, like other people, act upon motives. Why should they do anything for us if we will do nothing for them? If they stake their lives for us they must be prompted by the strongest motive—even the promise of freedom. And the promise, being made, must be kept." I am sure you will not, on due reflection, say that the promise being made, must be *broken* at the first opportunity. I am sure you would not desire me to say or to leave an inference, that I am ready, whenever convenient, to join in re-enslaving those who shall have served us in consideration of our promise.[17]

In a 19 August meeting with the former governor of Wisconsin and a judge, Lincoln said, "There have been those who have proposed to me to return to slavery the black warriors of Port Hudson & Olustee to their masters to conciliate the South. I should be damned in time & in eternity for so doing. The world shall know that I will keep my faith to friends & enemies come what will."[18] It was a restatement of the position that Lincoln had eloquently stated time and again since issuing the Emancipation Proclamation at the beginning of 1863. But in August 1864 these words must have begun to ring hollow to Abraham Lincoln, as he contemplated that having assumed the mantle of responsibility for freeing the slaves in the Confederate states, he was about to lose control of that office which had made it possible for him to undertake that task.

Upon receipt of Raymond's letter, Lincoln wavered. He composed the peace commission, which, if it became an official document, would reduce to meaningless rhetoric all those marvelous defenses of his policy that had been stated repeatedly over the previous twenty months.

To Henry J. Raymond   Washington, August 24, 1864

Sir:

You will proceed forthwith and obtain, if possible, a conference for peace with Hon. Jefferson Davis, or any person by him authorized for that purpose.

You will address him in entirely respectful terms, at all events, and in any that may be indispensable to secure the conference.

At said conference you will propose, on behalf of this government, that upon the restoration of the Union and the national authority, the war shall cease at once, all remaining questions to be left for adjustment by peaceful modes. If this be accepted hostilities to cease at once.

If it be not accepted, you will then request to be informed what terms, if any embracing the restoration of the Union, would be accepted. If any such be presented you in answer, you will forthwith report the same to this government, and await further instructions.

If the presentation of any terms embracing the restoration of the Union be declined, you will then request to be informed what terms of peace would, be accepted; and on receiving any answer, report the same to this government, and await further instructions.[19]

On 24 August 1864, Lincoln considered reneging on the demand for emancipation. It is true that he was as certain as Raymond was that the proposal would be rejected and that this would hurt the Confederate government with its constituents, while the Federal government would probably benefit politically. However, much of what was good and decent about the government, about the act of the president in issuing the Emancipation Proclamation, about the course of a nation seeking to achieve a better kind of democracy, one in which freedom and equality were goals to be sought, would have been lost. The Emancipation Proclamation would simply fade back into that realm of all other political acts, a pawn to be maneuvered on a chessboard of compromise. The single most noble and unselfish act ever undertaken by an American statesman would lose much of its lustre.

If *ever* there was a time when Abraham Lincoln would have withdrawn emancipation as a condition of peace, it would have been during that last week of August 1864. The Raymond commission, however, never became an official document, because by 25 August, when Henry Raymond arrived in Washington and came to the White House, Lincoln had decided that he could not proceed with the plan. The president had met with Secretaries Seward, Stanton, and Fessenden and discussed Raymond's proposition. They had concurred in the opinion that to send a peace commission to Richmond would be worse than losing the presidential contest; it would amount to an ignominious surrender.[20]

We will never know how seriously Lincoln considered the peace commission. In *Abraham Lincoln: A History*, the president's secretaries claim that he never considered the plan seriously, that he wrote the experimental draft of instructions solely to facilitate examination and discussion of the question.[21] After all, Henry Raymond was an important man, and it would be unwise simply to reject his suggestion without giving it serious consideration. Or the written appointment drafted by him on 24 August may simply have been another example of Lincoln's playing devil's advocate with himself regarding a difficult question. He had always applied Euclidean logic and argument as he attempted to make the case for every side of an issue, thereby eliminating the least meritorious as he developed what he considered the best position. Or possibly he intended on 24 August when he drafted the commission actually to assign Raymond to carry it out. If so, it was a very tenuous commitment, because twenty-four hours later he had changed his mind or been persuaded by others to hold to his original position.

It was the Raymond peace commission that has often been cited as evidence of Lincoln's lack of commitment to emancipation. The other item was his 17 August letter to a War Democrat, the editor of the *Green Bay Advocate*, to whom he wrote, "To me it seems plain that saying re-union and abandonment of slavery would be considered, if offered, is not saying that nothing *else* or *less* would be considered, if offered." He concluded the letter, "If Jefferson Davis wishes . . . to know what I would do if he were to offer peace and re-union, saying nothing about slavery, let him try me."[22] This was hardly a spread-eagle declaration that he would drop emancipation if the rebel president merely proposed peace and re-union. In fact, it was a "safe" statement for Lincoln, since he already knew from several Northern peace emissaries who had traveled to Richmond that nothing short of independence would satisfy Davis and the South. When historians suggest that Lincoln's 17 August letter evidenced his willingness to drop emancipation, if only Jeff Davis would have requested it, they descend into illogic and speculation. The president's political standing was no better on 25 August than it had been on 17 August. On the latter date he would not approve a peace commission that he was certain would not be acceptable to the rebel leader, because to do so would appear to compromise the commitment of the government to the freedom of the slaves. The idea that Lincoln would have been willing a week earlier, before he heard the bad news from Raymond, to drop emancipation if only his Southern counterpart would initiate the dialogue, simply makes no sense. Moreover, the 17 August letter, like the Raymond peace commission, never left Lincoln's office. The fact that it remained unmailed would indicate that the author determined that it would not be appropriate for publication as a statement of his position. Thus, Lincoln critics who questioned his commitment to emancipation in 1864 ultimately had to harken back to his letter to Horace Greeley on 22 August 1862, in which he had said, "My paramount objective in this struggle is to save the Union, and is not either to save or to destroy slavery."[23] That communication was sent more than four months before the issuance of the Emancipation Proclamation, and like anything else that occurred prior to 1 January 1863, is irrelevant to the question of whether Lincoln would or would not have withdrawn the promise of freedom once it had been made.

A RISE IN FORTUNE

With the end of August both Lincoln's and the nation's fortunes improved remarkably. Meeting in Chicago the last three days of that month, the Democrats seemingly tried to pull the Republicans back into the race by adopting a peace platform that condemned the war effort as a failure. That provision of the Democratic national platform which has often been referred to as the "war failure" plank was the plank the Democrats would walk to their political death in 1864.[24] Hardly had the Democrats adjourned in Chicago than the War Department received news from Georgia: "Atlanta is ours and fairly won." The fall of this second most important city still in Confederate possession was a victory of enormous strategic and symbolic importance. This victory, along with David Glasgow Farragut's dramatic victory at Mobile Bay several weeks earlier, meant that the war took on a whole new complexion in the North. The fall of Atlanta was the death knell of the Confederacy and everybody knew it.

Republicans who had been so ambivalent about their loyalties to Lincoln in August now started to work in earnest, campaigning for the reelection of their ticket. Zachariah Chandler undertook a whirlwind excursion between New York and Washington in an attempt to broker Fremont's withdrawal from the race.[25] The sacrificial lamb was the postmaster general, Montgomery Blair, who had long been despised by the Radicals. In return for Blair's resignation, Fremont reluctantly withdrew his name from consideration for the presidency. Then in October, having carried out a scorched-earth campaign in the Shenandoah Valley while inflicting a series of defeats on Jubal Early's Army of the Valley, diminutive Phil Sheridan made his famous ride at Cedar Creek, rallying his fleeing troops to return and inflict a devastating, and final, defeat on Early's army, which had earlier in the day achieved conspicuous success in surprising and routing the bluecoats. Sheridan's ride from Winchester became part of American folklore as songs and poems were composed about the general and his fire-breathing horse Rienzi.

In the West Copperhead plots to attack Federal camps housing Confederate prisoners, were revealed. These accounts lent credence to Republican accusations of domestic treason. In October state elections were held in the key states of Indiana, Ohio, and Pennsylvania. Since Indiana did not have absentee balloting for soldiers, thousands of Hoosiers were furloughed home to vote. Republicans were victorious in all three states, though the vote in Pennsylvania was very close and left the Keystone State in doubt for November. On 13 October Abraham Lincoln sat in the War Department telegraph office and wrote a prediction. He guessed that McClellan would carry New York, Pennsylvania, Illinois, New Jersey, Missouri, Kentucky, Maryland, and Delaware, for a total of 114 electoral votes. He would carry the rest, gaining 117 electors.[26] He was right about the outcome, but he missed the margin of victory by a mile.

On 8 November 1864, George McClellan won the states of Kentucky, Delaware, and New Jersey, gaining 21 electoral votes. Abraham Lincoln won the rest of the states, gathering 212 electoral votes and 55 percent of the popular vote.

The only presidential election that had been more one-sided had been Thomas Jefferson's reelection in 1804. The president treated the victory as a popular referendum on emancipation and set to work immediately to assure that the Emancipation Proclamation would never have to undergo Supreme Court scrutiny. He wanted to resolve the matter of slavery in those parts of the country that had been exempted from the proclamation, and he wanted to assure that no future president or court could undo the work he had begun.

In his State of the Union message in December, he addressed the lame-duck session of the Thirty-eighth Congress and challenged its members again to consider a proposed constitutional amendment abolishing slavery.

At the last session of Congress a proposed amendment of the Constitution abolishing slavery throughout the United States, passed the Senate, but failed for lack of the requisite two-thirds vote in the House of Representatives. Although the present is the same Congress, and nearly the same members, and without questioning the wisdom or patriotism of those who stood in opposition, I venture to recommend the reconsideration and passage of the measure at the present session. Of course the abstract question is not changed; but an intervening election shows, almost certainly, that the next Congress will pass the measure if this does not. Hence there is only a question of time as to when the proposed amendment will go to the States for their action. And as it is to so go, at all events, may we not agree that the sooner the better? It is not claimed that the election has imposed a duty on members to change their views or their votes, any further than, as an additional element to be considered, their judgment may be affected by it. It is the voice of the people now, for the first time, heard upon the question. In a great national crisis, like ours, unanimity of action among those seeking a common end is very desirable—almost indispensable. And yet no approach to such unanimity is attainable, unless some deference shall be paid to the will of the majority, simply because it is the will of the majority. In this case the common end is the maintenance of the Union; and, among the means to secure that end, such will, through the election, is most clearly declared in favor of such constitutional amendment.[27]

Lincoln had expressed the meaning and importance of that election. As he correctly stated, it was "the voice of the people . . . for the first time, heard upon the question." The people had spoken, and the president now determined to use their mandate to purge forever that institution which had caused such division and barred true progress toward the achievement of the democratic ideal. In January the enabling legislation for the proposed Thirteenth Amendment came before the House of Representatives for a vote. The previous June the amendment had fallen thirteen votes short of the two-thirds majority needed for the passage.[28] But during December and January, Lincoln and Seward had courted many lame-duck Democrats, using the patronage of the presidency, promising appointments to politicians who had been defeated at the polls in November. Sixteen of them voted for the legislation, and along with a unanimous yes vote from the Republicans, the final tally was 119 for, 58 against.[29] Abraham Lincoln's journey had been completed; it came less than two and one half months before the end of the war and his assassination.

THE POSSIBILITY OF McCLELLAN

Probably no event in American history has given rise to as many "what if" questions as the Civil War. Yet the most compelling question of them all, and the one that sets the 1864 election apart as a political event without peer, is what would have happened had George McClellan been elected president. Though any such question invites a certain amount of speculation, there are several aspects of McClellan's character that suggest that he would have proceeded very differently than Abraham Lincoln. He was no friend to the African American. In the immediate aftermath of the preliminary Emancipation Proclamation he wrote to his wife:

It is very doubtful whether I shall remain in the service after the rebels have left this vicinity. The Presdt's late Proclamation, the continuation of Stanton and Halleck in office render it almost impossible for me to retain my commission & self-respect at the same time. I cannot make up my mind to fight for such an accursed doctrine as that of a servile insurrection—it is too infamous.[30]

On 7 July 1862, while his defeated army huddled at Harrison's Landing in the aftermath of the Seven Days battles, George McClellan turned statesman as he offered advice to the visiting president of the United States. In a letter he presented to Lincoln that day, McClellan advised his commander-in-chief:

Neither forcible confiscation of property . . . or forcible abolition of slavery should be contemplated for a moment. . . . Military power should not be allowed to interfere with the relations of servitude, either by supporting or impairing the authority of the master. . . . A declaration of radical views, especially upon slavery, will rapidly disintegrate our present Armies.[31]

In July 1864, when McClellan's popularity as the potential Democratic candidate for president was peaking, he wrote that the original purpose of the war, "the preservation of the Union, its Constitution and its laws, had been lost sight of, or very widely departed from," and that other issues have been brought into the foreground which "either should be entirely secondary, or are wrong or impossible of attainment." He thought that the war had taken a course that "unnecessarily embitters the inimical feeling between the two sections, and much increases the difficulty of attaining the true objects for which we ought to fight." He concluded that he disliked "a policy which far from tending to that end tends in the contrary direction."[32]

That McClellan would have done nothing to advance the cause of emancipation is clear. What he might have done to retard or reverse it remains problematical. However, the larger question in terms of the future of the nation and the end of slavery was what he would have done regarding the continuation of the war. The second plank of the Democratic Party platform had called for immediate efforts to "be made for a cessation of hostilities." Though McClellan's letter of acceptance does not clearly reject the notion of a cease-fire (an event most Civil War historians agree would have meant the end of the conflict regardless of what followed thereafter), he also does not embrace it. His letter is ambiguous. Nevertheless, his possible course may be suggested by several letters written by others. The New York businessman S. L. M. Barlow, McClellan's principal adviser in the campaign, wrote to Manton Marble on the eve of the Democratic convention attempting to assure the substantial peace wing of the party as to the general's intentions if he were elected. "The General is for peace, not war. . . . If he is nominated, he would prefer to restore the Union by peaceful means, rather than by war."[33] And a St. Louis businessman who was well acquainted with McClellan wrote on 24 August that the candidate had told him, "If I am elected, I will recommend an immediate armistice and a call for a convention of all the states and insist upon exhausting all and every means to secure peace without further bloodshed."[34] It is virtually certain that McClellan's election to office without announcing an immediate cease-fire would have resulted in an open split within the Democratic Party ranks. The very sizable minority, and perhaps even a majority, of the party that had been calling for peace at any price would condemn the new president they had just helped to elect, and they might finally resort to the desperate tactics of insurgency, which had bubbled close to the surface for the previous two years. The prospect of four more years under a president determined to continue prosecuting the war, after they had demonstrated their party loyalty by supporting his candidacy, would probably have been regarded as the ultimate perfidy propelling them to armed insurrection against the government. If George McClellan had attempted to continue the prosecution of the war, he would have quickly learned that he had even fewer friends as president than had Abraham Lincoln. Even had he wanted to, President McClellan might have found it impossible to establish the consensus in support of his administration that would have made possible the successful conclusion of the war effort by the federal government.

A MANDATE FOR EMANCIPATION

Many political commentators and historians would disagree with Lincoln's interpretation of his reelection as a mandate for emancipation and the Thirteenth Amendment. They would argue that the sole determinant in how the decisive ballots were cast in 1864 was success or failure on the battlefield. That is an interpretation which probably gives less credit to nineteenth-century voters and to Lincoln than they should be accorded. Certainly the prospect of a successful conclusion to the war within the foreseeable future was a conditional precedent for many voters to support Lincoln. That should be obvious. Very few people would have voted to continue interminably the kind of devastating warfare that this conflict had brought to the North American continent. Nevertheless, if a successful conclusion to the war was foreseeable, then many of them would support the effort to achieve that end. Federal victory would obviously bring a revolutionary change in the social and economic relations between Americans of European descent and Americans of African descent. The Democrats had conducted a loud and virulently racist campaign in order to ensure that voters were fully aware of that. And Abraham Lincoln had never sought to mislead voters regarding his view of slavery and its relationship to the war, and the program of change that he employed in order to end the war.

Therefore, very few voters who cast a ballot for Abraham Lincoln in 1864 could claim to be unaware of what his reelection meant in terms of slavery. Since he had mandated the most revolutionary change in American political history during his first term in office, it was hardly a subject about which voters would not have been interested when they cast their ballots in 1864. A voter who opposed emancipation and yet cast his ballot for Lincoln knew that his vote helped to bring about the very thing that he opposed. Since this action is less logical than the conclusion that most voters casting their ballots for Lincoln also supported the president's racial policies, I would suggest the latter interpretation has greater merit.

In conclusion, most voters who supported Lincoln in the 1864 election also approved of his policies as to slavery. Many of those voters might have voted against him if they believed that emancipation was responsible for the continuation of the war and that the war would drag on for a long period of time and cost many thousands more lives. Thus the achievement of significant military successes in September and October made it possible for many voters to cast their ballots in accordance with their belief in the propriety of Lincoln's racial policies.

The 1864 election was the most important electoral event in American history. It was a watershed occurrence that determined the direction of the nation in the twentieth century and guaranteed that the American people would enter that century as one nation undivided. The election marked a division between the United States as it was prior to 1861 and the United States as it has been since 1864. Abraham Lincoln's insistence on the abolition of slavery as a condition of peace in the months before the election, particularly when his prospects for reelection were gloomiest, was an act of unsurpassed political courage and integrity. Such a singular act of human decency and political consequence should not lose its dignity to the ravages of revisionism.

NOTES

1. Francis B. Carpenter, *Six Months at the White House with Abraham Lincoln* (New York: Hurd & Houghton, 1866), 87, 269.

2. John G. Nicolay and John Hay, *Abraham Lincoln: A History* (New York: The Century Co., 1890), 8: 410–411, 421–424.

3. Richard N. Current, *The Lincoln Nobody Knows* (New York: Hill & Wang, 1958) chap. 10; James A. Rawley, *Turning Points of the Civil War* (Lincoln: University of Nebraska Press, 1966), 185–188.

4. Abraham Lincoln, *The Collected Works of Abraham Lincoln*, (New Brunswick, N.J.: Rutgers University Press in association with the Abraham Lincoln Association, 1953–55), 8: 459, 499–501, 501n, 506–508, 514n, 517, 517n (hereafter cited as *CWAL*).

5. Ibid., 8: 442, 459–460.

6. Ibid., 8: 435–436.

7. David Goodman Croly and George Wakeman, *Miscegenation: The Theory of the Blending of the Races, Applied to the American White Man and Negro* (New York, 1863), 7: 361.

8. Samuel S. Cox, *Memoirs and Speeches: Eight Years in Congress from 1857–1865* (New York: D. Appleton & Co., 1866), 361.

9. Ibid., 352.

10. Manton Marble Papers, Library of Congress.

11. James G. Randall and Richard N. Current, *Lincoln the President: Last Full Measure* (Chicago: Dodd, Mead & Co., 1955), 4: 213.

12. *CWAL*, 7: 517.

13. Ibid.

14. Ibid.

15. J. W. Schuckers, *The Life and Public Services of Salmon Portland Chase* (New York: D. Appleton & Co., 1874), 453–455.

16. *CWAL*, 7: 514.

17. Ibid., 7: 500.

18. Ibid., 7: 507.

19. Ibid., 7: 517.

20. Ibid., 7: 518n.

21. Nicolay and Hay, *Abraham Lincoln*, 9: 220.

22. *CWAL*, 7: 499–501.

23. Frank Moore, ed., *The Rebellion Record* (New York: Van Nostrand, 1871), 12: 482–483.

24. Nicolay and Hay, *Abraham Lincoln*, 9: 220.

25. Zachariah Chandler to Mrs. Chandler, 27 August 1864; 28 August 1864; 2 September 1864; 6 September 1864; 8 September 1864; 18 September 1864; 24 September 1864; Benjamin Franklin Wade to Zachariah Chandler, 15 September 1864; 2 October 1864. Zachariah Chandler Papers, Library of Congress.

26. *CWAL*, 8: 46.

27. Ibid., 8: 149.

28. Edward McPherson, *The Political History of the United States of America during the Great Rebellion, from November 6, 1860 to July 4, 1864* (New York: Philip & Solomons, 1864), 259.

29. Nicolay and Hay, *Abraham Lincoln*, 10: 80–90.

30. McClellan to Mary Ellen McClellan, 25 September 1862, McClellan Papers, Library of Congress.

31. McClellan to Abraham Lincoln, 7 July 1862, *The War of the Rebellion: A Compilation of the Records of the Union and Confederate Armies* (Washington, D.C.: Government Printing Office, 1890–1901), ser. 2, vol. 1, 567–568.

32. McClellan to Francis P. Blair, 22 July 1864, McClellan Papers, Library of Congress.

33. S. L. M. Barlow to Manton Marble, 24 August 1864, Barlow Papers, The Huntington Library. San Marino, Calif., reprinted by permission.

34. James Harrison to Louis V. Bogy, 24 August 1864, Clement C. Clay Papers, National Archives, quoted in *Confederate Operations in Canada and the North*, by Oscar A. Kinchen (North Quincy, Mass.: Christopher Publishing, 1970), 93.

6 Lincoln and Grant: A Reappraisal of a Relationship

Brooks D. Simpson

Perhaps the most important relationship that Abraham Lincoln formed during the American Civil War was the one with the man who would eventually lead the Union armies to victory—Ulysses S. Grant. For Lincoln, more than most people, knew that in the end the war would be won or lost on the battlefield. "Upon the progress of our arms," he admitted in his second inaugural address, "all else chiefly depends."[1] Yet the relationship between the president and the general has not received much scholarly scrutiny. Instead, the majority of historians and biographers have chosen to follow a rather standard account, one that places great emphasis on Lincoln's patience, foresight, and insight as he watched Grant develop into a great commander and stood unflinchingly behind his general. J. F. C. Fuller, one of the foremost experts on Grant's military career, proclaimed that Lincoln "unfailingly supported him" in dark times.[2] T. Harry Williams asserted that Lincoln "marked [Grant] as great" before Vicksburg and followed Grant's progress closely and approvingly during the general's western campaigns. Lincoln, according to Williams, "had little fear that Grant would fail."[3] Grant biographer William Brooks agreed, remarking that "Lincoln had stood by Grant through all the bitter clamor of the earlier years when he seemed his only friend."[4] William McFeely argued that as early as Fort Donelson Lincoln viewed Grant as a "pivotal figure" in the war.[5] More recently, Joseph T. Glatthaar has claimed that the Lincoln-Grant relationship offers a prime example of the cooperation necessary to succeed in war.[6]

A somewhat more contested part of the standard account is the notion that when Grant came east to assume supreme command, Lincoln gave him a free hand. Grant himself helped to create this image, writing that all Lincoln had ever wanted was a general to take charge. The publication of Williams's *Lincoln and His Generals* in 1952 changed that account somewhat, for Williams pointed to several instances where the president overruled the general. This view gave a twist to the old story:

henceforth most historians and biographers suggested that if Lincoln interfered at all, it was to save Grant from error. Still, old stories die hard: Warren Hassler contrasted Lincoln's restraint with Grant to his meddling with George B. McClellan, while Benjamin Thomas maintained that Lincoln, "for the most part," declined to interfere with Grant.[7]

A closer look, however, reveals that the traditional story is in need of modification. First, Lincoln did very little out of the usual to promote Grant's career. Grant's rise to command commenced as a result of the parceling out of patronage, and it gathered steam as a result of his battlefield accomplishments, not because of Lincoln's foresight. The president failed to remove Grant from command when the general came under attack, although he did not refrain from taking such action due to any especial confidence in him. Indeed, on several occasions Lincoln considered superseding Grant. Second, Lincoln most definitely did not give Grant a free hand as general in chief. Contrary to Williams's portrait of Lincoln as the wise and provident coordinator of strategy in the war's final year, it was the president's justifiable concern with politics that shaped Grant's planning in critical ways, not all of which enhanced military prospects. Finally, one key and often overlooked component of the Lincoln-Grant relationship is the role played by Grant—a role in which the general displayed shrewdness, patience, and common sense, as well as an understanding of Lincoln's position. Perhaps in trying to present Lincoln as a great military strategist we have overlooked the extent to which Grant understood the politics of civil-military relations and exploited them for his advancement.

LINCOLN'S ROLE IN GRANT'S CAREER

Lincoln did not pick Grant out of a crowd at the beginning of the war, although postwar tales attempted to suggest that such was the case. Grant's promotion to brigadier general in 1861 was owing to the political influence of Congressman Elihu Washburne, not to presidential prescience. Lincoln supposedly commented favorably on Grant's September 1861 proclamation to the citizens of Paducah, assuring that town's residents of the limited aims of the Union war effort; but after Grant had engaged a Confederate force at Belmont, Missouri, the following November, it was one of his subordinates, John A. McClernand, who received a warm letter from the president.[8] Indeed, to the extent that Lincoln paid special attention to Grant, it was not the sort of attention Grant welcomed. Much has been made of Lincoln's cavalier attitude toward stories of Grant's drinking. Yet that was not always true. When reports reached the president of Grant's drinking in early 1862, Lincoln submitted the reports to Washburne for comment.[9]

Lincoln's skepticism was justified, for he knew little of Grant. It would not be until February 1862 that Grant would take his place among the nation's heroes by accepting the surrender of Fort Donelson. Lincoln honored Grant with another promotion, this time to major general of volunteers. But it would be hard to argue that this post represented foresight rather than reward, just as Grant's promotion to brigadier was a byproduct of patronage rather than a sign of trust—and the president failed to offer the general his personal congratulations.[10] Before long Lincoln did help Grant out by protecting him from critics who urged his removal. When in March 1862 Henry W. Halleck attempted to put Grant aside by charging that he was irresponsible and possibly intoxicated, Lincoln stepped in and demanded that Halleck either prove his charges or drop them.[11] Lincoln also refused to remove Grant after Shiloh, when the general suffered heavy criticism, and in the early stages of the Vicksburg campaign, when Grant's inability to get at the Confederate fortress once again encouraged his critics.

The value of Lincoln's retention of Grant cannot be underestimated. Had the president sacked the general, Grant would have been lost to history—something that might also have happened to a Lincoln stripped of his greatest general. But even then Lincoln's relationship with Grant deserves closer scrutiny. Not all the stories stand up under examination. Nowhere is this more evident than in the account of the Lincoln-Grant relationship recounted by the Philadelphia politico Alexander McClure, who told what stands as the most vivid story of Lincoln's support of Grant. After Shiloh, newspaper reporters, soldiers, and politicians relentlessly criticized Grant, attributing the enormous bloodshed to his military incompetence. Some even suggested that Grant's direction of the battle was beclouded by a bout with the bottle. McClure went to the White House to urge that Grant be sacked. "When I said everything that could be said from my standpoint, we lapsed into silence," McClure recalled years later. "Lincoln remained silent for what seemed a very long time. He then gathered himself up in his chair and said in a tone of earnestness that I shall never forget: *'I can't spare this man. He fights.'* "[12]

It makes a good story. Certainly Lincoln may have uttered those words. Scholars accept this story without question. But McClure did not stop here, and what followed is open to serious question. Lincoln, McClure claimed, had decided to shield Grant from further criticism by ordering Halleck to take personal command of the armies in western Tennessee. Grant would serve as Halleck's second-in-command, a low-profile position; then, "when it was entirely safe to restore Grant to his command," Lincoln called Halleck east to assume the office of general in chief. Thus, concluded McClure, "It was Lincoln, and Lincoln alone, who saved [Grant] from disgrace" and protected him "from one of the most violent surges of popular prejudice that was ever created against any of our leading generals . . . by such well-concerted effort that he soon won popular applause from those who were most violent in demanding Grant's dismissal."[13]

The documentary record flatly contradicts this story. Halleck, on his own initiative, started for Pittsburgh Landing on 9 April upon receiving word of the clash from Grant—before word of the battle, let alone the storm of protest against Grant, reached Washington. In fact, Halleck had already planned to join Grant before news of Shiloh reached his headquarters. The first newspaper report of the battle appeared on 10 April in the *New York Herald*; Whitelaw Reid's report, which became the most noteworthy of the critical accounts, did not appear until the following week. Thus, Halleck's arrival at Shiloh had nothing to do with the criticism directed at Grant in the Northern press—nor was it ordered by Lincoln. Moreover, on 23 April, Secretary of War Edwin M. Stanton telegraphed Halleck: "The President desires to know . . . whether any neglect or misconduct of General Grant or any other army officer contributed to the sad casualties" suffered at Shiloh—not exactly a ringing endorsement of Grant's generalship. Halleck, acting again on his own initiative, reorganized his command at the end of April, naming Grant his second-in-command; Grant, believing that he had been shelved, first complained, then looked for another command, and at last became so despondent that he almost left the army. Lincoln decided to call Halleck because of McClellan's setbacks on the Virginia peninsula; Grant was restored to command, but only after Halleck had offered the command to another general.[14]

The most obvious evidence of Lincoln's doubts about Grant was his decision to outfit an expedition to capture Vicksburg under the command of John A. McClernand. Lincoln and McClernand had first met as political opponents in Illinois; the president, seeking as much bipartisan aid as possible, welcomed McClernand as an ally, and McClernand was not long in trying to turn this to his advantage. He served under Grant at Belmont, Fort Donelson, and Shiloh, gaining a reputation for self-promotion that irritated his superior, who often found his desk littered with McClernand's arrogant and condescending missives. Nor did McClernand refrain from complaining about Grant to Lincoln.[15] In August 1862 he traveled east to visit the president to secure an independent command with the mission to capture Vicksburg. The president thought McClernand "brave and capable, but too desirous to be independent of every body else."[16] Nevertheless, Lincoln, frustrated with the military situation elsewhere, approved McClernand's plan. David D. Porter, whose Mississippi flotilla was supposed to cooperate with McClernand, explained that Lincoln was convinced that McClernand was responsible for saving the day at Shiloh, an impression McClernand shared and most probably cultivated in the president's mind.[17]

Grant was not informed of the project and only got wind of it in November. Immediately he telegraphed Halleck to find out who was in charge of operations against Vicksburg. Lincoln might tell Lyman Trumbull that Grant "would be left alone except to be urged forward," but that was hardly the case.[18] With Halleck's encouragement, Grant and William T. Sherman commenced an offensive against Vicksburg. It was not until 18 December that Halleck told Grant that "it is the wish of the President" that McClernand "shall have the immediate command under your direction" of the Vicksburg expedition. As Grant had just informed Halleck that he found McClernand "unmanageable and incompetent," this arrangement was not promising; but as Sherman had already started for Vicksburg, the orders came too late.[19] Only in January was the chain of command clearly established with Grant in charge of operations, much to McClernand's disgust.

But the dispute was not over. McClernand denigrated Grant at every possible opportunity, sending officers to Washington with stories of Grant's drinking.[20] These stories made an impact, for the president continued to inquire of visitors whether Grant did indeed drink.[21] At one point, he supposedly contemplated offering Grant's command to Benjamin Butler; Chase and others urged the president to transfer Grant's men to William S. Rosecrans's Army of the Cumberland.[22] Finally, Lincoln, impatient at Grant's failure to take Vicksburg, urged Halleck to get Grant and Nathaniel P. Banks to cooperate. Banks outranked Grant; should the two join forces, Grant would once again have to take a back seat to one of Lincoln's "political generals," suggesting less than full confidence in Grant. And at the same time Lincoln worried, Grant was finding out that his status was a cause of concern with the arrival at headquarters of several visitors from Washington.

The first of these visitors, Adjutant General Lorenzo Thomas, was charged with overseeing the raising of black regiments. Rumor had it that Thomas was authorized to relieve Grant.[23] Reports had reached Washington that Grant and his subordinates were less than enthusiastic with the administration's policy of enrolling blacks in the Union army. At the same time Secretary of War Stanton directed his assistant, Charles A. Dana, to travel to Grant's army to inspect the pay service; this flimsy pretense did not fool Grant or his staff officers, who understood that Dana's real mission was to report on Grant. As Dana later put it, Stanton wanted Dana "to give such information as would enable Mr. Lincoln and himself to settle their minds as to Grant." Neither move reflected confidence in Grant.[24] Nor did Stanton's decision to dispatch a medical officer to investigate reports of sickness among Grant's troops.[25] Even Washburne and Illinois governor Richard Yates visited Grant's army to see what was going on.[26]

The positive reports of Dana, Thomas, and the medical officer reassured Lincoln about Grant's ability. But as the president watched Grant move down the Mississippi in late April and then cross south of Vicksburg, he began to worry again. Instead of turning south to join forces with Banks, Grant moved east and north into the interior of Mississippi. Within three weeks his forces had won several victories culminating with the containment of Confederate forces in Vicksburg. Lincoln believed the campaign "one of the most brilliant in the world."[27] The six weeks of siege that followed, coming at a time when Robert E. Lee's army was moving northward into Maryland and Pennsylvania, caused Lincoln some concern, but in the main he was relieved. "I rather like the man," he told one visitor. "I think I'll try him a little longer."[28] After Gettysburg, Lincoln confided to Daniel Sickles that he liked Grant because Grant did what he could with what he had.[29] Little did Lincoln know that at that very moment the news of Vicksburg's capitulation was on its way to Washington. An overjoyed Lincoln wrote Grant "a grateful acknowledgment for the almost inestimable service you have done the country." Recounting his own doubts about the campaign, he graciously added, "I now wish to make the personal acknowledgment that you were right, and I was wrong."[30]

After Vicksburg, Lincoln, for the most part, stood solidly behind Grant. He had declared that if the general captured the river citadel, he "is my man and I am his the rest of the war."[31] Certainly his decision to elevate Grant to command of the western theater in October suggested as much; Stanton hurried to Louisville to bestow the new office on the general. And Lincoln's decision not to contest Grant's removal of McClernand during the siege of Vicksburg also suggested that the president had found his man. But still doubts lingered. In November, as Grant made plans to attack Braxton Bragg's army outside Chattanooga, Major General David Hunter arrived for yet another look.[32] As Lincoln waited for Grant to commence operations, he became "a little despondent," according to John Hay. Only when news of the opening of the battle reached Washington did the president again take heart.[33]

Grant's victory at Chattanooga completed the case for his elevation to supreme command. In February 1864 Lincoln named Grant lieutenant general; the next month he formally installed Grant as general in chief. From that time until the end of the war Lincoln retained his confidence in Grant. But this confidence had not always been there; it grew during the war and was far more a product of Grant's accomplishments than of Lincoln's foresight. Grant's slow rise to top command reflected Lincoln's justifiable skepticism about Grant's uneven record from April 1862 to April 1863.

THE POWER LINCOLN GAVE GRANT

The second assumption that will not stand close scrutiny is that Lincoln gave Grant as general in chief a free hand in military operations. Other historians, who claim that the president's meddling in military affairs fatally handicapped field commanders, suggest that others, especially McClellan, would have enjoyed like success under such conditions.[34] The myth of the "free hand" was exploded by Williams. In *Lincoln and His Generals*, he demonstrated that Lincoln continued to supervise military operations after Grant took command. But Lincoln's decisions were always wise. In January 1864, in response to inquiries from headquarters, Grant outlined an overall plan of campaign. It featured a two-pronged offensive from Chattanooga and Mobile against Atlanta and an invasion of North Carolina to cut Richmond's rail links to the south, forcing Robert E. Lee's Army of Northern Virginia to abandon Virginia and contest the advance or face severed lines of communication and supply. The plan was bold, imaginative, and achievable, encompassing a broad view of the eastern theater beyond Virginia and promising to nullify Lee's defensive positions in the Old Dominion. But the administration turned Grant down. It viewed the North Carolina operation as too risky, for Lee might attack the Army of the Potomac, an army commanded by officers in whom the president lacked confidence. Lincoln preferred a direct confrontation with Lee on his home soil of Virginia. The idea of a campaign against Mobile also disappeared, because Lincoln wanted the troops assigned to that campaign to launch an offensive up the Red River—a maneuver designed with diplomatic and political concerns in mind, and to be headed by Banks, a political appointee. Moreover, as Grant came east in March to assume overall command, he also discovered that he would have to find places for two other general officers who held commissions owing to their political clout—Franz Sigel and Ben Butler.[35]

Thus Grant's original vision of a series of synchronized strikes slicing apart the Confederacy had to be abandoned. Banks's Red River expedition took precedence over the capture of Mobile; Grant's revamped Virginia plan bore the marks of Lincoln's political concerns. It looked to force Lee to fight by cutting off his supplies. The Army of the James, under Butler, would strike at Richmond from the James River, severing the rail link between the Confederate capital and Petersburg to the south. A Union column under Sigel would advance up the Shenandoah Valley to deprive Lee of that rich source of supplies. One looks in vain for signs of Grant the mindless butcher, who won by grinding up human flesh in a war of attrition. But the men selected to head these offensives owed their shoulder straps to their political influence rather than their military skill. The collapse of these two drives, which between them threatened Lee's supplies, his rear, and the safety of the Confederate capital, shaped the 1864 offensive, depriving Grant of an opportunity to crush Lee in a campaign of maneuver.[36]

Lincoln was also not above offering his own plans. As Grant recalled it twenty years later, the president rolled out a map of Virginia and suggested that Grant land a force between two streams that emptied into the Potomac—although a quick look at a map suggests that Lincoln was pointing to the Chesapeake. Grant listened quietly and said nothing and then went about his business. There was no need to point out possible flaws, for to do so might unnecessarily antagonize the president. Horace Porter merely recalled that Grant termed the president's plan "impracticable."[37] Williams dismissed these stories as the product of Grant's imagination; yet Lincoln had offered a similar plan to Halleck and Ambrose E. Burnside in November 1862.[38]

The political situation confronting Lincoln in 1864 put Grant in somewhat of a bind. The president was fighting for reelection, and the pressures of politics called for a military campaign that would achieve a timely victory with minimal casualties. "I cannot pretend to advise," Lincoln commented in June, after Grant had laid siege to Petersburg, "but I do sincerely hope that all may be accomplished with as little bloodshed as possible."[39] Yet political considerations also dictated the appointment of generals who held commissions for political reasons rather than military skill—and the actions of these men contributed to prolonging the conflict and increasing its cost, especially in Virginia. Thus Grant found himself looking to assault Lee's positions with an eye to achieving the kind of victory that would spark celebrations in the North, knowing full well that unless he achieved a decisive battlefield triumph, the casualties incurred would dampen Northern morale and Lincoln's electoral prospects.

Lincoln intervened yet again in Grant's efforts to wage war in the summer of 1864. As the Union army settled into the siege of Petersburg, Grant became convinced that George G. Meade, commander of the Army of the Potomac, might well have to be assigned to another command, for Meade's temper had caused problems with other generals. At the same time, Grant contemplated assigning Butler to a desk job, replacing him with William B. Franklin as a field commander in charge of the Army of the James. It proved impossible to move Butler, in large part because of Butler's political influence—Lincoln could not afford to alienate the radicals in his party still more in the aftermath of his veto of the Wade-Davis bill and the departure of Salmon P. Chase from the cabinet. Grant then considered placing either Meade or Franklin in charge of the Union forces protecting Washington, imposing unity of command where it was sorely needed, as the fumbling Yankee reaction to Jubal Early's excursion to the capital's outskirts suggested. Lincoln rejected both of these suggestions, although the president seemed willing to elevate McClellan to the post, effectively removing from contention his most probable opponent in the forthcoming presidential contest. In the end, Grant could not shift Meade or Butler, but he did secure the appointment of Philip H. Sheridan to head the forces around Washington with instructions to destroy Early's army. Lesser men would have assailed the president, but Grant persevered within the limits set before him. In the end, of course, it was the triumph of Grant's overall strategy elsewhere, at Atlanta and in the Shenandoah Valley, which brought forth the cheers and the hundred-gun salutes, while he engaged in the less glamorous but equally important job of pinning Lee down.[40]

These facts reinforce Williams's claim that Lincoln did not give Grant a free hand in planning and conducting military operations during the last year of the war. Political fortunes and preferences constrained Grant's planning and contributed significantly to the contours of the ensuing campaign in Virginia, but the general understood and accepted them without complaint. It was this characteristic that impressed Lincoln most. "He doesn't ask me to do impossibilities for him," he told a secretary, "and he's the first general I've had that didn't."[41]

GRANT'S ROLE IN THE
LINCOLN-GRANT RELATIONSHIP

Much has been made of Lincoln's handling of Grant; less has been said about Grant's handling of his relationship with the president, in which Grant displayed tact, political shrewdness, and an understanding of the nature of civil-military relations that did much to increase his influence with Lincoln. There is no better way to demonstrate this understanding than to compare a passage in one of Grant's letters to Lincoln to another from the pen of McClellan. During the Seven Days Battle in 1862, a rattled McClellan telegraphed Washington, "If I save this Army now I tell you plainly that I owe no thanks to you or any other persons in Washington—you have done your best to sacrifice this Army."[42] Compare this to the closing sentence of Grant's last letter to Lincoln before the start of the 1864 offensive: "Should my success be less than I desire and expect, the least I can say is, the fault is not with you."[43] The man who could write these words was worthy of Lincoln's confidence.

Through 1861 and 1862 Grant seldom communicated with Lincoln except in support of appointments and promotions. Congressman Washburne, Grant's political patron and a long-time associate of Lincoln, acted as a go-between, relaying information from headquarters to interested parties in Washington and vice versa. Grant's letters to Washburne were calculated to refute charges, to present the general as duty-bound to obey orders, and to portray him as being in step with administration policy. And Grant kept an eye on who might have Lincoln's ear. In November 1862 he heard that Leonard Swett, one of Lincoln's Illinois associates, was on the verge of becoming one of the president's advisers. Immediately he warned Washburne that Swett was one of his "bitterest enemies" because he had opposed Swett's efforts to control supplying the army in Southern Illinois in 1861.[44]

Grant also declined to question administration policy. He believed that it was his duty to execute administration directives, not create new policies that challenged established ones. Doing one's duty also meant keeping one's job. As one of Fremont's subordinates in 1861, Grant had witnessed first hand what happened when a general defied the administration. Grant had his own opinions about slavery and emancipation, but he confined his comments to private correspondence. "I have no hobby of my own with regard to the negro, either to effect his freedom or to continue his bondage," Grant told his father. "If Congress pass any law and the President approves, I am willing to execute it."[45]

In the winter of 1863, as Grant struggled to find a way to take Vicksburg, he knew that Lincoln was watching him closely. With McClernand poised to replace him, he had to watch his step. Although he made it clear to the administration that he, not McClernand, would direct operations against Vicksburg, he did not at this time press home his complaints against McClernand, aware that he was not arguing from a position of strength. Instead, he worked to shore up his support. He persisted in digging canals west of Vicksburg because Halleck told him that Lincoln was taking an interest in the project.[46] Grant knew that if he abandoned his position and returned to Memphis, as Sherman advised, it would be interpreted as a retreat if not a defeat, and the cry for Grant's removal might become too loud for Lincoln to resist.[47]

Grant responded shrewdly to the visits of Dana and Thomas. Instead of treating these visitors as unwelcome intrusions, reminding him of his precarious position, Grant saw an opportunity to reassure the authorities in Washington of his fitness for command and of his support for the administration. He received Thomas and Dana warmly and promised his full cooperation. Both men were won over. Dana's dispatches to Stanton praised Grant and criticized McClernand, eroding that general's standing in Washington. When during the Vicksburg campaign Grant found McClernand to be a serious hindrance to operations, Dana relayed that information to Washington; back came Stanton's telegram authorizing Grant to remove McClernand if necessary.[48] Grant waited for McClernand to trip over his own ego one more time; when McClernand accommodated him, by violating regulations by publishing one of his self-congratulatory orders, Grant immediately relieved him. Wisely waiting to decapitate McClernand until after he had secured a series of military victories, Grant had thus strengthened his hand immeasurably; to have demanded McClernand's removal during the dark days of early 1863 might well have resulted in his own replacement.

Grant reaped other benefits from his befriending of Dana and Thomas. No reports reached Washington of an intoxicated commander, although there are contested accounts that Dana witnessed Grant under the influence of alcohol. Thomas wired Washington that Grant gave him "every assistance in my work."[49] When

Dana returned to Washington after Vicksburg's fall, he praised Grant effusively and assured Radical senator Henry Wilson that Grant "is in favor of destroying the cause of this civil war—of overthrowing slavery."[50] Moreover, Dana declared that Grant harbored no political aspirations, a subject of some concern to Lincoln when it came to other generals.[51]

Grant also dispatched envoys of his own to Washington. His chief of staff, John A. Rawlins, arrived in Washington at the end of July. Lincoln invited Rawlins to a cabinet meeting, where the staff officer held forth for two hours about the fall of Vicksburg. Rawlins persuasively presented McClernand as "impracticable and unfit, . . . insubordinate . . . [and] an obstruction to army movements and operations." Navy secretary Gideon Welles noted that Grant had dispatched Rawlins "for a purpose," and that was "to enlist the President rather than bring dispatches"—a mission that Welles judged a success. That Rawlins had succeeded became apparent when Lincoln refused to accede to McClernand's call for a court of inquiry or a court martial.[52] Another one of Grant's subordinates, John Eaton, reaffirmed Grant's commitment to emancipation. In November 1862 Grant had put Eaton in charge of organizing camps for black refugees. Now Eaton described his progress to Lincoln, reminding the president that Grant had been a convert to the cause for some time. Lincoln, pleased, commented that Grant's handling of refugees "meets present exigencies without attempting to determine impossibilities." Reporting on his meeting with the president to Grant, Eaton added that Lincoln took great pleasure in the fall of Vicksburg: "Those who made such an effort to interfere with you, now are ashamed to aver it."[53]

Grant supplemented the reports of his envoys with letters of his own—the first extended discourses he had offered the president. He assured Lincoln that he was giving "the subject of arming black troops my hearty support." Aware of past rumors about his own commitment to administration policy, he added that the enlistment of blacks "is an order that I am bound to obey and do not feel that in my position I have a right to question any policy of the Government." But Grant made it clear that he supported the policy enthusiastically, arguing that "by arming the negro we have added a powerful ally. They will make good soldiers and taking them from the enemy weaken him in the same proportion they strengthen us." The president was so pleased with Grant's letter, in part because the general had echoed his own justification of black enlistment, that he referred to it in defending his policy.[54]

This correspondence capped the transformation of the relationship between Grant and Lincoln. After the fall of Vicksburg, the general relied less and less on Washburne as a go-between and more on direct personal contacts by letter or visitor. Dana's return to Washington, the visits of Eaton and Rawlins, and Grant's decision to correspond directly with Lincoln were all part of an effort to bolster his reputation with the president in the afterglow of victory. This endeavor proved successful; in October Grant was the logical choice to take command of operations in the West.

Chattanooga sparked talk of Grant's elevation to high command as general in chief with the newly revived rank of lieutenant general. Some observers, led by

New York Herald editor James Gordon Bennett, had the presidency itself in mind. Grant dismissed the idea, but it soon became apparent that if Lincoln believed that he harbored presidential ambitions, the promotion to lieutenant general would be jeopardized. Grant decided that letters to friends who conversed with Lincoln would do the trick. Writing to Frank Blair, one of his old subordinates currently in Congress as a spokesman for the administration, Grant declared that he had no po-litical aspirations, then added that Blair should "show this letter to no one unless it be the president himself"—an ill-disguised hint to do just that. Another letter to J. Russell Jones, an associate of Washburne and the president, denying any interest in politics, was also intended for Lincoln's eyes. Lincoln was relieved to discover that "the Presidential grub" had not been "gnawing at Grant." Secure in the knowledge that Grant would not contest his leadership, Lincoln supported the lieutenant gen-eralcy bill, opening the way for Grant to assume the position of general in chief.[55]

Finally, as general in chief, Grant understood and operated within the political constraints that Lincoln imposed upon him. He accepted Butler, Banks, and Sigel as generals; acquiesced in Lincoln's preference not to restore Franklin to command, despite Grant's great respect for him; and retained Butler in command for political reasons, only removing him (with Lincoln's approval) in the aftermath of a botched military operation at the end of 1864, long after the November election. He also responded to Lincoln's offers of advice and expressions of concern, assuaging the president's fears about Confederate threats to the capital and the conduct of other campaigns instead of dismissing them, as had McClellan. All of this was done in matter-of-fact, common-sense communications, without the melodramatics of McClellan's missives, reflecting the mutual respect of the president and the general. And at the war's end Grant demonstrated that he was a good listener. In March 1865 Lincoln had made it clear that he favored a lenient peace. "Let 'em up easy," the president urged. "Let them once surrender and reach their homes, they won't take up arms again. . . . Let them have their horses to plow with. . . . Give them the most liberal and honorable terms." On 9 April 1865, Grant, guided by these senti-ments, offered Lee terms that marked as much the beginning of a peace as the end-ing of a war. Later scholars pointed out that Grant apparently exceeded his authority when he stated that so long as Confederate soldiers and officers honored the terms of their parole, they were "not to be disturbed by United States author-ity." But Lincoln was delighted that his general had proved a statesman. "Good! . . . All right! . . . Exactly the thing!" he exclaimed as he perused the document.[56]

A warm personal relationship grew between the two men. Lincoln cheered Grant on, confided his fears and concerns, offered advice without pressing Grant to comply, and reiterated his confidence in his general. "The President has more nerve than any of his advisers," Grant once remarked.[57] And the general returned the favors. He received Lincoln warmly at headquarters several times, conducting reviews of black regiments for the president to watch. He celebrated Lincoln's re-election as a triumph for the Union and republican institutions. Early in 1865, he gladly satisfied Lincoln's request to place his son on the general's staff. Indeed, had it not been for his concern about the erratic behavior of Mary Todd Lincoln (whose repeated public tantrums in front of Grant and his wife at City Point and in Washington had caused the Grants great embarrassment), the general might well have accompanied the president to Ford's Theater on the night of 14 April 1865. Instead, he sat at Lincoln's coffin several days later, tears welling in his eyes.

Grant was not Lincoln's favorite from early on in the war; the president, even if he did not succumb to the doubts of others, had reservations about Grant. Stories that Lincoln shielded Grant have been exaggerated; indeed, at several points the president nearly replaced him. Lincoln's early doubts about him were understandable and justifiable, and they did not entirely dissipate until after the battle of Chattanooga. Nor did Lincoln extend Grant a free hand in military operations when the general assumed overall command. Lincoln oversaw operations, provided advice, and limited Grant's options when it came to planning and appointing subordinates. Much of the cooperation between the two was the result of a congruence in thought; much was also owing to Grant's understanding of the subordination of military to civil authority and his skillful handling of Lincoln's concerns. If Williams has taught us that Lincoln was an able strategist, Bruce Catton, William McFeely, and others have also reminded us that Grant practiced politics with poise and purpose.

Gradually these two men earned each other's trust and respect; ultimately, a friendship emerged. They discovered that they often saw eye to eye on the important issues raised by the war. And they also came to understand that their fates and that of the Union were inextricably linked. When Grant left Lincoln to launch his last campaign against Lee, Lincoln cried out, "Remember, your success is my success."[58] Side by side, the tall, lanky president and the short, cigar-smoking general must have seemed a comical pair to the observer. But they were indispensable to each other and to the survival of the nation through the transforming crucible of civil war.

NOTES

1. Abraham Lincoln, *The Collected Works of Abraham Lincoln*, ed. Roy P. Basler, 9 vols. (New Brunswick, N.J.: Rutgers University Press in association with the Abraham Lincoln Association, 1953–55), 8: 332 (hereafter cited as *CWAL*).

2. J. F. C. Fuller, *The Generalship of Ulysses S. Grant* (Bloomington: Indiana University Press, 1958), 134.

3. T. Harry Williams, *McClellan, Sherman, and Grant* (New Brunswick, N.J.: Rutgers University Press, 1962), 96–97; T. Harry Williams, *Lincoln and His Generals* (New York: Alfred Knopf, 1952), 225.

4. William Brooks, *Grant of Appomattox* (New York: Bobbs-Merrill, 1942), 206.

5. William S. McFeely, *Grant: A Biography* (New York: W. W. Norton, 1981), 104.

6. Joseph T. Glatthaar, *Partners in Command: The Relationships between Leaders in the Civil War* (New York: Free Press, 1994).

7. Williams, *Lincoln and His Generals*, esp. pp. 304–310; Warren W. Hassler, Jr., *Commanders of the Army of the Potomac* (Baton Rouge: Louisiana University Press, 1962), 207; Benjamin P. Thomas, *Abraham Lincoln* (New York: Alfred A. Knopf, 1952), 420.

8. Lincoln to John A. McClernand, 10 November 1861, *CWAL*, 5: 20.

9. Lincoln to Simon Cameron, 4 January 1862, in *The Collected Works of Abraham Lincoln: Supplement 1832–1865,* ed. Roy P. Basler (Westport, Conn.: Greenwood Press, 1974), 118.

10. Glatthaar, *Partners in Command,* 192.

11. Bruce Catton, *Grant Moves South* (Boston: Little, Brown, 1960), 206. In *Partners in Command,* Glatthaar mistakenly asserts (p. 192) that "Halleck's probe cleared Grant." In fact, Halleck launched no probe but rather backed down in the face of one proposed by Lincoln.

12. Alexander McClure, *Lincoln and Men of War Times* (1892; Philadelphia: Rolley and Reynolds, 1962), 191–194.

13. Ibid., 194–195.

14. Halleck to Ulysses S. Grant, 8, 9 April 1862, in *The Papers of Ulysses S. Grant,* ed. John Y. Simon, 18 vols. to date (Carbondale: Southern Illinois University Press, 1967—), 5: 20 (hereafter cited as *PUSG*); Catton, *Grant Moves South,* 252; McFeely, *Grant,* 116. McClure's other story about Lincoln and Grant is also shattered by other accounts. McClure claimed that in late October 1864, Lincoln hesitated to ask Grant to furlough Pennsylvania soldiers in order to guarantee a Republican victory in Pennsylvania's "home vote" because, he told McClure, "I have no reason to believe that Grant prefers my election to that of McClellan." George G. Meade and Philip H. Sheridan, according to McClure, provided the necessary furloughs between 20 October and election day (8 November). McClure, *Lincoln,* 199. It is hard to know where to start refuting this story. Meade, who would have been hard pressed to furlough 5,000 men at the same time he launched offensive operations south of the James, mentioned nothing about such a request; see George G. Meade, *The Life and Letters of George G. Meade,* 2 vols. (New York: Charles Scribner's Sons, 1913), 2: 235–241. It is hard to believe that Meade could have kept Grant in the dark about such a large furlough; moreover, Grant who had openly declared his support of Lincoln in a letter to Washburne, had furloughed Delaware soldiers to vote at Stanton's request—suggesting that either Lincoln was ignorant of Grant's willingness to help or that McClure was lying. Brooks D. Simpson, *Let Us Have Peace: Ulysses S. Grant and the Politics of War and Reconstruction, 1861–1868* (Chapel Hill: University of North Carolina Press, 1991), 64, 67. Grant and Lincoln exchanged telegrams about the October election; see Grant to Stanton, 12 October 1864 and Lincoln to Grant, 12 October 1864, *PUSG,* 12: 454. Finally, Lincoln had earlier expressed doubts about Grant's intentions in an August 1864 conversation with John Eaton. Eaton visited Grant's headquarters, learned of Grant's support for Lincoln, and returned to Washington within a week to inform Lincoln of Grant's support; John Eaton, *Grant, Lincoln, and the Freedmen* (New York: Longmans, 1907), 186–191. One must thus qualify Mark E. Neely's conclusion that McClure's book "is an important source for the political aspects of Lincoln's administration." (Neely, *The Abraham Lincoln Encyclopedia* [New York: Da Capo Press, 1982], 202) by raising questions about its veracity.

15. McFeely, *Grant,* 116.

16. David Donald, ed., *Inside Lincoln's Cabinet: The Civil War Diaries of Salmon P. Chase* (New York: Longmans, 1954), 161 (27 September 1862). Oddly enough, Neely's encyclopedia does not include an entry for McClernand.

17. Ibid., 170 (7 October 1862); David Dixon Porter, *Incidents and Anecdotes of the Civil War* (New York: D. Appleton, 1885), 122–123; Clarence Macartney, *Grant and His Generals* (New York: The McBride Co., 1953), 228. Gideon Welles remarked that Porter had advocated McClernand's appointment because of his distaste for West Point graduates like Grant and Sherman. Howard K. Beale, ed., *The Diary of Gideon Welles,* 3 vols. (New York: W. W. Norton, 1960), 1: 167 (10 October 1863).

18. Lyman Trumbull to Ulysses S. Grant, 24 November 1862, *PUSG*, 6: 288.

19. Kenneth P. Williams, *Lincoln Finds a General*, 5 vols. (New York: Macmillan, 1949–59), 3: 187–188; Ulysses S. Grant to Henry W. Halleck, 14 December 1862, *PUSG*, 7: 29; Halleck to Grant, 18 December 1862, *PUSG*, 7: 62; Army General Orders No. 210, 18 December 1862, *PSUG*, 7: 63.

20. McClernand to Lincoln, 15 March 1863, Robert Todd Lincoln Collection, Library of Congress. On the reverse of this letter Kountz scribbled that Grant "was Gloriously drunk" on 13 March 1863. Kountz had made similar charges earlier in the war when Grant relieved him from duty. See Catton, *Grant Moves South*, 120. However, a letter from Murat Halstead to Salmon P. Chase, dated 1 April 1863, which was shown to Lincoln, also charged that Grant had been intoxicated in mid-March. Halstead, who termed Grant "a jackass in the original package," reported that "about two weeks ago" Grant had been so drunk that staff officers shut him up in his cabin. Halstead to Chase, 1 April 1863, Robert Todd Lincoln Collection, Library of Congress. Of course, Halstead may have heard of the story from Kountz.

21. Ulysses S. Grant III, *Ulysses S. Grant: Warrior and Statesman* (New York: William Morrow, 1969), 178–179.

22. Benjamin F. Butler, *Butler's Book* (Boston: A. M. Thayer & Co., 1892), 550; draft order, dated 17 February 1863, Robert T. Lincoln Collection, Library of Congress; William M. Lamers, *The Edge of Glory: A Biography of General William S. Rosecrans* (New York: Harcourt, Brace & World, 1961), 262–263.

23. Beale, *Diary of Welles*, 1: 259 (2 April 1863); Sylvanus Cadwallader, *Three Years with Grant*, ed. Benjamin P. Thomas (New York: Alfred Knopf, 1955), 60; Porter, *Incidents and Anecdotes*, 182.

24. Charles A. Dana, *Recollections of the Civil War* (1898; New York: Collier, 1963), 41–42.

25. William C. Church, *Ulysses S. Grant and the Period of National Preservation and Reconstruction* (New York: Garden City Publishing, 1897), 181. The officer reported that the rates of disease and death did not differ from those in the Army of the Potomac.

26. Cadwallader, *Three Years with Grant*, 66; Porter, *Incidents and Anecdotes*, 181–82.

27. Lincoln to Issac N. Arnold, 26 May 1863, *CWAL*, 6: 230.

28. Church, *Grant*, 181.

29. Gene Smith, *Lee and Grant* (New York: McGraw-Hill, 1984), 168.

30. Lincoln to Ulysses S. Grant, 13 July 1863, *CWAL*, 6: 326.

31. James M. McPherson, *Battle Cry of Freedom: The Civil War Era* (New York: Ballantine Books, 1988), 638.

32. Simpson, *Let Us Have Peace*, 51; David Hunter to Edwin M. Stanton, 15 December 1863, Edwin M. Stanton Papers, Library of Congress.

33. Tyler Dennett, ed., *Lincoln and the Civil War in the Diaries and Letters of John Hay* (New York: Dodd, Mead, 1939), 125 (23 November 1863).

34. See Hassler, *Commanders*, 207; Richard N. Current, *The Lincoln Nobody Knows* (New York: Hill & Wang, 1958), 153–154.

35. Simpson, *Let Us Have Peace*, 54–55. Compare the discussions of these plans in Williams, *Lincoln and His Generals*, 295–297; Current, *The Lincoln Nobody Knows*, 158; Herman Hattaway and Archer Jones, *How the North Won: A Military History of the Civil War* (Urbana: University of Illinois Press, 1983), 511–515; Archer Jones, *Civil War Command and Strategy: The Process of Victory and Defeat* (New York: Free Press, 1992), 183–185; and Glatthaar, *Partners in Command*, 201–205. In *Abraham Lincoln and the Promise of America: The Last Best Hope of*

Earth (Cambridge: Harvard University Press and the Huntington Library, 1993), Mark E. Neely, Jr., asserts that "Lincoln's clear-sighted unwillingness to allow partisan concerns to interfere with decisions critical to the army was an admirable trait crucial to winning a major war in a democracy" (p. 90). The president's dalliance with McClernand in 1862–63 and his repeated interference with Grant's choice of commanders throughout the campaign of 1864 suggest a far different conclusion—that Lincoln made military decisions with partisan concerns in mind precisely because he thought they were necessary "to winning a major war in a democracy."

36. Simpson, *Let Us Have Peace*, 56–57.

37. Porter, *Campaigning with Grant*, 27. Grant recounted the conversation in greater detail in *Personal Memoirs of Ulysses S. Grant*, 2 vols. (New York: C. L. Webster, 1885–86), 2: 122–123.

38. Lincoln to Henry W. Halleck, 27 November 1862, *CWAL*, 5: 514–515. Williams's comments are in *Lincoln and His Generals*, 304–305. He omitted Porter's account of the story; his comments on Lincoln's 1862 letter are on p. 198, although he failed to see that these two plans were one and the same—a point of confusion due to Grant's reference to the Potomac River instead of the Chesapeake.

38. Porter, *Campaigning with Grant*, 223.

40. Bruce Catton, *Grant Takes Command* (Boston: Little, Brown, 1969), 326–348; Simpson, *Let Us Have Peace*, 57–69.

41. Catton, *Grant Takes Command*, 176–178.

42. McClellan to Edwin M. Stanton, 28 June 1862, *The Civil War Papers of George B. McClellan*, ed. Stephen W. Sears (New York: Ticknor and Fields, 1989), 323.

43. Catton, *Grant Takes Command*, 178.

44. Grant to Elihu B. Washburne, 7 November 1662, *PUSG*, 6: 273.

45. Simpson, *Let Us Have Peace*, 28–29.

46. Catton, *Grant Moves South*, 377. Ironically, Lincoln later expressed skepticism about the canal. Madeleine Dahlgren, *Memoir of John A. Dahlgren* (Boston: J. R. Osgood, 1882), 389.

47. McFeely, *Grant*, 130; Simpson, *Let Us Have Peace*, 35–37.

48. Dana, *Recollections of the Civil War*, 66.

49. Simpson, *Let Us Have Peace*, 44.

50. Ibid., 46.

51. Benjamin P. Thomas and Harold M. Hyman, *Stanton: The Life and Times of Lincoln's Secretary of War* (New York: Alfred Knopf, 1962), 269.

52. Beale, *Diary of Welles*, 1: 387 (31 July 1863).

53. Eaton to Grant, 23 July 1863, *PUSG*, 8: 343.

54. Donald, *Diaries of Chase*, 178 (29 August 1863).

55. Simpson, *Let Us Have Peace*, 53–54; McFeely, *Grant*, 162–164.

56. Simpson, *Let Us Have Peace*, 74–89.

57. Porter, *Campaigning with Grant*, 274.

58. Ibid., 426.

7 Abraham Lincoln and Southern White Unionism

William C. Harris

No Northern political leader during the Civil War had more confidence in Southern Unionism than Abraham Lincoln. From the beginning of the conflict until his death, Lincoln believed that Southern white loyalists held the key to the rapid restoration of the rebel states to their "proper practical relations with the Union."[1] Indeed, for Lincoln the main purpose of the war was to restore loyal men to power in the South and insure that rebel leaders did not regain control. By late 1862, emancipation had also become an objective of Lincoln, a goal he pursued carefully with the racial sensibilities and constitutional scruples of Southern white Unionists in mind, as well as those of border-state and Northern conservatives.

THE SIGNIFICANCE OF SOUTHERN LOYALISTS

Historians have failed to recognize the significance of Southern loyalists in Lincoln's approach to emancipation.[2] With rare exception, Unionists had been proslavery when the war began, and during the early stages of the conflict they expected Lincoln to make good on his repeated promise that he would not disturb the peculiar institution in the South. It was a remarkable achievement by Lincoln, aided by the exigencies of the war, that the majority of these Unionists either supported or acquiesced in emancipation and ultimately worked for the eradication of slavery in their state constitutions. By the end of the war, loyal governments in four former Confederate states had abolished slavery in their fundamental law; only in one of these states, Arkansas, had the president explicitly made emancipation a requirement for reconstruction. Federal-occupied parts of Louisiana and Virginia and all of Tennessee had been exempted from the Emancipation Proclamation. Lincoln's encouragement, however, was the catalyst for Unionist action toward ending slavery in these states. The president's success in restoring loyal governments in the

South and ending slavery, though not completed until Federal arms had triumphed, owed a great deal to the confidence that the president had in Southern Unionists, his sympathy for their plight, and the spirit of cooperation that emerged between them as the war progressed.

Lincoln's faith in Southern Unionism was based on his belief that the masses were never deeply committed to secession and that a smaller body of white Southerners remained staunchly devoted to the Union. Secession leaders, he concluded, had seized control in 1860–1861 by temporarily deceiving the people into believing that his election and determination to resist disunion had jeopardized their rights. Having gained power, he assumed that secessionists were resorting to military coercion to sustain the rebellion. In a message to Congress on 4 July 1861, soon after the beginning of the war, Lincoln declared that Southerners possessed "as much of moral sense, as much of devotion to law and order, and as much . . . reverence for the history and government of their common country, as any other civilized, and patriotic people." He told Congress that "there is much reason to believe that the Union men are [today] the majority in many, if not every other one [except South Carolina], of the so-called seceded States."[3]

It was his task, Lincoln said, to nurture the latent Unionism in the South and "call out the war power" to suppress the rebellion and restore loyal governments in the region. He assured Southerners that in using military force he would leave undisturbed their institutions and laws, which meant, when Lincoln made this promise, that he would not interfere with slavery.[4] Fearing anarchy even in the North, Lincoln did not want, as he later expressed it, to see the war for the Union "degenerate into a violent and remorseless revolutionary struggle." Such a struggle, he insisted would hurt the loyal as well as the disloyal and destroy the last, best hope of mankind, the republic of the founding fathers.[5]

Lincoln in 1861 overestimated the Southern commitment to the Union. A realist in most matters, the president must have recognized his error when Southern resistance became fierce on the battlefield and the war became long and bloody. He never abandoned, however, the notion that a solid nucleus of Unionists existed in the seceded states, a nucleus that included men of ability and prominence who could be counted on, as Federal armies penetrated the South, to reestablish loyal governments and influence wayward rebels to return to the fold.

Although it was not the groundswell that he initially thought, Lincoln was correct in believing that a relatively large number of Southerners remained loyal to the Union during the war. As evidence of their commitment, many Southerners from the seceded states served in the Federal army or in Union home-guard units. The standard compilation of United States troop strength during the war indicates that 54,000 Southern whites joined the Union army at some time during the war.[6] This figure is an undercount, since no troops are listed for Virginia and Georgia. Furthermore, only 5,000 troops are given for Louisiana, which is almost 5,000 fewer than what General Nathaniel P. Banks reported in 1864. A recent study by Richard N. Current puts the total figure at 104,000, but he counts 30,000 troops from West Virginia and probably slightly overcounts Federal troops from East Tennessee and

Arkansas. Including home-guard units in Federal-occupied areas of Louisiana, Arkansas, Tennessee, and Virginia, a fair estimate of men from Confederate states serving in Union armed forces would be 70,000.[7]

THE APPEAL OF UNIONISM

Unionism cut across class lines. One of the great historical misconceptions about the Civil War is that Southern planters were united in support of the Confederacy, and conversely the lower classes, who, supposedly had no real stake in the Southern cause, were misled into the rebellion by planter aristocrats. No doubt many poor whites were either Unionists or were unwilling to become involved in the conflict, but they had no monopoly on devotion to the old republic or did they provide the leadership for Southern resistance to the Confederacy. In semi-frontier Arkansas, a state that provided the Federal army with almost 10,000 white troops, the editor of the *Little Rock National Democrat* attempted to counter the already prevalent stereotype that Southern Unionists were poor and ignorant. He pointed to Arkansas volunteers as evidence that the majority of Unionists were from property-holding families. The Union troops from his state, he contended, though mainly from nonslaveholding counties, "in reality, with scarcely an exception, were owners of farms, of cattle and well to do in the world." They were also educated and subscribed to more newspapers than whites in the slaveholding counties.[8]

Planter support for the Union was impressive along the Mississippi River, where the Whig Party had been strong. Evidence of Unionism among the affluent classes can be found in the records of the Southern Claims Commission, which was created after the war to adjudicate loyalist claims for property losses. The law provided that only ironclad Unionists could be compensated. Of the 22,000 claims submitted to the commission, 7,000 were successful. These figures and the documents submitted to the commission suggest that thousands of Unionists were affluent and of the planter slaveholding class. Some of the wealthiest planters of the South, though admittedly a minority of their class, remained true to the Union during the war.[9] Even in loyal East Tennessee, where only four percent of the white population held slaves, most of the Union leaders were slaveholders, albeit small slaveholders. Whether slaveholders or not, Unionists throughout the South began the war as firm supporters of the institution of slavery and critics of antislavery elements in the North, which, they believed, in provoking Southerners had been equally to blame with Southern-rights fire-eaters for secession.

The Southern loyalist views of the Union and the initial purpose of the war were strikingly similar to Lincoln's. Most Unionists, like the president, were products of a rural Southern culture that was fundamentally conservative and individualistic. This conservatism was reinforced by a prewar affiliation with the Whig Party, whose members, both North and South, had great reverence for the founding fathers, the Constitution, and the national principles of Henry Clay. In Illinois, transplanted Southerners like conservative Whigs Orville Browning and Stephen

A. Hurlbut became confidants of Lincoln. Few Southern Unionists, however, had personally known Lincoln before 1861.

One such Southerner was John Minor Botts, a wealthy Virginia planter who had served in Congress with Lincoln. In a letter to a Northern friend during the war, Botts, who had been jailed by Confederates for his loyalty to the old flag, expressed his admiration of Lincoln the man. He wrote:

Mr. Lincoln is by nature a vigorous, strong-minded, and conscientious man, honest in his purpose, and indefatigable in the exercise of what he conceives to be the duties of his office. In natural endowments, I doubt if he is not quite equal, if not superior to any of those by whom he is surrounded. He is not so cultivated as many, because he had not the same advantages in early life, but he is what I always honor, an original and self-*made* man, and is what I have generally called one of God Almighty's educated men; that is, he gets what he knows chiefly from his Creator.[10]

One important quality, however, set Lincoln apart in 1860–1861 from the overwhelming majority of Southern Unionists. This quality was Lincoln's moral abhorrence of slavery and his determination to resist its expansion. Proslavery Unionists, however, who in most cases supported John Bell for president in 1860, recognized that, though Lincoln was the candidate of a sectional and antislavery party, he was not an abolitionist. In an effort to head off secession, they repeatedly told Southerners that they had nothing to fear from Lincoln regarding slavery. Oliver P. Temple told a large Tennessee audience that the president-elect's "opinions on the whole subject of slavery are nearly identical with those entertained by Mr. Clay to the day of his death. He expressly denies the power, the right, or any intention to interfere with it in the states." Then, Temple asked, "Why fret ourselves with alarms, when it is evident Mr. Lincoln neither has the power nor the inclination to interfere with slavery?"[11] Almost all Unionists predicted that war would follow secession and slavery would be destroyed in the ruin that would be the South's fate. The best protection for slavery, they insisted, was not in the Confederacy but in the Union and under the Constitution.[12] Lincoln's promise in his inaugural address not to interfere with the institution in the South provided the kind of reinforcement that they needed on the issue to sustain them in their commitment to the Union after Fort Sumter and the secession of four upper South states.

Southern Unionists, like Lincoln, feared that the war would unleash destructive revolutionary forces upon their communities and states, particularly racial conflict. As Carl Degler has pointed out, "Within the South, Unionism may have been a form of dissent, but it was also a defense of the old order."[13] The main concern of Unionists was the preservation of their society. To Unionists, secession itself was revolutionary, and rebels in their armed resistance to the United States were leading the country beyond revolution and into anarchy.[14] Like Lincoln, Unionists viewed the rebellion as immoral and a violation of the principle of self-government, since, they believed, the secessionists had seized power through subterfuge and were sustaining their control through military force. Also like Lincoln, they downplayed the war as primarily a sectional conflict. Both Unionists and the president found "traitors" in the North as well as in the South. Unionists especially deprecated the use of the words *Northerner* and *Southerner* to describe the combatants in the war. A correspondent to the *Nashville Union* wrote that such distinctions fostered a continuation of sectional animosities and "prevented that [national] unity which should pervade the heart of every American."[15]

Yet most Unionists still identified with the South and its interests. They claimed that true Southerners were those who resisted the rabid secessionists of the South and the fanatical abolitionists of the North. William G. "Parson" Brownlow, a fearless champion of East Tennessee Unionists and a postwar Radical Republican, declared in 1862 that "I am a southern man, and all relatives and interests are thoroughly identified with the South and southern institutions, including slavery."[16] In an "Appeal to the People of the South," James W. Hunnicutt, a Baptist minister-editor who also would affiliate with the Radicals during Reconstruction, wrote that he was "a Southern man." "I love the South," he said, "and shall until I die. I am no traitor. . . . The only friends the South has are the *uncompromising union men of the South, and of these United States.* Jefferson Davis and his accursed clique of arch traitors are the enemies of the South."[17]

LINCOLN'S CONFIDENCE IN
SOUTHERN UNIONISTS TESTED

Lincoln's confidence in Southern Unionists and his theory that only a nucleus of loyal men were needed to restore civil governments in the South were tested early. Three days after the Virginia convention voted to take the state out of the Union, John S. Carlile, a leading spokesman of western Virginia Unionists, visited Lincoln and reminded him of his constitutional duty to guarantee a republican form of government for his state. The president encouraged Carlile to go home to Clarksburg and rally opposition to secession. Lincoln promised to give Virginia's Unionists what aid he could. Acting on the president's advice, Carlile obtained the call for a convention that created the "Restored Government of Virginia" and selected as governor Francis H. Pierpont. Lincoln gave his hearty approval to what he considered to be the legitimate government of Virginia. The Restored Government, consisting at first of the western counties, immediately sent two senators and three representatives to Congress. All of them were seated in these, the first heady months of the war when most Northerners agreed with Lincoln that the South had never left the Union and the loyal population should be recognized as the body politic of the states.[18] Later, in 1862, when the Restored Government gave its consent to statehood for the western counties—an action that Lincoln initially opposed because it was highly irregular—Pierpont moved his Virginia government to Alexandria, where he presided over an even smaller domain than in the west. Because of its Lilliputian size, the Restored Government became the target of ridicule both in the South and in the North. Nevertheless, Lincoln continued to support it. One of the last acts of his life was to reaffirm this support, and when the war ended Pierpont was installed in the governor's mansion in Richmond.[19]

UNIONISM IN EAST TENNESSEE

Lincoln thought that the Virginia model would work elsewhere, particularly in Tennessee, where the eastern counties were a hotbed of Unionism. East Tennessee, he believed, could serve as a nucleus for the restoration of a loyal government in the whole state. Unlike western Virginia, that bordered on the North, East Tennessee was isolated and virtually surrounded by mountains, creating severe problems for the Washington administration's plans to aid local Unionists. Early in the war Confederates assumed control of the area and prepared to defend it from any Unionist uprising or Federal assault through Cumberland Gap. In Washington, Senator Andrew Johnson, Congressman Horace Maynard, and other Tennessee Unionists worked assiduously during the summer of 1861 to obtain arms for their compatriots in East Tennessee. They frequently met with President Lincoln and quickly developed a special relationship with him. John Hay, Lincoln's secretary, noted after a presidential meeting with the Tennessee loyalists in 1863: "I never saw him more at ease than when he is with [these] first rate patriots of the border. He is of them really, . . . [and] they [are] full of admiration for the President's way of doing things."[20]

In September 1861, East Tennesseans conceived of a plan, which was approved by Lincoln, to send a military force through Cumberland Gap to liberate the area. Simultaneous with the movement, Union guerrillas, who would be supplied with weapons by the War Department, were to destroy all the bridges on the railroads running through East Tennessee from Bridgeport, Alabama, to Bristol, Tennessee. At the designated time in November, Unionists burned five major bridges and attacked Confederate outposts. But the Federal force, consisting primarily of East Tennessee exiles and Kentuckians, never reached Cumberland Gap. General William Tecumseh Sherman, who commanded in Kentucky, called off the advance because of severe logistical problems in the mountainous terrain and the apparent inadequacy of the small army charged with the task. East Tennessee Unionists, consisting of two-thirds of the population of the area, were left to face the wrath of Confederate authorities, who summarily hanged several guerrillas, imprisoned others, and established martial law. Many East Tennesseans fled the area and joined the Federal army in Kentucky.[21] Some, like Parson Brownlow, went north where their thrilling but frequently embellished tales of persecution and escape gained the sympathy of the border and Northern people.

Lincoln was deeply moved by the plight of his East Tennessee friends. When General Don Carlos Buell replaced Sherman in command, the president, in consultation with East Tennessee leaders, immediately pressed him to launch another campaign to liberate the region. To facilitate the operation, he asked Congress to provide funds "as speedily" as possible for the construction of a railroad from Kentucky into East Tennessee. Congress, with other financial needs to meet, refused the request.[22] Meanwhile, Buell delayed his movement, which brought forth a rebuke from the president, who reminded him that "our friends in East Tennessee are being hanged and driven to despair." If you do not act, "we lose the most valuable stake we have in the South."[23] For sound military reasons, Buell still did not move; instead he made preparations for a campaign into middle Tennessee. Lincoln, whose policy was not to interfere with military decisions in the field, threw up his hands in frustration and lamented: "As everything else, nothing can be done."[24] His interest in the early liberation of East Tennessee Unionists, however, did not die, and it would be rekindled before the end of 1862.

The Federal occupation of parts of Tennessee, North Carolina, and Louisiana (New Orleans and environs) during the spring of 1862 spurred Lincoln to appoint military governors for these states. Before the end of the year he had also selected military governors for Arkansas and Texas, though Federal forces had only a weak foothold in those states. The military governors, the most notable of whom was Andrew Johnson of Tennessee, were charged with the responsibility of reorganizing civil government as soon as possible in the occupied regions and using this base to restore the states to their proper practical relationship in the Union. The success of the president's policy, of course, depended upon the progress of the Federal military in suppressing Confederate arms. It also depended upon the resurgence of loyal sentiments among the people, which in turn would be influenced by the course of the war and the policies of the Lincoln administration and its surrogates in the South. Lincoln expected Southern Unionists to take the initiative and provide the leadership for the work of reorganization. He permitted local Unionists a great deal of freedom in the restoration of civil authority, though with the stipulation that their efforts were not to conflict with military operations. Reorganization, however, proceeded slowly, mainly due to the failure of the Federal army to expand the occupied area and provide security for Unionists and war-weary Confederates who might be ready to give up the fight.

EMANCIPATION AND UNIONISM

Lincoln's emancipation policy, which was announced during the second year of the war, complicated efforts for an early restoration of the South to the Union. The preliminary proclamation of 22 September 1862, issued as a war measure, promised only to emancipate areas in rebellion. Proslavery Union leaders, however, were distressed by its implications, and they immediately sought its reversal. Congressman Horace Maynard declared that the enforcement of the proclamation against loyalist East Tennessee, an area still in rebel hands and thus conceivably subject to emancipation, "would be such a cumulative outrage upon their rights" that support for the Union would be in jeopardy in the area.[25] Thomas A. R. Nelson, another East Tennessee leader who had been elected to Congress but had not been able to take his seat, issued a printed address to his constituents attacking Lincoln's "infamous" proclamation and calling on them to resist "the tyrants and usurpers of the Federal administration who have blasted our hopes and are cruelly seeking to destroy the last vestige of freedom among us."[26] Faced with the prospect of losing the support of his East Tennessee friends, Lincoln placated them by exempting all of their state from his final proclamation of 1 January 1863. John-

son wrote Lincoln and expressed relief at the president's action. Even Nelson returned to the Union camp.

North Carolina, however, received no such concession from Lincoln. Military
Governor Edward Stanly had earlier met with the president to protest the issuance
of the preliminary Emancipation Proclamation, arguing that it would destroy latent
Union sentiment in his state. At that time Lincoln had assured him that occupied
North Carolina could avoid emancipation by holding a congressional election
prior to 1 January when the Emancipation Proclamation would become effective.
Stanly, however, failed to meet the deadline, and when Lincoln applied emancipa-
tion to North Carolina, the governor resigned.[27]

Most Southern Union leaders, if not their followers, eventually made their peace
with Lincoln on emancipation. Viewed as traitors by staunch Confederates,
Unionists had tied their fortunes and perhaps their lives to the Washington government. Despite their own racial prejudices and their fear that returning Southern
loyalty would be seriously retarded by it, the majority of Union activists in the
South realized that they could not oppose a major policy of the administration that
controlled the government and served as their protector. Unionists also knew that
their opposition to the president's emancipation policy would give encouragement
to the rebels and contribute to division over the war in the loyal states. Historians
have long commented on Lincoln's need to move carefully on emancipation lest he
lose support for the war in the border and Northern states. They have neglected
the importance of Southern Unionists in Lincoln's approach to emancipation and
the future status of blacks in Southern society. Lincoln understood that in order to
prevent large numbers of Unionists from deserting the cause, and thus dashing his
hopes for the early reorganization of their states, he must not push too quickly or
too hard on emancipation or black rights. A strong believer in self-government,
which he thought could best be exercised at the state level, Lincoln did not think
that he could or should require much beyond fundamental freedom for blacks.

Taking their cue from the president, Unionists justified their newfound support
of emancipation as necessary to save the Union. Unlike Lincoln, however, they frequently used racist language in their arguments, which they probably not only felt
but also hoped would mollify fellow Southerners regarding emancipation. Editor
James R. Hood of the *Chattanooga Gazette* wrote that he favored "blotting the institution" of slavery "from the face of the earth, . . . not because we love the negro,
but because we love the Government and hate the domineering fiendish spirit that
slavery breeds."[28] Virginian James W. Hunnicutt announced that he had been a
proslavery man, but circumstances "have made me a thorough anti-slavery man.
When traitors to God and their country threw African slavery into one end of the
scales and their country to the other end, and asked me which I would choose,
slavery without my country, or my country without slavery, my answer was, is, and
always will be, my country."[29]

Military Governor Johnson of Tennessee, a slaveholder until the Confederates
confiscated his slaves, repeatedly declared that he favored the president's Emancipation Proclamation because it freed white men, not blacks. At Franklin, Tennessee,

in August 1863, Johnson avowed that in order to end the rebellion if "slavery must go, I say, let it go! I am for my Government with or without slavery; but if either the Government or slavery must go, I say give me the Government and let the negroes go. . . . Rather than have [the Union] destroyed I would send every negro back to Africa, and see Africa itself swept beyond the line where gravitation ceases to exist."[30]

Other Unionist defenders of Lincoln's Emancipation Proclamation argued that the war itself was rapidly destroying the institution, and Southerners should accept this new reality before greater dislocations occurred. S. M. Arnell told a large rally at Columbia, Tennessee, in early 1864 that though he had "all of the prejudices in favor of southern institutions," he could not "resist the evidences of [his] senses in the matter." "The rude hands of the war," he declared, "have unsettled the [slavery] institution. It is a small matter now either in money or comfort to its owners. . . . The great question today is not the future of the southern slave, but the future of the southern white man." His future, Arnell contended, depended upon "the immediate restoration of civil Government in our midst" and the end of the destructive war.[31] Prominent Vicksburg Unionist Armisted Burwell informed Lincoln in August 1863 that the end of slavery in the Mississippi Valley was being accomplished by "the practical operation of war" and offered no real barrier to reconstruction. A similar report from Union General John M. Thayer appeared in the *Washington Chronicle*, Lincoln's newspaper organ in the national capital. Writing from Little Rock, Thayer indicated that "the leading Union men here, now take the ground that Arkansas must come back a free State. This conviction is fast spreading, not only in Arkansas, but in Louisiana, Tennessee, and Mississippi."[32]

Lincoln was overjoyed by the growing support for emancipation among Southern Unionists. He wrote Johnson on 11 September 1863, soon after the governor's Franklin speech: "I see that you have declared in favor of emancipation in Tennessee, for which, may God bless you. Get emancipation into your new State government—Constitution—and there will be no such word as fail for your case."[33] The support by Johnson and important Union leaders elsewhere encouraged Lincoln to take another step not only toward ending slavery but also toward the restoration of the Southern states to the Union. Influenced also by numerous reports of great disaffection in the Confederacy, the president, on 8 December 1863, issued a Proclamation of Amnesty and Reconstruction, outlining a new initiative in the reorganization of the Southern states.

UNIONISM AND THE REORGANIZATION
OF THE SOUTH

Lincoln's 8 December proclamation set forth a simple plan by which Southerners could "resume their allegiance to the United States" and "re-inaugurate loyal State governments." He made it clear in his annual message to Congress that his proclamation should not undercut the work of reorganization already occurring in the occupied South. His plan, which required 10 percent of the 1860 electorate to form a loyal government, retained the core concept of Unionism for the reorganization of the states, but it also provided a liberal amnesty policy by which Confederates, except for certain categories of leaders, could regain all of their rights, including the right to vote and hold office. The great majority of Confederates in order to obtain amnesty must swear a simple oath of future loyalty to the Union and pledge to abide by all federal measures regarding emancipation. Although his plan did not expressly require that states or parts of states that had been exempted from the Emancipation Proclamation abolish slavery, Lincoln made it clear that he expected them to do so. In a separate paragraph, however, he indicated that he would accept, as a temporary arrangement, an apprenticeship system for newly freed blacks, provided that they were given the benefits of education.[34]

Southern Unionists, having come to terms with emancipation, had no important reason to complain about Lincoln's reconstruction plan. Furthermore, the president in his appointments to federal offices in the South had demonstrated his preference for homegrown Unionists to outsiders. Indeed, he had expressed a strong aversion to "obnoxious strangers," or what the postwar generation would refer to as carpetbaggers, in public positions in the South. In early 1864 thousands of war-weary and demoralized Confederates took Lincoln's oath. Elections to constitutional conventions were held in occupied Louisiana, Arkansas, and Virginia. All three states abolished slavery in their constitutions, and Louisiana and Arkansas elected new state governments and sent representatives to Congress. Virginia's Restored Government under Pierpont continued to function as the recognized authority in that state. In Tennessee, Lincoln in 1863 had renewed his pressure on his field commanders, for both military and political reasons, to liberate the eastern part of the state. Indeed, he placed a high premium upon the redemption of East Tennessee. He wrote General William Rosecrans on 4 October that if Federal forces could win East Tennessee, "I think the rebellion must dwindle and die." Meanwhile, he encouraged Military Governor Johnson to hold elections and move toward the restoration of civil government.[35] Johnson, however, refused to act until East Tennessee had been completely redeemed by Federal forces, which, he believed, was needed to assure a loyal majority at the polls. Not until early 1865 did Tennessee hold a convention and adopt a new constitution abolishing slavery and restoring civil government.

Lincoln recommended in a remarkable 13 March 1864 letter to Governor Michael Hahn of Louisiana, which he marked *Private*, that the state convention enfranchise certain classes of blacks, who he believed were qualified for suffrage. Despite this suggestion, he refused to impose a voting requirement on a Southern state. Prior to the Reconstruction era, suffrage qualifications were viewed strictly as a matter for the states to determine, a constitutional position that Lincoln supported. Furthermore, he did not want to alienate his Southern Unionist supporters in Louisiana by imposing black suffrage on their state. He told a delegation of New Orleans blacks that sought his support for voting rights for their race that he would not interfere unless their enfranchisement was necessary to suppress the rebellion.[36] To Lincoln, who had no personal objections to the ballot for some blacks, emancipation, not voting rights, was required to win the war. Had he lived, the realities of Reconstruction and the need to preserve the fruits of Union victory in the war might have caused him to change his mind. At any rate, Louisiana rejected his suggestion of black suffrage, though the state convention went further than most Northern states in granting other rights to blacks.[37]

ELECTION OF 1864

By the summer of 1864, Reconstruction had virtually ground to a halt, having fallen victim, at least temporarily, to military reversals, a growing opposition to the Lincoln administration in the North, and factionalism among Southern Unionists. For the first time, Congress seriously challenged Lincoln's control of Reconstruction. Divisions over the war, emancipation, civil liberties, and Reconstruction were played out in the presidential contest of that year. Southern Unionists in the occupied areas fully expected to participate in the election. Like the rest of the country, they were divided over the issues and the candidates, especially during the early part of the campaign. From the beginning, however, support for Lincoln was a great deal stronger among Unionists in the South than in the North and in the border states. Furthermore, Unionists, who would suffer a harsh fate if the Confederacy won its independence, unlike Northerners, were united in their opposition to a peace short of reunion with loyal men in control of the South.

In Louisiana, an early challenge to the president by friends of Salmon P. Chase threatened to win control of the state's delegation to the national Republican convention. Supporters of the president's Reconstruction policy, led by Michael Hahn and encouraged by General Nathaniel P. Banks, organized a Lincoln party and obtained the quiet encouragement of their benefactor, particularly in matters of patronage. Hahn's *New Orleans True Delta* claimed to be the first newspaper in America to place Lincoln's name on its masthead. On 1 January 1864, Hahn, who would soon be elected Louisiana's first Union governor, declared that he would "use his whole influence to maintain power in the hands of the patriot who stands immovably at the head of the national administration." The *True Delta* soon waxed warm in its praise of Lincoln. On 12 March it boldly proclaimed that "when history comes with impartial pen and writes the account of his administration, the name of Abraham Lincoln will be enrolled among the world's great. . . . Calm and pure as was Washington, quick and indomitable as was Jackson, shrewd and cunning like Van Buren, he is eminently qualified to fill the position of President of the United States in this the greatest crisis of the world's history."[38] The failure of the Chase candidacy in the spring left the Hahn forces in complete control, and they sent a Lincoln delegation, headed by Cuthbert Bullitt, an old friend of the president, to the Republican national convention.[39]

A different division among Unionists occurred in Tennessee, where conservatives, still smarting over emancipation, challenged the hardline policy of Military Governor Johnson. In 1863 conservatives had sought to elect state officers under the old constitution, but Johnson refused to order an election on the grounds that state reorganization would be premature until East Tennessee had been liberated and provisions made to prevent rebels from regaining power. When conservatives appealed to Lincoln to override his military governor, he declined to intervene, though he continued to press Johnson to hold elections preparatory to the restoration of civil government. In early 1864 Johnson further alienated conservative Unionists when he required a more stringent loyalty oath than Lincoln's for participation in local elections. Although much of East Tennessee was under Federal control by the spring of 1864, the governor still refused to authorize state elections.[40]

Meanwhile, Johnson's star had risen among Northern Republicans, who believed that the Tennessean, in addition to his influence with Union Democrats, would serve on the national ticket as a useful counterweight to the soft and indecisive president. Lincoln also favored Johnson for vice president because of his Democratic background and the legitimacy that the Tennessean as his running mate would give to his Southern policy. The president, however, did not dictate his choice to the delegates. Some Radicals in the convention complicated matters for Johnson's nomination by questioning the seating of the Southern delegates. They argued that these delegations represented rotten boroughs that were created to secure Lincoln's nomination and election. Radicals, who never had much confidence in Southern Unionism, also objected to the seating of the delegates on the ground that such action would be a recognition of the president's Reconstruction governments. The convention, however, agreed to seat the Southern delegation, except for South Carolina's, but granted voting rights only to Tennessee, Louisiana, and Arkansas. Inexplicably, Virginia's delegation was denied a vote, though the Pierpont government had been recognized by Congress as well as by the president.[41] The convention, having conferred legitimacy upon some of the Southern delegations, went on to nominate Johnson for the vice presidency on the Lincoln ticket.

Southern Unionists overwhelmingly rallied to the Lincoln-Johnson standard. Privately, some Southern Lincolnites, like their political brethren in the North, expressed displeasure with the president. Governor Pierpont of Virginia wrote a friend that "Old Father Abraham is running the machine to the Devil just as fast as possible. The man seems to have forgotten every thing except his re-election."[42] The Democratic peace platform, however, which threatened to leave Unionists at the tender mercies of the rebels, scared Southern loyalists to the marrow, inspiring them to campaign aggressively for the president. Even some Unionists who still opposed emancipation, announced their support for Lincoln. John Minor Botts, a wealthy planter and a former Whig colleague of Lincoln in the House of Representatives, wrote from Confederate Virginia that though he thought the president had no constitutional right to abolish slavery, Lincoln was "entitled to the gratitude of the people of the North" for his efforts to suppress the rebellion. Botts lamented that he would not be able to cast a vote for this "vigorous, strong-minded, and conscientious man."[43]

In the 1863 state and local political contests, several Southern Unionists had campaigned for the Republican party in the critical lower North. The *Washington*

Chronicle, Lincoln's newspaper organ in the capital, had hailed the "glorious consequences [of] their eloquent appeals in favor of the Government and against the rebellion" that followed the Southern Unionist efforts. They had especially won support for the administration of many old Whigs and Democrats.[44] In 1864 Unionists speakers, including Pierpont, again went north to campaign for the war party and its candidate for president.[45] Pierpont, who consulted with the president before leaving for a campaign swing, undertook the most grueling canvass in Lincoln's behalf of any Southern speaker. He stumped for eight weeks in the Northeast, sometimes speaking twice a day to crowds of 3,000 or 4,000.[46] In the South, Union newspapers, of which there were about twenty, with a few exceptions devoted their columns to the promotion of the Lincoln ticket. Even Southern radicals, who were in a minority, fell in line and supported Lincoln after the collapse of the movement to replace him on the Republican ticket. In Arkansas, the *Little Rock Unconditional Union*, the organ of the radical faction, carried Lincoln's name on its masthead while attacking his Reconstruction program and his conservative subordinates in the state.[47]

In Tennessee, however, a vigorous opposition to the Lincoln-Johnson candidacy arose. Here, conservative Unionists aligned themselves with Northern Democrats and border-state conservatives in an effort to defeat the Republicans, though they too deplored the Democrats' peace platform. Their main target was Johnson, whose highhanded methods as military governor had alarmed them, convincing them that he was intent upon perpetuating his power in the state. Prewar political rivalries also played a part in the opposition to Johnson. The conservative leaders were old Whigs of Middle Tennessee who had long battled Johnson for control of the state. They organized what they styled Conservative Union clubs and selected an electoral ticket for George B. McClellan, the Democratic candidate for president. In raising the standard of "the hero of Antietam," conservatives hoped not only to get rid of the Johnson regime and restore civil government but also reverse emancipation.[48]

When Governor Johnson on 30 September announced a more stringent oath for voting in the presidential election, the Tennessee conservatives objected to Lincoln. John Lellyett, one of the conservative leaders, delivered the protest to the president. When Lellyett insisted that he override Johnson's action and provide protection for McClellan supporters in the state, Lincoln refused and evidently treated the Tennessean in a rough way. Lellyett immediately wrote an account of the interview and sent it to the *World*, the Democratic organ in New York. He charged that Lincoln in abruptly ending the exchange with him declared: "I expect to let the friends of George B. McClellan manage their side of this contest in their own way; and I will manage my side of it in my way." The publication by the Democratic press of Lellyett's account created considerable grist for the McClellan campaign mills in the North and border states. The Republican press ignored it.

A few day after the appearance of Lellyett's account in the *World*, Lincoln sent a sharply worded letter to the Tennessee protesters. He again indicated that he could not "perceive any military reason for . . . interference in the matter" of the election. The president, he said, "is charged with no duty in the conduct of a presidential election in any State" except "to give protection against violence," which, he contended, Governor Johnson could provide.[49] The Tennessee conservatives indignantly replied that "in view of the fact that our people are overawed by military power [and] the laws set aside and violated with impurity" they were withdrawing the McClellan ticket in the state.[50]

The election under Johnson's stringent voting requirements, however, was held. Despite the official withdrawal of the McClellan ticket, the Democratic candidate received approximately 5,000 to Lincoln's 30,000 votes. About one-half of Lincoln's ballots came from recently liberated East Tennessee.[51] The state's electoral votes for Lincoln, along with those of Louisiana, which were cast by the legislature, were not counted by Congress. Loyal governments in Virginia and Arkansas offered no electoral slate, though Unionists in both states held Lincoln rallies and in other ways supported his candidacy.[52] Since Lincoln won 212 electoral votes to 21 for McClellan, he did not need the Southern votes.

The Republican victory at the polls not only insured the success of Lincoln's war aims, including complete emancipation, it also meant that his control over Reconstruction had been strengthened. As the war came to an end, Lincoln probably saw no good reason to make a major change in his Southern policy. In what seemed designed to spur Southerners to resume their allegiance to the Union, Lincoln in his annual message to Congress in December declared that the time might come when he would be forced to change his liberal amnesty policy. Still, he admitted that some Southerners were not yet in a position to make a free choice regarding their loyalties. In early 1865 Lincoln objected to the congressional postponement of a resolution to seat senators and representatives from Louisiana and Arkansas, but this action did not portend of a serious conflict with Congress over his Southern policy.[53]

The president in his last speech praised the new Louisiana constitution and expressed the hope that the state legislature would confer "the elective franchise . . . on the very intelligent [blacks], and on those who serve our cause as soldiers." However, he made it clear at this time, at least to the satisfaction of Secretary of Navy Gideon Welles, that he would leave the matter of suffrage for the states to decide. The statement in his last address that he might "make some new announcement to the people of the South" did not necessarily mean that he would develop a new plan of Reconstruction. He probably had in mind a proposal that Secretary of War Edwin M. Stanton was drafting for the temporary military control of states preparatory to the holding of elections. States that had been reorganized or were in the process of reorganization, namely Tennessee, Louisiana, Arkansas, and Virginia, would not be affected except where military assistance was needed to sustain the Union governments and provide local security.[54]

Lincoln still expected Southern Unionists to direct the work of reorganization. But after the war when a large number of former Confederates took his amnesty oath and regained their political and civil rights, Lincoln, had he lived, would have encountered the problem that he raised with his secretary in 1863: how could "the rebellious populations" be prevented "from overwhelming and outvoting the loyal minority" in the South?[55] Despite his faith in self-government, by which he meant the majority of whites in the South who had sworn allegiance to the Union, Lincoln's nonintervention policy after the reestablishment of civil authority would have been sorely tested by postwar realities. Although we cannot be certain what course he would have taken after the war, we can confidently assume that he would have done a better job of sustaining Unionist control and protecting black freedom than did his successor, Andrew Johnson.

NOTES

1. Lincoln to Lyman Trumbull, 8 January 1865; Abraham Lincoln, *The Collected Works of Abraham Lincoln*, ed. Roy P. Basler, 9 vols. (New Brunswick, N.J.: Rutgers University Press in association with the Abraham Lincoln Association, 1953–55), 8: 207, (hereafter cited as *CWAL*).

2. See, for example, Kenneth M. Stampp, *The United States and National Self-Determination: Two Traditions*, 30th Annual Robert Fortenbaugh Memorial Lecture, (Gettysburg, Pa.: Gettysburg College, 1991), 18–21; and James M. McPherson, *Battle Cry of Freedom: The Civil War Era* (New York: Ballantine Books, 1988), 352–354, 502–506, 562–563. Hereinafter the designation *Southern loyalists* or *Southern Unionists* will refer to whites. Most Southern blacks, of course, especially after the Emancipation Proclamation, were loyal to the Union but were not free political agents as were Southern whites.

3. "Message to Congress in Special Session, July 4, 1861," in *CWAL*, 4: 432–433, 437. At one point, as president-elect he had actually expressed support for the military preparations that were being made in the South, since, as he said, with arms in their hands, "it will enable the people the more easily to suppress any uprisings there." "Passage Written for Lyman Trumbull's Speech at Springfield, Illinois, November 20, 1860," in *CWAL*, 4: 141–142.

4. *CWAL*, 4: 426, 439–440.

5. "Annual Message to Congress, December 3, 1861," in *CWAL*, 5: 48–49.

6. Frederick H. Dyer, *A Compendium of the War of the Rebellion*, 3 vols. (New York: T. Yoseloff, 1959), 1: 11–12.

7. Nathaniel P. Banks, *The Reconstruction of States. Letter of Major-General Banks to Senator Lane* (late 1864) (New York: Harper & Brothers, 1865), 13; Richard N. Current, *Lincoln's Loyalists: Union Soldiers from the Confederacy* (Boston: Northwestern University Press, 1992), 217–218. James M. McPherson (*Battle Cry of Freedom*, 306n) estimates that between 850,000 and 900,000 troops served in the Confederate army. This means that 7.6 percent of Southerners who fought in the Civil War fought on the Federal side.

8. *Little Rock National Democrat*, 13 August 1864.

9. Frank W. Klingberg, *The Southern Claims Commission* (Berkeley and Los Angeles: University of California Press, 1955), 17–19; Carl N. Degler, *The Other South: Southern Dissenters in the Nineteenth Century* (New York: Harper & Row, 1973), 177–182. A revealing statement of the strength of Unionism among the planter class was made by Union Governor Francis H. Pierpont to the legislature of the Restored Government of Virginia meeting at Wheeling in 1861. "Secession has not originated among the large slaveholders of the South," he declared, "nor has it found among that class its busiest and most ardent advocates." The latest election returns in Virginia, he said, "will show that the slaveholders themselves considered the safety of their property as dependent upon the maintenance of the

Union." Virginia, *Journal of the House of Delegates of the State of Virginia, for the Extra Session, 1861* (Wheeling: Daily Press Book and Job Office, 1861), 6.

10. John Minor Botts to John B. Frey, 22 January 1864, Abraham Lincoln Papers, Robert Todd Lincoln Collection, Library of Congress (hereafter cited as Lincoln Papers). This letter can also be found in John Minor Botts, *The Great Rebellion: Its Secret History, Rise, Progress, and Disastrous Failure* (New York: Harper & Brothers, 1866), Appendix, 311.

11. Excerpt from late November 1860 speech, in *East Tennessee and the Civil War*, by Oliver P. Temple (1899; reprint, Freeport, N.Y.: Books for Libraries Press, 1971), 133.

12. Temple, *East Tennessee and the Civil War*, 134–135; James W. Hunnicutt, *The Conspiracy Unveiled: The South Sacrificed, or, The Horrors of Secession* (Philadelphia: J. B. Lippincott & Co., 1863), 29; Virginia, *Journal of the House of Delegates, Extra Session, 1861*, 6; *Nashville Daily Union*, 14 February 1864; Botts, *Great Rebellion*, Appendix, 248–254.

13. Degler, *Other South*, 186.

14. Hunnicutt, *Conspiracy Unveiled*, 34, 74; "Speech of Andrew Johnson, at Franklin, Tennessee, August 22, 1863," in *The Papers of Andrew Johnson*, vol. 6, 1862–1864, ed. Leroy P. Graf and Ralph W. Haskins (Knoxville: University of Tennessee Press, 1983), 335 (hereafter cited as *JP*).

15. *Nashville Daily Union*, 6 April 1864. See also Joseph S. Fowler to Andrew Johnson, 6 April 1862, *JP*, vol. 5, 1861–1862 (Knoxville: University of Tennessee Press, 1979), 272.

16. As reported in the *New York World*, 25 March 1862.

17. As reported in the *New Bern North Carolina Times*, 20 April 1864. See also Hunnicutt, *Conspiracy Unveiled*, 73.

18. Francis H. Pierpont, "History of the Reorganization of the Restored Government of Virginia and the Formation of the State of West Virginia," in Governor Francis H. Pierpont Papers, Box 578, Virginia State Library, Richmond; a version of Pierpont's "History" was printed in the *New York Times*, 26 June 1864; Virgil A. Lewis, ed., *How West Virginia Was Made: Proceedings of the First Convention of the People of Northwestern Virginia at Wheeling, May 13, 14, and 15, 1861, and the Journal of the Second Convention of the People of Northwestern Virginia at Wheeling* (Charleston: State of West Virginia, 1909), 34.

19. Richard G. Lowe, *Republicans and Reconstruction in Virginia, 1856–70* (Charlottesville, VA: University of Virginia Press, 1991), 14–20.

20. Salmon P. Chase to Andrew Johnson, 29 June 1861, *JP*, vol. 4, 1860–1861 (1976), 522–523; entry for October 21, 1863, in *Lincoln and the Civil War in the Diaries and Letters of John Hay*, ed. Tyler Dennett (New York: Dodd, Mead, 1939), 104–105.

21. Temple, *East Tennessee and the Civil War*, 370–371, 374–375, 378; Andrew Johnson to Gideon Welles, 30 September 1861, *JP*, 5: 12–13; William Tecumseh Sherman to George H. Thomas, 8 November 1861, *War of the Rebellion: A Compilation of the Official Records of the Union and Confederate Armies*, 73 vols., 128 parts; (Washington, D.C.: Government Printing Office, 1880–1901), ser. 1, vol. 4, 347, (hereafter cited as *OR*). On 13 December 1862, a history of the futile effort to aid East Tennessee Unionists was given to the House of Representatives by Horace Maynard. *OR*, ser. 1, vol. 20, pt. 2, pp. 167–171.

22. Andrew Johnson and Horace Maynard to Don Carlos Buell, 7 December 1861, *JP*, 5: 43–44; "President Lincoln's Annual Message to Congress, December 3, 1861," in *CWAL*, 5: 37.

23. Lincoln to Don Carlos Buell, 4, 6 January 1862, *CWAL*, 5: 90, 91.

24. Lincoln to Simon Cameron, 10 January 1862, *CWAL*, 5: 95.

25. Statement of Horace Maynard, 13 December 1862, *OR*, ser. 1, vol. 20, pt. 2, p. 171; William G. Brownlow to Lincoln, 25 December 1862, Lincoln Papers.

26. Address of Hon. T. A. R. Nelson to the People of East Tennessee, 3 October 1862, in *OR*, ser. I, vol. 16, pt. 2, pp. 909–911.

27. Edward Stanly, *A Military Governor among Abolitionists: A Letter from Edward Stanly, to Charles Sumner* (New York: n.p., 1865), 167–68; *Washington Daily National Intelligencer*, 6 August 1863.

28. *Chattanooga Daily Gazette*, 5 (quotation), 20 March 1864.

29. As reported in the *New Bern North Carolina Times*, 20 April 1864. See also *Nashville Daily Union*, 24 February 1864.

30. William C. Harris, "Andrew Johnson's First 'Swing Around the Circle': His Northern Campaign of 1863," *Civil War History* 35 (June 1989): 158, 161, 168; Speech at Franklin, 22 August 1863, in *JP*, 6: 337–338. An exception to the blatant Unionist racism on the emancipation question was Governor Francis H. Pierpont of Virginia. In a letter to Lincoln (3 September 1863, Lincoln Papers), Pierpont argued the military necessity for freeing the slaves and avoided racist comments. He also took the initiative in late 1863 to call a state constitutional convention whose main purpose would be to abolish slavery.

31. Newspaper clipping from *Columbia* [Tennessee] *Sentinel*, 6 February 1864, in Lincoln Papers.

32. Armisted Burwell to Lincoln, 28 August 1863, in Lincoln Papers; *Washington Chronicle*, 1 December 1863. See also Address of Brig. Gen. E. W. Gantt, C.S.A., at Little Rock, Arkansas (n.p., 1863), and the *Little Rock National Democrat*, 26 December 1863. Ex-Confederate General Gantt also visited Washington and met with Lincoln. E. W. Gantt to Lincoln, 15 July 1863, 29 January 1864, Lincoln Papers.

33. Lincoln to Andrew Johnson, 11 September 1863, *CWAL*, 6: 440.

34. Proclamation of Amnesty and Reconstruction, 8 December 1863, in *CWAL*, 7: 53–56.

35. Lincoln to William S. Rosecrans, 4 October 1863; Lincoln to Andrew Johnson, 11 September, 28 October, 1863, *CWAL*, 6: 440, 448, 498; Lincoln to Johnson, 10 December 1863, *CWAL*, 7: 59. For his opposition to "obnoxious strangers" in Southern positions, see Lincoln's first inaugural address, 4 March 1861, in *CWAL*, 4: 266, and Lincoln to George S. Shepley, 21 November 1862, *CWAL*, 5: 504.

36. Lincoln to Michael Hahn, 13 March 1864, *CWAL*, 7: 243; *New York Principia*, 10 March 1864.

37. Lincoln himself labeled the Louisiana document "an excellent constitution—better for the poor black man than we have in Illinois." Lincoln to Stephen A. Hurlbut, 14 November 1864, *CWAL*, 8: 107.

38. *New Orleans True Delta*, 1 January, 12 March 1864.

39. Hahn to Lincoln, 23 May 1864, Lincoln Papers. After the convention, Bullitt returned to Washington and went to Philadelphia with the president, where Lincoln addressed the "Great Central Sanitary Fair." Rush Plumly to Lincoln, 16 June 1864, copy in Nathaniel P. Banks Papers, Library of Congress.

40. *Nashville Daily Press*, 3 October 1863; Emerson Etheridge to Lincoln, 28 September 1863, Lincoln Papers; *Nashville Daily Union*, 8 October 1863.

41. For the debate over the seating of the Southern delegations, see Richard H. Abbott, *The Republican Party and the South, 1855–1877: The First Strategy* (Chapel Hill: University of North Carolina Press, 1986), 35–36. The conclusion that Lincoln favored Johnson for the nomination because of the legitimacy it would bring to his Southern policy is mine.

42. Francis H. Pierpont to Arthur Boreman, 18 May 1864, Arthur Boreman Papers, West Virginia University Library, Morgantown. See also J. D. Hale to Horace Maynard, 25 June 1864, Lincoln Papers.

43. John Minor Botts to John B. Frey, 22 January 1864, Lincoln Papers.

44. *Nashville Daily Union*, 11 October 1863; *Washington Daily Chronicle*, 27 January 1864.

45. *Knoxville Brownlow's Whig*, 11 June 1864; *New Bern North Carolina Times*, 20 July 1864.

46. Julia Pierpont to Will Robertson, 27 January 1865, *Calendar of the Francis Harrison Pierpont Letters and Papers in West Virginia Depositories* (Charleston: State of West Virginia, 1940), 251.

47. *Little Rock Unconditional Union*, 15 September 1864; *Little Rock National Democrat*, 17 September 1864.

48. John Lellyett to William B. Campbell, 15 September 1864; Jordan Stokes to Campbell, 24 September 1864, both in Campbell Family Papers, Duke University Library; *Nashville Daily Press*, 3, 15, 24 October 1864.

49. Lincoln to Campbell, 22 October 1864, *CWAL*, 8: 58–72. Most of these pages contain Johnson's election proclamation of 30 September, the conservative protest, and Lellyet's account of his interview with Lincoln. For the reaction in the North to the Lincoln-Lellyet incident, see the *Washington National Intelligencer*, 25 October 1863. The Tennessee conservatives also complained that at least one McClellan rally had been broken up, with Johnson's approval, by Tennessee troops stationed at Nashville.

50. *CWAL*, 8: 59–61n. See also Balie Peyton to Campbell, 25 October 1864, Campbell Family Papers.

51. Andrew Johnson to Lincoln, 18 November 1864, *JP*, vol. 7, 1864–1865 (1986), 301 and 301n; *New York Times*, 21 November 1864.

52. Thomas B. Alexander, *Political Reconstruction in Tennessee* (Nashville: Vanderbilt University Press, 1950), 16; Michael Hahn to Lincoln, 11 November 1864, Lincoln Papers; *Little Rock National Democrat*, 26 November 1864.

53. "Annual Message to Congress, December 6, 1864"; Lincoln to Lyman Trumbull, 9 January 1865, both in *CWAL*, 8: 152, 206–207. For a full account of Lincoln's Reconstruction policy during the last five months of his life, see my forthcoming book *Mystic Chords of Memory: Abraham Lincoln and the Southern Restoration*, chapter 11. My account challenges the view of recent historians that Lincoln and Radical Republicans in Congress were close to agreement in early 1865 on a more stringent plan of Reconstruction than the 1863 plan, one that would provide for black suffrage in the South.

54. "Last Public Address, April 11, 1865," in *CWAL*, 8: 402–405; entries for 13, 14 April 1865, in *Diary of Gideon Welles: Secretary of the Navy under Lincoln and Johnson*, with an introduction by John T. Morse, Jr., 3 vols. (Boston: Houghton Mifflin, 1911), 2: 279–282; *Selected Essays by Gideon Welles: Civil War and Reconstruction*, compiled by Albert Mordell (New York: Twayne Publishers, 1959), 190–192, 205–206.

55. Entry for 1 November 1863, Dennett, *Hay Diary*, 113.

8 Lincoln and Idaho: A Rocky Mountain Legacy

David H. Leroy

The shortest communication Abraham Lincoln wrote on the last day of his life was confined to a single word: "Appoint." The delegate from Idaho Territory, William H. Wallace, had given the president the letter upon which the response was written. "I would respectfully recommend James H. Alvord for the office of Marshal of the Territory of Idaho, made vacant by the removal of Dolphus S. Payne." Lincoln's one-word endorsement was directed to Attorney General James Speed for action.[1]

A second letter from Wallace accompanied the first. In it he recommended the appointment of Milton Kelly to fill a vacancy of an associate justiceship on the Supreme Court of Idaho Territory. A resignation by Samuel C. Parks had created the opening. On this document Lincoln wrote, "If it is definitely concluded to accept Judge Parks' resignation, as I understand it is, let the within appointment be made. April 14, 1865. A. Lincoln."[2]

Despite the fact that Wallace had been one of the political managers for Lincoln's second inaugural on 4 March 1865, by 13 March he was complaining that he had been unable to obtain an interview with the president.[3] On Friday, 14 April 1865, however, William Henson Wallace was able to arrange to appear in person at the White House before the president. They were friends of long standing, and Lincoln occasionally called Wallace, who had served as both governor and delegate to Congress from Idaho Territory, by the nickname Old Idaho.[4] After Wallace had finished his presentation and the president had concluded to grant the appointments, an important social opportunity was extended:

Then, according to the story handed down to the Wallace family, the President asked Mr. Wallace if he and Mrs. Wallace would join the theater party President and Mrs. Lincoln were having that evening. Because of a slight indisposition of Mrs. Wallace, the Colonel declined the invitation, and the President closed the interview by patting the Colonel on the shoulder and saying, "Now, 'Old Idaho' come down in the morning, Monday between 9 and 10 o'clock and get your second commission, and you can have everything for Old Idaho as you want it."[5]

While it is only a coincidence that two of the three presidential appointments made by Lincoln on the Friday of his assassination related to the Territory of Idaho, it is not well understood how closely Lincoln himself was tied to Idaho as a political creator. Lincoln's relationship with Wallace spanned more than a quarter of a century. The same was true of Sam Parks, the judge whom Wallace sought to replace. The study of these two territorial figures helps initially to illustrate that Idaho has a Lincoln legacy beyond mere coincidence.

RELATIONSHIPS WITH WALLACE AND PARKS

The Lincoln-Wallace relationship reportedly went back to days of mutual political activities in Illinois or in Indiana, where Wallace resided until he left for Iowa in 1837. Even after he moved from Fort Wayne, Wallace continued to visit both Illinois and Indiana from time to time.

In the Wallace family there is the tradition that such a friendship began when Wallace was able to arrange for Lincoln to make a political speech at a public meeting at a time when Lincoln was practically unknown. The time usually assigned is in the 1850's. . . . Lincoln is supposed to have made several speeches while in Indiana, but the time and place cannot be identified as all accounts are in the form of recollections recorded years after the events and are wholly unreliable as to time and place. I believe, therefore, that William, in campaigning with his brother, David, was able to arrange for one of these speeches. Lincoln never forgot this kindness, and so "never failed to grant any request made by William Henson Wallace."[6]

Lincoln visited a number of Indiana cities in the 1830s, 1840s and 1850s. They included Petersburg, Rockport, and Vincennes in 1830; Washington in 1834; Bruceville, Gentryville, Vincennes, and Washington in 1844; and Indianapolis in 1859.[7] Although Wallace remained a resident of Iowa from 1837 until 1853, it is possible that he may have encountered and introduced Lincoln at a speech in either Indiana or Illinois during that period. A particularly likely opportunity would have occurred in 1844, when both tradition and travel records report that young Lincoln stumped and gave Whig speeches in the Hoosier state from October to 4 November.[8] After serving as the Speaker of the House of Representatives in the Iowa Territorial legislature in 1838, Wallace became a member of its council in 1842. He was the Whig nominee for congressional delegate in 1843 and for United States senator in 1848. Though unsuccessful in both these nominations, he served as a colonel in the Iowa militia and held office as Zachary Taylor's appointee for "Receiver of Public Monies at Fairfield, Iowa." He remained in that post until the spring of 1853, when he moved to the West Coast, settling in the new Territory of Washington.[9]

While the commencement of the Lincoln-Wallace relationship may have become obscure, it is clear that it remained a sufficiently strong connection that Wallace immediately determined to capitalize upon it when Lincoln was elected to the presidency. By 2 February 1861, Colonel Wallace had arrived in Washington, D.C., seeking the removal of disloyal territorial officers and his own appointment as governor of Washington Territory. On 9 April 1861, Wallace secured the gubernatorial appointment from Lincoln. As of 17 April, Wallace was already en route back to the territory, but he learned when his ship docked in San Francisco in early June that he had been nominated to run for another office—delegate to Congress as the candidate of his Republican Party. After the campaign and when the canvass of votes was completed and announced in June 1861, Governor Wallace had at least realized his political dream of becoming a member of Congress by a margin of just over 300 votes.[10]

Wallace, Lincoln's friend, returned to the national capital and was present in the fall and winter of 1862 when proposals began to surface about subdividing the existing Washington Territory to carve out still another new territory in the Northwest.

Samuel C. Parks of Logan County, Illinois, had an even longer, closer connection to the president of the United States than Wallace. "I became acquainted with Mr. Lincoln the year of 1840, in Springfield, Illinois,—when he was 31 years of age and I was 20. For more than 10 years my relations with him were intimate and confidential."[11]

Beginning in the spring of 1840, Parks began law training under John T. Stuart and Ninian W. Edwards in Springfield. By 1846, Parks had established a law practice in Logan County and frequently was associated in trials with Lincoln in that jurisdiction. As a delegate to the first Republican national convention in 1856, he participated in Lincoln's attempt to be nominated for the vice presidency. Again in 1860, Parks worked for Lincoln's nomination at the Republican national convention, this time helping to make his friend successful as the presidential nominee.[12]

Parks's contact with Lincoln on the judicial circuit had given him unique insights into the character and temperament of the president:

Lincoln's conscience, reason, and judgment worked out the law for him. It would not do to call him a great lawyer, for he is not; but it is fair to state that he was a good lawyer under conditions. He was not as quick as some men—in fact, required more time to study his case and thus arrive at the truth. But above all things he must feel that he was right. For a man who was for a quarter of a century both a lawyer and a politician, he was the most honest man I ever knew. He was not only morally honest, but intellectually so. At the bar he was strong if convinced he was in the right, but if he suspected he might be wrong, he was the weakest lawyer I ever saw.[13]

Apparently Parks gained these insights from actual courtroom circumstances. Lincoln reportedly once urged Parks to give the closing argument in a criminal case instead of doing it for the client himself because Lincoln was convinced that the defendant was guilty.[14]

Parks took these insights into various political roles during Lincoln's prepresidential campaigns.

In 1854, I became a member of the Illinois Legislature at the request of Mr. Lincoln and I did all I could for his election to the United States Senate. To facilitate my labor with the members of the House and Senate on his behalf, he took a small blank book and wrote down the name and politics of every member as "Whig," "Democrat" or "Anti-Nebraska Democrat." Occasionally when there was anything notable in the position of any member he would mention it in a short note. I believe that his is the only book of the kind that he ever made.[15]

In the 1858 senatorial campaign, Lincoln urged that Parks speak on his behalf in Tremont, Illinois. At an appearance for the candidate in the town of Lincoln, Parks introduced him. [16]

In the presidential campaign of 1860, it fell to Parks, the man who believed in Lincoln and knew him well, to undertake two special political tasks. At the 1860 convention in Chicago, he was assigned by Judge David Davis, the campaign's manager, to organize support for the nominee among the delegation from Vermont, Parks's native state.[17]

The second mission for Parks in the 1860 campaign was of his own making. On 5 July 1860, the publishing house of Follett, Foster, and Company published a book called *The Lives and Speeches of Abraham Lincoln and Hanibal Hamlin*, written by William Dean Howells. Early advertising by the publishers promised that Lincoln himself had "authorized" the edition. In a 19 June confidential letter Lincoln stressed that he was astounded by that public announcement, as the book was not upon his authority.[18] Perhaps familiar with Lincoln's anguish over the promotion of this volume, Parks later explained why he took a unique step with his own copy of the book:

Soon after his nomination for the Presidency, I bought Howell's campaign "Life of Lincoln," which I wish to use in the canvass, and asked Mr. Lincoln to correct it for me. He went through it carefully, speeches and all, and returned it to me with about twenty corrections on the margin over the signature of "L." in pencil.[19]

The extent to which Parks actually used the Lincoln annotated biography during the 1860 campaign remains unreported. Nevertheless, the importance of the volume as a biography of Lincoln's life is unparalleled. During his lifetime, Lincoln authored two relatively brief autobiographical essays; but because the Howell's book is greater in length and contains many more facts and descriptions than either of Lincoln's personal efforts, it becomes the definitive statement of Lincoln's history when read together with his corrections. Thus Parks's act, together with Lincoln's response, established the "authorized" edition of Lincoln's life, whether the candidate intended it to be so or not.[20]

In February of 1861, Sam Parks also went to Washington to see his friend Abraham Lincoln. However, instead of urging his own appointment to some federal post, Parks strongly recommended to the president that Simon Cameron from Pennsylvania be placed in a Cabinet post to firm up support for the new administration within "the great border state of Pennsylvania." Since the Republicans of Illinois could not agree upon any local man to insist on for Cabinet service, Parks urged that an Illinois aspirant, Norman Judd, should be satisfied with a foreign post. After a stint as a minor functionary in Cameron's War Department, Judd was, indeed, appointed by the president to the post of minister to Prussia.[21] Thus, apparently, Lincoln took Parks's advice. By the fall of 1862, Parks was once again in his native Illinois.

CREATING IDAHO TERRITORY

At the same time, Lincoln's friend from Indiana, William H. Wallace, now territorial delegate to Congress from Washington Territory, began to work with other politicos to split his territory in two. With the discovery of gold in the Rocky Mountains some 400 miles east of the capital at Olympia, more than 20,000 people had moved inland. The hardships of travel and communication began to create a movement seeking separate territorial status for the Eastern District of Washington Territory and the state of Oregon. By 1861, the discontent had focused in the form of deannexation bills introduced before the legislature of Washington Territory.[22] Knowing that any successful proposal ultimately would have to be presented for congressional action and would require the signature of the president, Wallace involved another Lincoln intimate in conceiving the proposal for territorial division.

Anson G. Henry graduated from medical school in 1827. He moved his practice to Springfield in October of 1832. Soon afterward he met Abraham Lincoln, and they both became active in public affairs there. Henry was one of three commissioners supervising the building of the new state capital in Springfield in 1837. When Lincoln became despondent after he and Mary Todd broke off their first engagement in January of 1841, it was Henry who undertook to cure Lincoln's melancholy. By 1848, he was speaking on platforms beside Lincoln on behalf of presidential candidate Zachary Taylor. When Taylor was elected, Henry received an appointment as Indian agent for Oregon Territory. He did not arrive in the West, however, until 1852. Within a year he was a member of the Oregon legislature and by 1856 he had received a second federal appointment as deputy United States surveyor for the Territory of Washington.[23]

Henry maintained a correspondence with Lincoln even from the West Coast. After the 1858 defeat by Stephen Douglas in the contest for the Senate, Lincoln wrote Henry from Springfield on 19 November words that showed a depth of both perspective and friendship:

I am glad I made the late race. It gave me a hearing on the great and endurable question of the age, which I could have had in no other way; and though now I sink out of view, and shall be forgotten, I believe I have made some marks which will tell for the cause of civil liberty long after I am gone.[24]

By 22 September of 1860, Lincoln is writing to tell Henry: "It all looks very favorable to our success. No one this side of the mountains pretends that any ticket can be elected by the people, unless it be ours."[25]

In July 1861, for one of his earliest appointments after taking office in March, Lincoln specified Henry for the office of surveyor general of the Territory of Washington.[26] In that position, Henry was drawn into the concerns about the size and ungovernability of the existing territory.

To begin to work with Wallace on the issue of dividing the territory, Henry traveled by sea and across the isthmus of Panama on a journey of four months, arriving in Washington, D.C., in April 1863. While in the nation's capital, he enjoyed significant and interesting access to the president because he lived with the Lincolns in the White House. On 3 April he accompanied the president, Mrs. Lincoln, their son Tad, and others on a river boat trip to visit General Joseph Hooker in Fredricksburg, Virginia.[27]

With this kind of access and historical relationship, Wallace and Henry were able to engage the president's personal participation and support for the idea of creating a new territory. Working sessions for the project were held at Wallace's three-story brownstone town house at 322 Indiana Avenue, Northwest. According to Wallace family recollections, President Lincoln himself was present at the meeting where it was determined to call the proposed new territory by the name of Idaho.[28]

By 22 December 1862, Congressman James M. Ashley, chairman of the House Committee on Territories, had introduced a bill to create a temporary government for the Territory of Idaho. In January 1863 a good deal of wrangling began to take place about the name of the new area, the duties of its various officers, the eligibility of electors, and even the prohibition of slavery in the territory. On 12 February 1863, however, by a vote of 85 to 39, the House of Representatives agreed to Bill 738 establishing the Territory of Montana. In the Senate, James H. Lane of Kansas introduced a similar measure. After debate and carrying an amendment by Senator Henry Wilson of Massachusetts to strike out the word "Montana" and insert "Idaho," the bill was adopted by a vote of 25 to 12. The House did not take up the issue of concurrence in the Senate amended bill until late in the evening of 3 March 1863, the last night of the Thirty-eighth Congress. With some angry debate, but because it was too late to utilize the typical device of a conference committee, the House agreed to the Senate changes and approved the bill for presidential consideration.[29]

President Lincoln's actions on the evening of 3 March signaled his own special interest in the Idaho legislation. It was between ten and eleven o'clock in the evening when the Idaho bill, as amended, was taken up by the House of Representatives for its final action. The Senate vote did not come until just before midnight. Just off the floor of the Senate, in his Capitol building office, President Lincoln awaited the passage of the Idaho bill and other legislation. John R. McBride, a representative from Oregon, wrote of his recollection of Lincoln's persistence in attending the Idaho bill:

During the evening, William H. Wallace, Dr. A. G. Henry, and I were working hard to push the Bill through. We were indebted to the California Delegation, especially Aaron A. Sargent, to members of the Pennsylvania Delegation, and especially to Speaker Grow, for the ultimate passage of the Bill. Within half an hour after it had been enrolled, it was placed in President Lincoln's hands. It was, of course, closing night of the session and President Lincoln was at his chambers in the Capitol.[30]

In fact, McBride was inaccurate about the length of time that Lincoln had to wait to sign the Idaho bill. It was much longer than "half an hour." After passing the bill, the House of Representatives took a recess from 12:20 to 1:50 A.M. on the morning of 4 March. Only after it reassembled was the Idaho bill enrolled and signed by the Speaker. Some time after 4.15 A.M., a message from the House announcing that the Speaker had signed the Idaho bill and others was received in the Senate. The president pro tempore of the Senate then signed the enrolled bill, which was taken immediately to the president. Thus, the actual delay during which Lincoln apparently remained in the Capitol was more than four hours.[31] Abraham Lincoln thus signed the Idaho bill at dawn on 4 March 1863, experiencing his first Idaho coincidence, for the name of the new territory is generally given the meaning of "sun coming over the mountains."[32]

With every expectation that Lincoln would fulfill the role they had long ago discussed in the house on Indiana Avenue by signing the Idaho bill, Wallace, Henry, and Congressman McBride went out to a late dinner celebration at Hanunark's restaurant on Pennsylvania Avenue. It was an establishment and an occasion "where good eating and champagne were prominent."[33] Without a doubt, the diners spoke of the next step that Lincoln would have to take in the organizing of Idaho Territory, the selection and nomination of its officers. From some source, Wallace seemed to have a strong indication of his own likely participation. When he returned to his Indiana Avenue residence after the meal, he informed his wife, "Well, Lue you have your territory and I am its Governor."[34] For Lincoln's part, he had a newly created territory, the largest in the United States, encompassing some 310,000 square miles—nearly all of the land mass of the states we now know as Idaho, Montana, and Wyoming. It was also an area in which slavery was specifically prohibited by the most recent act of Congress. The president may also have recognized a further opportunity for himself and his friends and political loyalists with appointments to be made for positions in Idaho. Neither Wallace nor Lincoln wasted any time in accepting the challenge and reaping the benefits.

OFFICERS FOR IDAHO TERRITORY

Within a week a group of seven congressmen and senators, including Wallace, had recommended a proposed slate of territorial officers for the president's consideration. Among those making the recommendations were Henry and McBride, both fresh from helping steer the Idaho bill through Congress. The suggested slate included William Wallace, as governor; William B. Daniels, as secretary; Dolphus

S. Payne, as chief justice; Sidney Edgerton and Alleck C. Smith, as associate justices; and Richard Williams, as United States attorney; no recommendation was made for the office of United States marshal.[35]

Lincoln apparently met in consultation with Wallace, Henry, and McBride to make the final selections.[36] At this session Lincoln made some changes in the list before forwarding the nominations to the Senate for confirmation. He struck the proposed Supreme Court chief justice, Dolphus Payne, from that post and advanced Edgerton to it from the position of associate justice. He moved Payne's name to the vacant office of United States marshal. That left an opening in one of the associate justice slots.[37] Thereupon Lincoln fashioned a highly personalized solution to fill the remaining vacancy.

Mr. Lincoln appointed me, in March 1862, Associate Justice of the Supreme Court of Idaho Territory. The manner of doing this was peculiar and characteristic. He took the list of officers which the Pacific Coast people had agreed upon for the territory and presented to him for appointment, and told them they must let him have one place on it for his old friend, Sam Parks of Illinois. He then struck out the name of one of the Judges and substituted mine. Dr. Henry, of Washington Territory, who was one of the party presenting the list, is my authority for this statement.[38]

Thus, Lincoln further cemented his own guardianship over the new Territory of Idaho. Likewise, he had foreshadowed the day just over twenty-five months in the future when Wallace, on Lincoln's last day, would come to see the president about filling the vacancy created by Judge Parks's resignation. Meanwhile, the next two years would be filled with numerous communications and contacts between Lincoln and Idaho.

The Senate confirmed Governor Wallace's appointment on 10 March 1863. Wallace, a week later in a letter to Secretary of State William Seward, replied: "I accept the trust." For the next two weeks Wallace prepared himself by collecting information and directions regarding Indian affairs and other business that he anticipated would be of importance in the new territory. On 1 April 1863, Governor and Mrs. Wallace, together with their young son, sailed from New York via Panama, San Francisco, and Portland, Oregon, toward the new territory.[39]

In 1863 the journey west was difficult for both men and information. News of the 4 March signing by Lincoln had not reached the frontier town of Lewiston, Idaho Territory, until 22 March 1863. The enthusiastic citizens there had fired a one-hundred-gun salute without being certain that their city was even within the new territory because of the confusion created by the last-minute boundary amendments in the Senate bill. It was not until the middle of April that Lewiston was able to ascertain definitely that it was indeed part of Idaho Territory. It was to Lewiston that Wallace went to organize the new government, arriving on 10 July 1863, exactly one week after the Battle of Gettysburg had been concluded.[40]

The value of Wallace's special access to and friendship with the president was not lost on the local Republicans in the Northwest's newest territory. In 1863 two Republican conventions were held to nominate a candidate for the delegateship to Congress, one on 15 September and the other on 18 September. Although the contest was close, Governor Wallace received the nomination of his party at both gatherings. In a potential repetition of his maneuver to make the transition from an appointed governor to an elected delegate to Congress, just as he had done previously in Washington Territory, Wallace now stood before Idaho voters at election in October 1863. When the official canvass was completed 2 December 1863, Wallace had been elected with a majority of 3,910 votes to 3,543 cast for John M. Cannaday, the Democrat. Serious allegations were raised that United States Marshal Dolphus S. Payne had manufactured 479 fraudulent votes for Wallace from the Fort Laramie area. Nevertheless, by 10 December 1863, Governor Wallace was headed down the Columbia River toward his new responsibilities in Congress. William B. Daniels, the territorial secretary who had certified the election results, remained behind to carry on as acting governor.[41]

Meanwhile, President Lincoln had begun to increase his own consciousness and information level about Idaho and the western regions of the country. From the Library of Congress, the Lincolns borrowed four treatises that dealt with explorations to the West in the weeks that followed the creation of Idaho Territory and the appointment of its officers: Mollhausen's *Pacific* (two volumes), on loan 2 July 1863 to 14 July 1863; Thornton's *Oregon and California* (two volumes), 2 July 1863 to 14 July 1863; Parkman's *Oregon Trail*, 2 July 1863 to 11 June [*sic*] 1863; and Fremont's *Oregon Explorations*, 2 July 1863 to 4 October 1863.[42]

Perhaps this kind of background information, together with firsthand reports from trusted friends like Wallace, helped make the president comfortable in including references to Idaho in both his 1863 and 1864 messages to Congress. On 8 December 1863, the president observed:

The condition of the several organized territories is generally satisfactory, although Indian disturbances in New Mexico have not been entirely suppressed. The mineral resources of Colorado, Nevada, Idaho, New Mexico, and Arizona proving far richer than has been heretofore understood.[43]

On 6 December 1864, the president mentioned Idaho again, even more selectively, in that year's message to Congress:

The territories of the Union are generally in a position of prosperity and rapid growth. Idaho and Montana, by reason of their great distance and the interruption of communication with them by Indian hostilities, have been only partially organized: But it is understood that these difficulties are about to disappear, which will permit their governments, like those of the others, to go into speedy and full operation.

As intimately connected with and promotive of, this material growth of the Nation, I ask the attention of Congress to the valuable information and important recommendations relating to the public lands, Indian affairs, the Pacific Railroad, and the mineral discoveries contained in the report of the Secretary of the Interior, which is herewith transmitted.[44]

Throughout his first and second terms, President Lincoln would appoint more than fifteen men to various federal positions in Idaho, filling the offices of governor, secretary, chief justice and associate justices of the Supreme Court, United States marshal, United States attorney, and Indian agent. After the initial round of appointments made necessary upon the creation of the territory in March 1863, Lincoln next exercised this executive authority in February 1864. Upon Wallace's return to Washington as delegate, it had become necessary to nominate another territorial governor. Lincoln made a most curious choice.

Even the congressional directories of the day promised that Caleb Lyon of Lyonsdale, New York, "writes poetry, lectures on the East, translates Oriental literature and is a member of several historical societies with a passion for archaeologic and antiquarian lore." The New York native was born in 1822, graduated from the University of Vermont in 1841, and was appointed by President Polk as United States consul at Shanghai, China. He became secretary of the California constitutional convention and later took credit for designing that state's official seal. Completing a tour of duty as the youngest member of the New York Senate, he was elected as a representative to the Thirty-third Congress in 1852.[45]

Lyon lost his seat in Congress after the campaign of 1856 and eventually left the Whig Party to become a Republican. In 1861 he came to Washington looking for an appointment. There was some discussion of a diplomatic post. On 2 May 1863, Lincoln wrote his secretary of state to inquire, "Have we any committal as to the vacant consulate at Havanna? If we have not, I am for giving it to Hon. Caleb Lyon, and of doing so at once."[46]

When none of the foreign posts seemed available, Lyon took advantage of his friendship with Secretary of the Interior John Usher to obtain Lincoln's promise to appoint him to the vacancy created when Wallace resigned the governorship of Idaho in December 1863. After Wallace arrived in Washington, he attempted to urge Lincoln not to choose Lyon for the Idaho appointment. Wallace preferred Idaho Marshal Dolphus Payne for the job. Lincoln, however, advised Wallace that his promise to Lyon was "absolute." When Wallace could not talk Lyon out of taking the position, the president made the appointment, and the Senate confirmed Lyon as Idaho's second territorial governor on 26 February 1864.[47]

Lyon was notoriously unsuccessful, his administration was fraught with both pomposity and scandal. He gave flowery speeches full of mythical references to hard-rock miners.[48] He became a leader in the intrigue to move the capital of Idaho southward some 300 miles from Lewiston to Boise. He actually commenced that removal by sneaking out of town under the guise of taking a duck hunting trip on the Snake River.[49] The angry people of Lewiston refused to turn over the territorial seal and records, protecting them by locking them in the local jail. The territorial government had thus come to an outrageous impasse under Lyon.

On 4 July 1864, Lincoln appointed a new territorial secretary. C. DeWitt Clinton was able to break the deadlock by commandeering the territorial property from the jail while accompanied by an armed escort of Federal troops from Fort Lapwai. On 30 March 1865, Associate Justice Smith left Lewiston on the Clearwater River ferry bound for Boise. By coincidence, Smith arrived with the seal and the archives in the new territorial capital on 14 April 1865, the same day Lincoln was shot.[50]

It was against that background of controversy and strife during the Lyon administration that Wallace was meeting with Lincoln to seek appointments replacing Judge Parks and Marshal Payne. Because of the Lyon controversies it is also possible that Wallace talked to Lincoln about resuming his former position as governor of the territory. Wallace's son is one source for that opinion:

Father was rather happy in his introductory speech for Mr. Lincoln at the Illinois meeting, and Mr. Lincoln never forgot it. So far as the affairs of the north Pacific Coast were concerned, father had great influence with Mr. Lincoln, and during his four years in Congress—1861 to 1865—was never refused a single request which he made to the president. Father was almost the last public man to hold an interview with Mr. Lincoln. He called on him late in the afternoon on the day of Lincoln's assassination. Mr. Lincoln told father on that occasion that he would reappoint him governor of Idaho. Andrew Johnson failed to carry out the expressed wish of Mr. Lincoln in this matter of appointment.[51]

Lincoln's contacts with Idaho Territory continued to deepen with more involvements of various types through 1864 and 1865. His official family was becoming very well represented in Idaho. Territorial Governor Caleb Lyon had brought Secretary of the Interior Usher's seventeen-year-old son, Arthur, with him to the territory as his private secretary.[52] Associate Justice Smith was married to one of the daughters of Lincoln's doctor, Anson Henry.[53] The new territorial secretary C. DeWitt Clinton had been appointed because Lincoln had received pressure from Attorney General Edward Bates to make that particular nomination at a time when Smith was serving as a clerk in the attorney general's office. Smith replaced the original territorial secretary, William Daniels, the brother-in-law of the same Congressman McBride from Oregon who had lobbied the Idaho Territory bill with Lincoln.[54]

In addition to the growing collection of Lincoln "people" serving there, Lincoln had the customary contacts with Indian tribes in the territory. On 7 January 1864, he reported to the Senate the number of Indian treaties, including "a treaty made at Soda Springs, in Idaho Territory, on the 14th day of October, 1863, between the United States and the Chiefs of the mixed bands of Bannacks and Shoshonees, occupying the Valley of the Shoshonee River."[55]

Likewise, Wallace continued to involve the president in various matters on the behalf of Idaho Territory. Sidney Edgerton was the original chief justice appointed by Lincoln in March 1863, who had been moved up to that slot by the president's personal preference. An acquaintance of Wallace's, Edgerton was a lame duck member of Congress from Ohio, who had voted for the Idaho bill just as his term had expired.[56] In late 1863 and early 1864, Justice Edgerton began to work with settlers in the most eastern part of the vast territory in support of further dividing it once again. By horseback to Salt Lake, stagecoach to Denver and Kansas, and then railroad to Washington, Edgerton went to see William Wallace and President

Lincoln on the question. Wallace agreed that the territory should be divided once more and helped Edgerton lobby in Congress. Ultimately, both the House and the Senate passed a bill creating Montana Territory. It was signed by President Lincoln on 26 May 1864. The former Idaho official was given a post in the new territory: Edgerton became governor.[57]

CONTROVERSY OVER PARKS

Meanwhile, back in Idaho, Sam Parks had been busily dispensing both justice and politics. Illness in his family, however, began to be a concern. From Lewiston on 15 December 1863, Parks wrote Wallace in Washington:

When I left Illinois the health of my wife was poor and is so still. I wish very much to go to see her as soon as my court is over in Bannock and to bring her out here if she is able to come. I am told that by some law passed in 62 . . . it is necessary to get leave of absence from the President. If this is so, I wish you would see to the matter for me.[58]

Unknown to Parks then was the fact that his son would soon die. Wallace did, indeed, present the matter to the president. On the back of this document, inscribed in Lincoln's hand, and signed and dated 5 March 1864, is the following note: "The writer of this—a Judge in Idaho,—is personally known to me to be very reliable— Is a leave necessary, when the service does not interfere with a term? And if yes, may not Judge Parks have the leave he asks?"[59]

On 7 March 1864, Parks again wrote Wallace, this time from Idaho City in the southern part of the territory. Enclosing a letter to the secretary of the treasury requesting that a draft for his salary be sent to his home in Lincoln, Illinois, Parks certified that he had done everything that the law or his instructions required by holding court throughout Idaho. Asking for Wallace's assistance in obtaining the money promptly, Parks wrote, "I need it very much."[60]

By 19 June 1864, Parks had been to Illinois and was returning through Atchison, Kansas, when he wrote to thank Wallace for a letter previously received and again to request assistance in the matter of obtaining his salary. In this letter he also had time for a bit of Idaho politics: "We *must* have a good man in place of Edgerton. He ought by all means to be appointed and enter upon the duty of his office immediately. You have no idea of the amount of business in the Territory."[61]

As the political campaign of 1864 began, it was again time for the territory to vote for a president and a delegate to Congress. Wallace's own image and popularity had slipped during his absence from the region. By August 1864, a radical element had assumed control of the Republican Party in Idaho. The Union Party convention nominated none other than Sam Parks as its candidate for delegate. Even so, Wallace left Washington, returned to Idaho, and campaigned for the Union ticket. Despite that effort, on election day, 10 October 1864, Democrat E. D. Holbrook defeated Parks by a margin of 600 votes to win the right to begin service as Idaho's next delegate to Congress for a term beginning in 1865.[62]

Even though he eventually had returned from Illinois to Idaho, Judge Parks had set in motion by his requests for salary and leave of absence the conflict that would bring Wallace into contact with President Lincoln on the last day of his life. Though the illness of Parks's wife and the death of his child in Illinois seemed a more than reasonable justification for leaving his post of duty temporarily between sessions of the court, and despite Lincoln's personal note of inquiry and endorsement, trouble was brewing in the Department of Justice. While in Illinois, Parks had asked Judge David Davis to write Lincoln's newly appointed Attorney General James Speed to obtain the official leave of absence that would allow him to draw his salary during his absence from the territory. When Davis received no reply from the attorney general, he followed up with a letter to the president stating that Speed had "treated my communication with contempt, and did not reply."[63]

On 12 April 1865, Attorney General Speed wrote a lengthy reply to Judge Davis apologizing and explaining the circumstances of his position regarding Parks's absence. Apparently, when Speed had received Davis's letter, he had taken it directly to the president, who had asked the attorney general to "hold on to it because we cannot break our rule so soon." Afterwards, Parks apparently came to Washington, where the attorney general explained to him "frankly and plainly how the matter stood." Speed's letter explained what had happened next:

The Judge [Parks] did express a wish to see the President to which I may have made no reply. I do not re-collect whether I did or not; If I did not, it was because I understood him as desiring me to get an interview or audience. That I could not do under my privilege, whilst Judges of the supreme court, Senators and members of the House of Representatives were waiting in the ante-room. Knowing that I would have to see the President that morning, I promised Judge Parks that I would mention the matter to the President and report to him at one o'clock. According to promise I saw the President and reported to him what was said. Judge Parks instantly drew up his letter of resignation and handed it to me. I did not file it amongst the papers of the office till after I had shown it to the President, which I had no opportunity of doing till after his return from City Point.[64]

Thus, one of the final internal controversies of the Lincoln administration dealt with Idaho Territory and a rift between Lincoln's official family and long-time friends. Attorney General Speed prudently gave his letter to the president for review before it was sent to former campaign manager Davis back in Illinois. On the reverse of the Speed letter Lincoln himself penned three sentences to Judge Davis:

Seeing your letter was about our friend Sam Parks, I handed it to Mr. Speed without reading into it far enough to discover that you were a little sharp on him. He answers, however, in good temper, and I send it to you. It will never do for you and Mr. Speed to be on other than good understanding. Yours truly, A. Lincoln. April 13, 1865.[65]

The day after Lincoln wrote that note, Wallace came to see him about Parks's replacement. It was not until two weeks after the assassination, however, that Davis received the letters.[66]

LINCOLN'S CONTINUING RELATIONS WITH IDAHO

Even the closing of the controversy related to Sam Parks and the death of the president did not terminate Lincoln's continuing relationship with Idaho. President Andrew Johnson made the two appointments sought by Wallace from Lincoln and authorized at the afternoon conference before he went to Ford's Theater. Furthermore, on 18 July 1865, Johnson appointed Wallace to the post of governor of Idaho Territory once again. However, Wallace's successor, Caleb Lyon of Lyonsdale, still governor and still controversial, used the influence of Thurlow Weed and Senator Edward Morgan of New York to have Wallace's commission stopped in the Department of State.[67]

Idaho's fellow territorial sponsor, Anson G. Henry was in Richmond, Virginia, when Lincoln was assassinated. He returned to Washington and rode in the funeral procession in the third carriage as one of the family. Henry remained in residence at the White House for six weeks, while he cared for Mrs. Lincoln in her deep grief. When Mary Lincoln finally was able to leave Washington and move to Chicago, Henry accompanied her. Afterward, returning to Washington Territory by steamship, he was lost when *Brother Jonathan* was sunk off the coast of San Francisco on 30 July 1865.[68] Upon hearing of his death, Mrs. Lincoln wrote to Mrs. Henry stating, "We consider that we have lost our best and dearest friend."[69]

The other principal proponent of Idaho Territory, John R. McBride, the congressman from Oregon, also maintained connections. In 1866 he sought and was appointed by President Johnson to the post of chief justice of Idaho Territory.[70]

After the assassination, "Old Idaho" Wallace determined that he would accompany the president's body back to Springfield. He likely participated in some of the public memorial services and viewing ceremonies that took place in Washington between 18 and 21 April. For some reason, however, Wallace did not immediately board the president's funeral train when it departed from the Washington station on Friday, 21 April. The train made initial stops in Baltimore; York, Pennsylvania; and Harrisburg. It then proceeded to Philadelphia, where it arrived at the Broad Street Station at 4:30 P.M. on Saturday, 22 April.[71] In Philadelphia, Wallace joined the senators, congressmen, and official representatives of the states. With them he occupied space in the coaches immediately behind the first carriage of the train and apparently remained with the entourage all the way to Springfield. At Chicago on 1 May, Wallace represented Idaho Territory as a member of the mounted guard of honor.[72]

Even after Lincoln was buried on 4 May, fate continued to tie the former president's friends and intimate acquaintances to the Territory of Idaho. None was more grief stricken and guilt ridden than Ward Hill Lamon, the president's personal body guard who had been made marshal of the District of Columbia. Familiar with Parks from their mutual days as lawyers in Illinois and as participants in the 1860 convention, Lamon was no doubt cognizant of Lincoln's relationship with Idaho. The marshal had frequently warned Lincoln to take more precautions about his personal safety, especially when attending the theater. At the time of the assassination, Lamon was on a mission for the president in Virginia. Despondent over Lincoln's death, Lamon resigned as marshal of the district and tried to obtain a new federally appointed position, the governorship of Idaho Territory. He was unsuccessful in doing so.[73]

Other Lincoln friends and acquaintances were more successful in seeking continuing Idaho connections. Mason Brayman had come to Illinois in 1842 to practice law. When Lincoln went to Congress in 1848, Brayman and his wife, Mary, and daughter, Ada, took over the lease on the Lincoln house and made it their residence for more than one year, from 1 February 1848 until Congressman Lincoln returned to Springfield on 31 March 1849. Brayman was late in paying the first quarter's rent of $22.50, which fell due on 1 May. It was not paid until 4 August. Nevertheless, the Brayman family was happy in the house. On 8 June 1848, Mason wrote his sister Sarah that "We have an excellent house and garden—with plenty of cherries and currants, and peaches growing—with vegetables of my own raising."

When Brayman paid another six months' rent of $45.00 with $50.00 in cash on 18 November, Lincoln wrote out a receipt for a $55.00 payment, giving the tenant additional credit for money expended in repairing a fence.

The Lincolns moved back into their home in the spring of 1849 and the Braymans took possession of another house nearby on the northwest corner of Eighth and Edwards streets. Brayman made a final rental payment to Lincoln on 9 May 1849, which generated another receipt. By 1853, Brayman, as a solicitor for the Illinois Central Railroad, was in a position to hire his friend Lincoln as a lawyer for the company in a taxation case. That single effort brought attorney Lincoln the handsome fee of $4,800. Through Brayman's connections and his own talents, Lincoln represented the Illinois Central throughout the 1850s in a variety of cases including property damage, livestock injury, trespass, right of way, and condemnation.[74]

When Lincoln traveled to New York City in 1860 to give his notable address at the Cooper Institute, his friend Brayman, while doing financial and legal business for the railroad, was also staying at the Astor House on Monday, 27 February. Of their contact in the metropolis, Brayman wrote:

We went to his room. Then came a Black Republican to take him up Broadway "to show him the fine buildings" but I guess it was to show him to the fine buildings. On his heels came a delegation from Patterson and Orange in New Jersey, begging him to go over and make speeches in those places. Thus, you perceive the fame of Ancient Abraham has extended even into foreign lands. To these unsophisticated heathens he presented me with a caution to be careful what they said, as I was a Democrat. Then came a Young Mans Committee of five whereupon I bolted for the door taking another man's coat in my haste.[75]

When Lincoln made his address at Cooper's Union Hall, he arranged for Brayman to sit in the back of the auditorium with instructions to raise his tall hat on a cane if the speaker's voice was not sufficiently audible. Thus, no man was in a better position to see, or hear, Lincoln's improbable, meteoric rise to the presidency in 1860 than Mason Brayman.[76]

As he had during the 1840s and 1850s, Brayman kept up his contacts with President Lincoln through correspondence as a general of the Illinois volunteers during the Civil War.[77] In 1876, President Ulysses S. Grant appointed Lincoln's friend, Mason Brayman, to the governorship of Idaho Territory.[78]

Even after Lincoln contemporaries such as Brayman were gone from the Idaho scene, their descendants continued to carry on a unique legacy of influence by the sixteenth president within Idaho Territory. One of them reported:

My father, Jesse K. Dubois, was the youngest son of a second marriage. My father pioneered a little more and went from Indiana to Illinois. While Indiana was a territory, he did his full part of the development of that great state where I was born. My father went into politics early and was in the Legislature in Illinois with Abraham Lincoln. Lincoln was 23 years of age and my father 21. He and Mr. Lincoln were close, intimate friends till the very hour of Mr. Lincoln's death. The Republican Party of Illinois was organized in 1856 at Bloomington, and was absolutely managed and controlled by Mr. Lincoln. Mr. Lincoln was a Whig and so was my father. When it came to the nomination of State Auditor, Mr. Lincoln himself put my father in nomination—this place going to the Whigs. All the Whigs and enough Democrats joined the new party, which was called the Republican party, to elect the ticket.[79]

Fred T. Dubois had his own recollections of Lincoln:

The front fence of Mr. Lincoln's Springfield home, then and now, was about three feet high, and stood on a brick wall, which was about five feet high. Almost directly in front of the steps leading up from the sidewalk to the home was a tree planted by Mr. Lincoln himself which still stands there. At that time it was about eighteen or twenty feet high.

Mr. Lincoln, as I recall, invariably wore a high hat, commonly called a "plug" hat. During the time of his great debates with Douglas and just preceding and after his nomination for the Presidency, Mr. Lincoln was much preoccupied in mind. When at home he usually went up to the State House after his evening meal to consult with his party associates. He was quite regular in his habits and usually came back about 8:30 in the evening. His daily habits were so well fixed that the boys could calculate on his movements, and we tied a string from the tree to the fence at just such a height as to strike Mr. Lincoln's plug hat about the center. We hid ourselves behind the fences in the adjoining yard, behind the wall, around the corner, and various places.

When Mr. Lincoln, with his arms folded behind his back and evidently in deep thought, would be suddenly aroused by having his hat knocked off by some unseen power, we would raise a mighty yell, rush out from our hiding places, grab hold of him wherever we could find a place and shout for joy. All his serious thoughts would vanish instantly and he would laugh and romp with us, and not infrequently march up the street with all the boys clinging around him until he could find a place to buy us some nuts or fruit.[80]

Fred Dubois came to Idaho from Illinois in 1880, when his brother "Dock" received a position at the Fort Hall Indian Agency. By 1882, Fred had been appointed U.S. marshal of Idaho Territory. In 1886, he was elected territorial delegate to Congress. Fred Dubois was not merely content to serve out his time representing a territory, however. More than any other man, he was instrumental in helping achieve statehood for Idaho and admission to the Union in 1890. Thus, through Dubois, the boy who romped with the man who became president, Lincoln's legacy was translated from the Territorial Act, which he signed, to a statehood, which he inspired a quarter of a century after his death. Dubois's efforts were recognized, too, by his election from the State of Idaho as its first United States senator.[81]

When Lincoln had completed his service as a congressman from Illinois in 1849, he sought a federal appointment as a means of continuing his service in politics. President Zachary Taylor chose him on 10 August 1849 to be secretary and later offered him the governorship all the Territory of Oregon. At that time, Oregon Territory included all the land mass of what we now know as Idaho. On 27 September Lincoln wrote a response declining that governorship. For the purpose of forwarding it through the correct political channels, he sent the letter to a friend in Springfield. The conduit was a man who would one day be further linked with Lincoln, Idaho, and the Northwest—Dr. Anson G. Henry.[82]

Because Lincoln declined to become the governor of the area that included Idaho, his history and the nation's took quite another course. Despite Congressman Lincoln's early disinclination to govern there, Idaho in the Rocky Mountains, became and remains one of President Lincoln's most direct legacies.

NOTES

1. Abraham Lincoln, *The Collected Works of Abraham Lincoln*, ed. Roy P. Basler, 9 vols. (New Brunswick, N.J.: Rutgers University Press in association with the Abraham Lincoln Association, 1953–55), 8: 412 (hereafter cited as *CWAL*). Alvord was subsequently nominated for the post by President Johnson on 20 December 1865. The Senate confirmed the appointment on 18 January 1866.

2. *CWAL*, 8: 412. Kelly was also nominated by Andrew Johnson on 20 December 1865, and confirmed to the judgeship by Senate action on 15 January 1866.

3. Harry E. Pratt, *Concerning Mr. Lincoln* (Springfield, Ill.: Abraham Lincoln Association, 1944), 118, quoting a letter from Anson G. Henry, the presidential family physician, to his wife dated 13 March 1865.

4. Anne Laurie Bird, "Portrait of a Frontier Politician," *Idaho Yesterdays*, 2, no. 3 (fall, 1958): 18.

5. Bird, "Portrait," *Idaho Yesterdays* 3, no. 1 (spring 1959): 30. Not all historical accounts report Wallace's face-to-face meeting with the president on 14 April. W. Emerson Reck in his book *A. Lincoln: His Last 24 Hours*, (Jefferson, N.C.: McFarland, 1987), 15 reports the signing of the endorsements but states that Lincoln executed them "before dressing and going to breakfast." By contrast, an obviously erroneous newspaper account carried in the *Boise* [Idaho] *Capital News* issue of 19 July 1936 reports that "The President went to Wallace's hotel and invited the Colonel and his wife to accompany him to the theater."

6. Bird, "Portrait," *Idaho Yesterdays* 1, no. 1 (spring 1957): 23, 24.

7. Lewis A. Warren, ed., "Dr. Henry Lauds Mrs. Lincoln, Chides Sec. Chase," *Lincoln Lore*, (Fort Wayne, Ind.: Lincoln National Life Insurance, 8 January 1934) 248: 1.

8. Earl Miers, ed., *Lincoln Day by Day: A Chronology 1809–1865*, 3 vols. in one, (Dayton, Ohio: Morningside House, 1991), 1: 237–238.

9. Bird, "Portrait," *Idaho Yesterdays* 1, no. 3 (fall 1957): 12–17.

10. Anne Laurie Bird, "William Henson Wallace, Pioneer Politician," *Pacific Northwest Quarterly* 49, no. 2 (April 1958): 73–76.

11. Leroy H. Fischer, "Samuel C. Parks's Reminiscences of Abraham Lincoln," *Lincoln Herald* (spring 1966), 11.

12. Ibid., 15–16; and Warren, *Lincoln Lore* (11 October 1948) 1018: 1.

13. Jesse W. Weik, *The Real Lincoln: A Portrait* (Boston: Houghton Mifflin, 1922), 128.

14. Jesse W. Weik, ed., *"Bulletin"* The Abraham Lincoln Association, no. 35 (June 1934).

15. Sam C. Parks to J. G. Nicolay, 25 September 1895. The book is in the historical collections of Lincoln College, Illinois.

16. Miers, *Lincoln Day by Day*, 2: 224, 233.

17. Willard L. King, *Lincoln's Manager David Davis* (Cambridge: Harvard University Press, 1960), 135–136.

18. W. D. Howells, *Life of Abraham Lincoln* (Springfield, Ill.: Abraham Lincoln Association, 1938), ix–x.

19. Fischer, "Park's Reminiscences," 14–15, 18–19. In Kansas City, Missouri, in May 1901, Parks inscribed the volume with these words, "This Life of Lincoln was corrected by him for me, at my request, in the summer of 1860, by notes in his handwriting, in pencil, on the margin. It is to be preserved by my children, as a lasting memorial of that great man and of his friendship for me." The book is now in the collection at the Illinois State Historical Library in Springfield.

20. Ibid., 12–14.

21. Leroy H. Fischer, *The Western Territories in the Civil War* (Manhattan, Kans.: Journal of the West, 1977), 28–29.

22. Harry C. Blair, M.D., *Doctor Anson G. Henry, Physician, Politician, Friend of Abraham Lincoln* (Portland, Ore.: Western Orthopedic Association, 1950), 5–15.

23. *CWAL*, 3: 339.

24. Ibid., 4: 118–119.

25. Blair, *Doctor Anson G. Henry*, 14–15.

26. Ibid., 16–17.

27. Bird, 2, no. 3 (fall 1958): 18.

28. Ibid., 18–20.

29. Thomas Donaldson, *Idaho of Yesterday* (Caldwell, Idaho: Caxton Printers, 1941), 397.

30. Ibid., 398.

31. Merle W. Wells, "The Creation of the Territory of Idaho," *Pacific Northwest Quarterly* 40 (April 1949): 117–20; and Ronald H. Limbaugh, "The Idaho Spoilsmen: Federal Administrators and Idaho Territorial Politics, 1863–1890," (Ph.D. diss., University of Idaho, 1967), 3.

32. Donaldson, *Idaho*, 397–398.

33. Bird, 2, no. 3 (fall 1958): 20.

34. Bird, 3, no. 1 (spring 1959): 8.

35. Merrill D. Beal and Merle W. Wells, *History of Idaho*, 3 vols. (New York: Lewis Historical Publishing, 1959), 1: 337.

36. Bird, 2, no. 1 (spring 1959): 8.

37. Fischer, "Samuel C. Parks's," *Lincoln Herald*, 14.

38. Bird, 3, no. 1 (spring 1959): 8.

39. Beale and Wells, *History of Idaho*, 1: 336–337.

40. Bird, 3, no. 1 (spring 1959): 15–20.

41. Warren, *Lincoln Lore* (28 September 1931), 129: 1.

42. *CWAL*, 7: 30.

43. Ibid., 8: 145–146.

44. Charles Lanman, *Dictionary of the United States Congress* (Washington, D.C.: Government Printing Office, 1864), 237.

45. *CWAL*, 6: 195.

46. Donald H. Limbaugh, *Rocky Mountain Carpetbaggers: Idaho's Territorial Governors 1863–1890* (Moscow: University of Idaho Press, 1982), 37–48.

47. Thomas G. McFadden, "Caleb Lyon: We'll All Wear Diamonds," *Idaho Yesterdays*, vol. 10, no. 2 (summer 1966): 3.

48. Limbaugh, *Rocky Mountain Carpetbaggers*, 52.

49. Beal and Wells, *History of Idaho*, 1: 350–354.

50. Donaldson, *Idaho*, 228.

51. Limbaugh, *Rocky Mountain Carpetbaggers*, 48.

52. Ibid., 29.

53. Ibid., 41.

54. Ibid., 40–41.

55. *CWAL*, 8: 112–113.

56. Limbaugh, *Rocky Mountain Carpetbaggers*, 29.

57. Bird 3, no. 1 (spring 1959): 25–26.

58. William H. Wallace Papers, University of Washington Libraries, General Correspondence File (1863), box 1, folder 10.

59. Ibid. (December 1863), box 1, folder 10.

60. Ibid. (March 1864), box 1, folder 16.

61. Ibid. (October 1864), box 1, folder 16.

62. Limbaugh, *Rocky Mountain Carpetbaggers*, 39–50.

63. King, *Lincoln's Manager*, 228–229.

64. *CWAL*, 1st supplement, 286–287.

65. Ibid., 286.

66. King, *Lincoln's Manager*, 228.

67. Beal and Wells, *History of Idaho*, 354–355.

68. Blair, *Doctor Anson G. Henry*, 18–23.

69. Warren, "Dr. Henry," *Lincoln Lore* (2 January 1950) 1082: 1

70. Limbaugh, *Rocky Mountain Carpetbaggers*, 61.

71. Ralph G. Newman, *In This Sad World of Ours Sorrow Comes to All: A Time-Table of the Lincoln Funeral Train* (Springfield: State of Illinois, 1965), 3–6.

72. Victor Searcher, *The Farewell to Lincoln* (New York: Abingdon Press, 1965), 121.

73. Benjamin P. Thomas, *Portrait for Posterity: Lincoln and His Biographers* (New Brunswick, N.J.: Rutgers University Press, 1947), 33.

74. *Journal of the Illinois Historical Society* 48 (1955): 69; Wayne C. Temple, *By Square and Compasses: The Building of Lincoln's Home and Its Saga*, (Bloomington, Ill.: Ashlar Press, 1984), 32–35; and Robert M. Sutton, "Lincoln and The Railroads of Illinois," *Lincoln Images: Augustana College Centennial Essays* (Rock Island, Ill.: Augustana College Library, 1960), 48–49.

75. Andrew A. Freeman, *Abraham Lincoln Goes to New York* (New York: Coward-McCann, 1960), 67–68.

76. Ralph G. Newman, ed., *Lincoln for the Ages* (Garden City, N.Y.: Doubleday, 1960), 138; and Freeman, *Lincoln Goes to New York*, 83.

77. *CWAL*, 7: 308–322.

78. Limbaugh, *Rocky Mountain Carpetbaggers*, 109.

79. Louis J. Clements, ed., *The Making of a State*, (Rexburg: Eastern Idaho Publishing, 1971), 21–22.

80. Emanuel Hertz, ed., *Lincoln Talks: A Biography in Anecdote* (New York: Halcyon House, 1939), 114–115. The Dubois family residence in Springfield still stands across the street from the Lincoln home and is preserved as a part of the historical park setting.

81. Clements, *Making of a State*, 11–12.

82. Miers, *Lincoln Day by Day*, 2: 65.

Part III

Coda: A Cross-National View

9 Lincoln and Leadership: An International Perspective

Frank J. Williams

Most students of American history have ignored world leaders and events beyond the boundaries of the United States during the Civil War. Yet, the dynamics of leadership as exercised by President Lincoln's contemporaries in other countries continued. Such issues as liberalism, nationalism, emancipation, formation of governments, unification, economics, war, and social upheaval were churning in many areas of the world during Lincoln's presidency.

Some would argue that after 1850, liberalism and nationalism, for example, were dead, as the rebellions in Germany, France, and Italy had been viciously quelled. Some leaders and followers of this press for democracy gave up hope and migrated to America—in Lincoln's words, "the last best hope of earth." Carl Schurz, who was to befriend Lincoln and play a major role in the events of the day is an example of this migratory spirit. But something happened around the time of the American Civil War to encourage nationalism, if not liberalism, as in the cases of Giuseppe Garibaldi for Italy and Otto von Bismarck for Prussia. Is this what Lincoln was doing—forging a new kind of nationalism—or was he trying to achieve a different end than other world leaders? Garry Wills, in his *Lincoln at Gettysburg*, says that the president used "sleight of hand" to "smuggle an abolitionalist view" of the Constitution into the mainstream of American political thought by giving priority to the Declaration of Independence over the Constitution.[1] Remember, even with his brevity at Gettysburg, Lincoln existed before sound bites. He may have been a tough politician and disingenuous at times, but he usually said what he meant.

Were the international leaders similar to Lincoln in style or prose or is this a case where we would never find anyone like our sixteenth president? And what role does leadership play in this? It seems to me that in the real world, leadership is the most important quality for measuring success for heads of state. While honesty, intelligence, eloquence, and success in foreign policy may be important, they are irrelevant in measuring achievement. How do the leaders stand on democratic issues and how successful were they in nurturing them with the support of the people?

If we were to poll the people, academicians, and government leaders today, how would they rate the world leaders in Lincoln's time? We know from William D. Pederson and Ann M. McLaurin in *The Rating Game in American Politics: An Interdisciplinary Approach* that all polls of academics place Abraham Lincoln as the greatest of all U.S. chief executives in the category that includes George Washington, Franklin D. Roosevelt, Thomas Jefferson, and Theodore Roosevelt.[2] Historian David L. Porter asks, "Would voters today recognize a candidate like Lincoln or reject him for his multiple past failures?"[3]

The work of political scientists and historians suggests guidelines for evaluating the leadership of chief executives, and the research in this volume contributes to understanding why Abraham Lincoln outscores both his contemporaries and most leaders since his administration.[4] He was a democrat rather than an autocrat who tended to be flexible rather than inflexible in pursuing his democratic vision for the nation. Moreover, though he was a traditional Whig by affiliation, he was energetic in promoting the spirit of the "last best hope of earth." In short, his "classical prudence and magnanimity" enabled him to maneuver through the political arena, understanding the Machiavellian reality without ever abandoning America's democratic vision.

His leadership becomes clearer when it is contrasted to that of the leaders of his day in terms of their views on specific issues: suffrage, constitutional restraints, civil liberties, especially in a time of nation building. How did other mid-nineteenth century leaders stand on these issues? Granted, not all these issues predominated in every country at the time of Lincoln's administration, but to the extent they did, a cross-national perspective may be helpful in forming judgments about world leaders.

At the time of Lincoln's administration most of the world was in ferment, including America's neighbors to the north and south. The Canadian assembly was arguing the need for confederation of upper and lower Canada under John MacDonald's leadership, Benito Juárez and his generals had captured Mexico City. General Garibaldi and his Thousand Redshirts invaded Sicily and crossed to Naples, and the Kingdom of Italy was formed under Victor Emmanuel II. In France, Napoleon III, nephew of Bonaparte, caused his country to intervene in the Piedmont-Austrian War. The papal states and Turkey were considered the weakest of the European states. In 1862 Bismarck became head of the Prussian ministry, beginning his drive to unite the German states. In Great Britain reform pressed by Prime Minister William E. Gladstone continued to excite the populace and the government. The Taiping Rebellion was in its twelfth year in China with millions of fatalities and Japan was still resisting westernization. A common thread runs through the turmoil—unification and the forming of nations. How did leaders respond to the efforts of people to govern themselves? The personalities and style of the leaders, as well as the cultural contexts in which they operated, require examination.

GREAT BRITAIN AND ITS EMPIRE

There was, as between President Lincoln and other world leaders of his day, a difference in leadership and cultural style. Within a month of Lincoln's first inauguration, *Harper's Weekly*, described three processions involving the leaders of Great Britain, France and the United States. In Great Britain, Queen Victoria was surrounded by "every kind of pageantry in which the military is most conspicuous." In France, Napoleon III was described as "the wise head of a military despotism as he marche[d] to his assembly through his bright camp in Paris." By contrast, as Lincoln passed through New York on the way to Washington, he appeared as "the plainest and simplest of citizens, without badge or decoration, without a soldier or a drum . . . with bare head, in an open carriage."

Their style as they assumed their respective responsibilities of leadership in the early weeks of 1861 were, however, more important in accentuating their differences. The queen of England opened Parliament on February 5 with these words:

My lords and gentlemen,—it is with great satisfaction that I again meet you in Parliament, and have recourse to your assistance and advice. My relations with foreign powers continue to be friendly and satisfactory . . . serious differences have arisen among the States of the North American Union. My heartfelt wish is that these differences may be susceptible of satisfactory adjustment.

To his assembly Napoleon III said:

I have endeavored to prove, in my relations with foreign powers, that France sincerely desires peace . . . she does not pretend to interfere in any place where her interests are not concerned; and, finally . . . she does not hesitate to condemn every thing which violates international right and justice.[5]

The first inaugural address of Abraham Lincoln was delivered at 1:30 P.M. on 4 March from a platform of unsightly planks and boards with little attempt at decoration, a far cry from the splendor of London and Paris:

Fellow citizens . . . ,—in compliance with a custom as old as the government itself, I appear before you to address you briefly, and to take, in your presence, the oath prescribed. . . .

I hold, that in contemplation of universal law, and of the Constitution, the Union of these States is perpetual. . . .

Physically speaking we cannot separate. . . .

We are not enemies, but friends. . . . The mystic chords of memory, stretching from every battle field and patriot grave . . . will yet swell the chorus of the Union when again touched . . . by the better angels of our nature.[6]

In Great Britain the leading principle during the American Civil War was nonintervention—thanks to foreign minister John Russell. Albert, the prince consort, who died just as the Lincoln administration was taking shape, deserves great credit for keeping peace between his country and the United States. It was he who significantly toned down the angry message prepared by the British government, threatening war for the embarrassing Trent affair, when two Confederate commissioners were seized by the U.S.S. *San Jacinto*. The president also recognized the futility of confrontation, saying, "Those prisoners will prove about as useless to us as white elephants."[7]

Until his death, Victoria accepted Albert's guidance, although there was a prejudice against him because of his supposed influence in politics. His cooperation with the queen in dealing with her political responsibilities represented a conscientious and self-sacrificing labor, and his wisdom and counsel were not known except to a very small circle. He was a man of cultured and liberal ideas, well qualified to take the lead in many reforms that Britain sorely needed.

Like Lincoln, Lord Palmerston, prime minister of Great Britain, wanted to be minister of a nation rather than just leader of a political party. Even his opponents agreed that he held office with great general acceptance. He was the irreconcilable enemy of slavery, despite his pro–Confederate leanings; and he labored with inexhaustible energy for maintenance of the empire. His philosophy was to take advantage of the weakness of his opponents. Ironically, he was more hostile toward Lincoln's government, the first U.S. administration to suppress the slave trade, than he was to any earlier administration.[8] In short, the traditional empire was the guiding light of his administration, as well as Machiavellian advantage over political opponents.

His foreign minister, Lord Russell, was a liberal himself, beginning his long career as a reformer in 1820. He supported Catholic emancipation and helped prepare and introduce the Reform Bill of 1832, insuring fairer representation in Parliament and extending the right to vote. In 1855, Russell represented England in Vienna in an unsuccessful conference to end the Crimean War. He worked brilliantly for the liberation of Italy. Not without failure, Russell introduced unsuccessful parliamentary reform bills on four separate occasions. As prime minister between 1846 and 1852, Russell used public works, grants, and other relief to help the Irish during the potato famine.

Lincoln, too, wanted to extend the franchise, first to women very early in his political career, and then to blacks, writing to Louisiana Governor Hahn in 1864:

Now you are about to have a convention which, among other things, will probably define the elective franchise. I barely suggest for your private consideration, whether some of the colored might not be let in—as, for instance, the very intelligent, and especially those who have fought gallantly in our ranks.[9]

Queen Victoria's essential achievement is as plain as it is simple. She received a crown that had been tarnished by ineptitude and vice, and she wore it for sixty-three years, making it a symbol of private virtue and public honor. If a monarchy, dignified and popular, is of value to the nation and empire, then it was Victoria who gave back these values to the crown. Her achievement was one of tradition more than intellect. Unlike a clear verdict in Lincoln's favor, opinions differ as to the queen's political acumen and the soundness of her understanding of her duty toward her ministers. Though no one can question her intense devotion to duty as wife, mother, and queen nor the transparent honesty of her character, she was hardly a modern democrat.

The Reform Bill of 1867, by which the vote was given to most of the working class, caused many to believe that England became, at last, a democracy. The Reform Bill was put through by the two great Parliamentary leaders and the two greatest rivals, Gladstone and Benjamin Disraeli, working together for once in their lives.

Disraeli, the Conservative leader, did not want reform. The year before when Gladstone had introduced a reform bill, he had fought against it and helped defeat it throwing his Liberal Party out of office. But Gladstone kept saying, "You cannot fight against the future." The rule by the people and for the people was bound to come. Disraeli was shrewd enough to see that, even though he did not want it. Since he knew it was coming he thought his party might as well get some credit for it. So when the Conservatives came into power, he did an about face and introduced a reform bill to which Gladstone kept adding until it suited him and then Disraeli manipulated the bill to passage.

ITALY: THREE LEADERS RATHER THAN ONE

Palmerston and his foreign minister Russell supported, while Victoria and Albert disliked, the actions of Cavour and Garibaldi which led to the union of Italy. Garibaldi, while a good military leader, needed the political calculations of Cavour to unify Italy under Victor Emmanuel. Lincoln came to the White House with great political skills and developed military skills as president. Thus, nation building in Italy required three leaders where only one was needed in America. Like Lincoln, Garibaldi and Cavour have become folk heroes. Cavour, ill from overwork like Prince Albert, died by the end of 1861. Thanks to the efforts of Giuseppe Garibaldi and Count Cavour, the Italian Parliament officially declared Italy a kingdom under Victor Emmanuel II, all as a result of French support and the taking of Naples and Palermo by Garibaldi's "Redshirts." The belated Italian experience in creating a nation is analogous to the German experience.

Victor Emmanuel II, King of Sardinia and first king of Italy, was bluff, hardy, good-natured and simple in his habits. He always had a high idea of his own kingly dignity and, like Lincoln, his statesmanlike qualities often surprised foreign diplomats, who were deceived by his homely exterior. He was a brave soldier, but he did not show great qualities as a military leader and had a great weakness for female society.

Napoleon III, to satisfy a vow he made when he became French emperor to assist in the unification of Italy, provoked the Austrians and won two major battles—Magenta (where the blood spilled caused a new word to be added to the English language) and Solferino, where one out of six soldiers lost their lives. He saw himself as another Bonaparte. At Villafranca, Napoleon III met Franz Josef, the young emperor of Austria, who was to rule for sixty-eight years—to arrange for peace—without telling his Italian allies. Support for Italian unity from France and the

Palmerston government had more to do with their hatred of the papacy than with promises made or any liberal or democratic leanings.

Pope Pius IX was disliked because he lived in the past and was unwilling to accept the present. With him in mind, Lincoln cautioned patience on emancipation early in the war, saying, "I do not want to issue a document that . . . must . . . be inoperative, like the Pope's Bull Against the Comet." No one had aided Protestantism more, since the Renaissance popes, than Pius IX, who through his inept leadership of the papal states, assisted in the creation of the Italian kingdom. The war of the French and the Sardinians against Austria in 1859 and the popular vote of 1860 incorporated a great part of papal territory with the Italian kingdom, but Pius always refused to recognize the unification.[10]

His is a tragic case. For two years after his election to the papacy, he pursued a progressive policy and even granted a constitution. But with the rioting of Italian nationalists in 1848, he was driven from Rome. He returned 12 years later with support of Napoleon III.

MEXICO UNDER A NATIONALIST WITH MALICE

Benito Juárez returned from exile in the United States to Mexico in 1855 to assist in the successful revolt against President A. L. de Santa Anna. As minister of justice, Juárez supported a liberal Constitution created in 1857, precipitating civil war with the Conservatives, who wanted no change. His government was recognized by the United States in 1859, and two years later he was elected president. Napoleon III, aware that the United States could only handle one war at a time, was intent on defying the Monroe Doctrine to undertake his expansionist views in Mexico. Outrageous demands for the repayment of the Mexican debt to France were a part of Napoleon's plot to establish an empire in Mexico. This scheme had been suggested by his brave and intellectual, but willful and impatient empress, Eugenie. French soldiers were dispatched to Mexico in 1861. Two years later Austrian Archduke Maximilian and his wife, Carlotta, were designated the new rulers of Mexico by a purported "election" and in April 1864 were acclaimed emperor and empress of Mexico. Maximilian's position was impossible. The country was opposed to him; the liberals refused to recognize his government, though he made several attempts to conciliate them, and such efforts only alienated the Conservatives and clerics. Financially, politically, and militarily he was wholly dependent upon France.

By the spring of 1865 there were 30,000 French soldiers in the country, and Juárez had been driven northward to the U.S. border with his armies shattered and his government almost penniless. By the end of the year, however, Maximilian was bankrupt and Napoleon saw the futility of his imperial project now that the United States, its Civil War over, demanded the withdrawal of French troops. In February 1867 the last French troops left from Vera Cruz and Maximilian was captured. Despite pleas from other governments for mercy, Juárez insisted on execution. This harsh treatment contrasts with Lincoln's lack of vindictiveness and willingness to allow the Confederate leaders to leave the country after Appomattox.[11]

Juárez's genius was not equal to the problem of reconstruction. With his death in 1872 one stage of Mexican history ended. He did not, as did Lincoln, wholly dominate his epoch, but during the most momentous period of Mexico's history he was, like Lincoln, the guiding genius, and he is often called Mexico's national hero. Each had the good fortune of saving his homeland, Lincoln, from disunity, and Juárez, not only from disunity but from foreign invasion.[12]

FRANCE UNDER A MACHIAVELLIAN DICTATOR

Napoleon III, obstinate and hesitating, held the throne of France for eighteen years. As president of the Second Republic, Louis Napoleon carefully prepared his eventual seizure of dictatorial powers, while pretending to defend democracy against the legislative assembly. Late in 1849, his administration took a decidedly dictatorial turn. The assembly was dissolved in 1851. An attempted workers' uprising was brutally repressed, anticipating the methods of more modern dictators. A plebiscite overwhelmingly favored constitutional revision. The new Constitution of 1852 gave the president dictatorial powers and created a Council of State, a Senate, and a Legislative Assembly subservient to the president. Subsequent decrees barred Republicans from the ballot and muzzled the press. In November 1852, another plebiscite confirmed the dictator's new title, Napoleon III, emperor of the French. For eight years Napoleon continued to exercise dictatorial rule, which, however, was tempered by considerable material progress. By 1860, having lost much of his popularity, the emperor inaugurated a more liberal domestic policy, widening the powers of the Legislative Assembly and lifting many restrictions on civil liberties.

The sudden rise of pressure under the leadership of Bismarck caused Napoleon to have a misplaced confidence in French military might. The Franco-Prussian War brought ruin to the Second Empire. He was caught in the disaster of Sedan on 1 September 1870, captured by the Prussians, and declared deposed by a bloodless revolution in Paris.

Both Lincoln and Napoleon III were enigmatic and complex figures, puzzling to historians. Yet Napoleon's policy was significantly more contradictory than Lincoln's —swaying from ruthless self-aggrandizement and rank imperialism to idealistic schemes and generosity. However, he was mostly unsuccessful in both. The true cultural leaders of the period, among whom Victor Hugo was outstanding, opposed his regime—unlike Walt Whitman, who praised Lincoln as the true representative of the people. Liberal intellectuals in France also respected Lincoln. Their expressions of pro-Lincoln sentiment were probably as much anti-Napoleon as pro-American. To praise Lincoln was to condemn Napoleon III.

CANADA LED BY A TRADITIONAL CONSERVATIVE

John MacDonald is remembered as the first premier of the Dominion of Canada, the person most responsible for the union of a loose confederation of the several Canadian provinces under the British North America Act of 1867. The difficulties of organizing the new dominion, the questions arising from federal rights, diverse claims, and the various conditions of the country, called for infinite tact and resource on his part. His theory was best summed up by his cardinal policy, "A British subject I was born, a British subject I will die." MacDonald's wish was to hold Canada for Great Britain; Lincoln's was to maintain an independent Union, saying, "the Devil takes care of his own. Much more should a good spirit—the spirit of the Constitution and the Union—take care of its own. I think it cannot do less and live."[13] The former reflects a traditionalist with a conservative spirit, the latter a conservative who understood the democratic spirit of a new nation.

GERMANY UNDER A MACHIAVELLIAN AND A KAISER

Bismarck, while a political genius of the highest rank, lacked the essential quality of the constructive statesman—he had no faith in the future or in the people. He clung to the privileges of his class and rank until the 1848 revolution. Recognizing that the old order could not be preserved unchanged, he went with liberalism and democracy in an effort to reduce their threat. While sometimes compared to Lincoln, who also made a compromise with liberalism and democracy, there was a basic difference. In Lincoln's America, there was a genuine compromise and in Germany only a facade. With German politics devoid of meaning and sincerity, the way was cleared for the triumph of demagogic dictators—resulting in two kaisers and a fuhrer.

While Lincoln may have deferred calling the Congress into session following the outbreak of civil war, he never prevented it from meeting. Bismarck, in direct violation of the Constitution, dissolved Parliament in 1862 and assumed control of the government and the budget. In contrast, Lincoln always understood the proper role of a legislature in a Republic; though he was willing to take extraordinary constitutional measures, he always later asked Congress to ratify those actions.

Bismarck was a clever Machiavellian. In order to weaken the Social Democrats, he instituted a program of sweeping social reform with laws passed providing for accident, sickness and old age insurance, and better working conditions.

Carl Degler sees elements of Bismarck in Lincoln. While admitting that the president's record was not comparable to Bismarck's deliberately editing a report so as to provoke the French declaration of war that Bismarck needed to create the Franco-Prussian hostilities and France's ultimate surrender at Sedan, he does argue that Lincoln maneuvered the South into firing the first shot of the Civil War.[14] He also points out that American nationalism was "incomplete" at the time of Lincoln's administration. "Lincoln emerges as the true creator of American nationalism, rather than as the mere savior of the Union."[15] Lincoln, then, comes considerably closer to the Bismarck who "laid the foundations for German nationalism." Yet, Degler's view distorts Lincoln's overall political achievement. Though he understood Machiavellian measures, he was at heart a democrat in tune with the spirit of the framers of the Constitution. His style was hardly that of an emotional nationalist—he respected reason too much.

Kaiser Wilhelm I was decidedly conservative and traditional in his politics. On the outbreak of revolution in 1848 he saw that some concessions were necessary but not before order was restored. While not possessing Frederick the Great's intelligence, he believed in the ultimate union of Germany and in Prussia as its instrument. His alien attitude to the liberal temper of contemporary Germany was tempered by shrewd common sense and wisdom in his choice of advisers. Even though his tenure remained in the shadow of his chancellor, Bismarck, whom he appointed in 1862, Wilhelm I was not a cipher.

As a symbol of reborn German unity, he was very popular, but his reactionary policy brought him the hatred of the radical elements. Unlike Lincoln he survived two assassination attempts. Like Bismarck, William H. Seward had begun his duties by supposing that he would be premier, and had proposed a startling program where he would lead the United States. Lincoln's answer to his secretary left no doubt as to who was president, but his words were without malice. "If a certain thing must be done," he said simply, "I must do it."[16] Though Wilhelm often disagreed with Bismarck's policies, he ultimately was always persuaded by his chancellor.

RUSSIA UNDER GOVERNMENT BY GRACE

Alexander II, czar of all the Russians, up to the moment of his accession in 1855, never gave anyone reason to believe that he would be known to posterity as a great reformer. While leaning, as a rule, to liberals, he never went so far as they desired and always sought some middle course by which conflicting interests might be reconciled—just as Lincoln dealt with emancipation. On 3 March 1861, the sixth anniversary of his accession as czar, the emancipation law for serfs was signed. Other reforms followed in quick succession. Alexander also suffered bouts of mental depression produced by the disappointments which he experienced in his foreign and domestic policy. Overall, rule by the czar, including reforms, always was exercised within the parameters of his grace rather than in terms of classical magnanimity which Lincoln epitomizes for the modern age.

On 24 August 1855, Lincoln wrote to his friend, Joshua F. Speed:

As a nation, we began by declaring that "all men are created equal." . . . When the know-nothings get control it will read, "All men are created equal, except negroes, and foreigners and Catholics." When it comes to this I should prefer emigrating to some country where they make no pretence of loving liberty—to Russia, for instance, where despotism can be taken pure, and without the base alloy of hypocrasy.[17]

Six years later, following Russian emancipation, Lincoln's opinion changed, and he even suggested to the recently returned secretary to the U.S. legation in St. Petersburg, Bayard Taylor, that he give a lecture on "serfs, serfdom, and emancipation in Russia," ending his request with, "Could not you get up such a thing?"[18] Unfortunately, Russia remained a traditional backward state. Early in 1881, during the twenty-sixth year of his reign, and on the very day in which he signed a Ukasi creating a special commission to prepare reforms in government, Alexander fell victim to assassins. He was too much a product of a political system which did not understand constitutional limitations.

Though the issuing of the Emancipation Proclamation remains one of the most memorable of Lincoln's acts, the stereotyped picture of the emancipator suddenly striking the shackles from millions of slaves by a stroke of the pen is incorrect. Lincoln's policy, like that of Alexander II, was a matter of slow development. When Union generals, Fremont in Missouri and Hunter in the lower South, attempted emancipation by military edict, Lincoln overruled them. Answering Horace Greeley's antislavery appeal on 22 August 1862, he wrote, though with the proclamation already in his desk, that his "paramount object" was to "save the Union," not "either to save or to destroy slavery."[19] Notwithstanding, Europe and the rest of the world considered his Emancipation Proclamation to be the "greatest achievement of his administration."[20]

The new governments of Prussia and Italy were considerably more conservative and traditional than Lincoln's. Where Bismarck was known for governing with "blood and iron," Lincoln spoke about "government of the people, by the people, for the people." Even though liberals in Germany and Italy admired Lincoln (Garibaldi who while discussing the possibility of taking a command in the Union Army could speak of "this holy battle" and "universal freedom"), nationalism remained the stronger force in both disunited Italy and disunited Germany.[21]

Without urging special laws against treason as he infrequently used such laws as existed, Lincoln had under the suspension of the habeas corpus, thousands of persons arrested on suspicion after which, usually without trial, they were kept in prison for a time and then released. In this policy, his purpose was precautionary and preventive, unlike the punitive and vindictive European treatment of dissidents. When confronted with antiwar or anti-administration agitation in speech or press, Lincoln usually showed toleration.

JAPAN UNDER DIVINE GOVERNMENT

In the East, the old ways were crumbling, yet its traditions were even more medieval than Russia's. On 8 July 1853, four American steamships under the command of Commodore Matthew Perry entered Yedo Bay (now called Tokyo) in what was to be a successful beginning for the Japanese to open their long closed door. Four years later a trade agreement was made between the nations, and then only because of the foresight and courage of Lord Naosuke—the Shogun's prime minister. For that he was called a traitor and a rebel and was murdered in March 1860 by hostile Samurai while on the way to a meeting with the Shogun. Shogun is actually a title for all the military dictators who were the actual rulers of Japan from the twelfth to the nineteenth centuries. Naosuke's death preceded by seven years the overthrow of the Shogun in 1867 and the beginning of modern Japan, in part, because of the intrusion of foreigners, initiated by Commodore Perry.[22]

Lincoln himself was concerned about Japan in his annual message to Congress in 1864:

the action of that empire . . . is inconstant and capricious. Nevertheless, good progress has been affected by the Western powers, moving with enlightened concert. . . . There is reason . . . to believe that these proceedings have increased rather than diminished the friendship of Japan towards the United States.[23]

In 1868, the power of government was placed in the hands of Japanese western-izers and the renovation of Japan on Western lines was accomplished. Feudalism was abolished and a new constitution was prepared and adopted. Japan was re-made into an industrial, modern state, though its culture kept the old military traditions that dreamt of empire and an emperor (a Sun God) even more out of touch than Russian czars.

CHINA'S TRADITIONAL GOVERNMENT

As for China, Abraham Lincoln wrote in the same 1864 message to Congress:

The rebellion which has so long been flagrant in China, has at last been suppressed, with the co-operating good offices of this government, and of the other Western commercial states. . . . China seems to be accepting with hearty good-will the conventional laws which regulate commercial and social intercourse.[24]

The year 1864 was the fifteenth year of a revolt to overthrow that emperor and his Manchu dynasty—a ruinous civil war known as the Taiping Rebellion. The dam-age wrought by the rebels and the unrest they incited were large factors in the fall of the Manchu dynasty in 1912.

THE CONFEDERACY: A REACTIONARY REBELLION

On 17 October 1862, William E. Gladstone, then chancellor of the Exchequer, said:

We may have our own opinions about slavery; we may be for or against the South; but there is no doubt that Jefferson Davis and other leaders of the South have made an army; they are making, . . . a navy; and they have made what is more than either, they have made a na-tion.[25]

If the Confederate rebellion had indeed been successful we would be comparing Lincoln to Jefferson Davis.

Historians generally believe Lincoln had the "capacity to grow" while Davis is thought of as being somewhat rigid. However, Davis ironically grew, too—from states rights conservatism to instituting state socialism in the Confederacy.[26]

Although Davis had superior military training and a formal education, Lincoln had stronger skills as a politician. Also their personalities were different. One is amazed to read Davis's letter of 31 March 1864 to North Carolina Governor Zebulon Vance, requesting that Vance cease sending him any correspondence at all except on official matters. Compare this to Lincoln's letter to Joseph Hooker on 26 January 1863:[27]

I have heard, in such way as to believe it, of your recently saying that both the army and the government needed a dictator. Of course, it was not for this, but in spite of it, that I have given you the command. Only those Generals who gain successes, can set up dictators. What I now ask of you is military success, and I will risk the dictatorship.[28]

Hooker, showing the letter to newspaper correspondent Noah Brooks, described it as "just such a letter as a father might write to his son." Instead of cutting off all but official correspondence with this vexatious general, President Lincoln turned his criticism to respect for him. Lincoln handled criticism much better than the thin-skinned Davis. In short, Lincoln had a democratic personality, while Davis leaned toward the tradition of the inflexible autocrat. Even their writing styles were different. Alistair Cooke believes that "Lincoln exemplified better than any statesman until Churchill, the Churchillian line: 'The short words are best, and the old words are the best of all.' "[29] Davis wrote like a bureaucrat.

CONCLUSIONS: A CLASSICAL "DEMOCRAT" IN THE MODERN ERA

Lincoln, while fighting the status quo, sought emancipation, "shrewdly" prevented British and French recognition of the Confederate States of America and thus their intervention, and showed great integrity by following his democratic convictions without being controlled by a concern for personal popularity and the dictates of his political party.[30] He was a conservative who could think "anew."

The sixteenth president was among the "consummate masters of statecraft" and such was the impression he left. In the list of the leaders of his time he takes preeminent place. His hold upon his acquaintances, his friends, and the affections of his own people and the world has not been due merely to the fact that he rose to America's highest office. Can the same affection rise among the people for Bismarck, Garibaldi, Cavour, Victor Emmanuel II, the Shogun, Emperor Hien Feng, Napoleon III, Alexander II, and even Queen Victoria, who gave her nation and the world the name of an era? They leaned toward tradition—relied on it. Lincoln, by contrast, encouraged responsible, democratic government through his leadership style. He was a person who would not be a dictator, autocrat, monarch, or mere Machiavellian. He acted to preserve and promote the democratic values of the framers of self-government.

It is doubtful whether any other leader of his time could have matched him in politics, in shaping language, in smoothing personal difficulties by a classical magnanimous touch or a tactful gesture, in avoiding domestic and international complications, in courageously persisting in the face of almost unendurable discouragements, and in maintaining war morale while refusing to harbor malice. Lincoln not only passes the test of leadership, he has become a symbol for democracy and union.[31]

NOTES

1. Garry Wills, *Lincoln at Gettysburg, The Words That Remade America* (New York: Simon & Schuster, 1992), 38.

2. Ann M. McLaurin and William D. Pederson, "Dimensions of the Rating Game," in *The Rating Game in American Politics*, ed. William D. Pederson and Ann M. McLaurin (New York: Irvington Publishers, 1987), 5.

3. David L. Porter, "American Historians Rate Our President," in *The Rating Game in American Politics*, ed. William D. Pederson and Ann M. McLaurin (New York: Irvington Publishers, 1987), 14.

4. See chapters by Barbara Tuchman, James MacGregor Burns, James C. Davies, James David Barber, as well as the introductory chapter by Pederson and McLaurin in *The Rating Game*. Also see William D. Pederson and Kenneth G. Kuriger, Jr., "A Comparative Test of Jimmy Carter's Character," in Herbert D. Rosenbaum and Alexej Ugrinsky, eds., *The Presidency and Domestic Policies of Jimmy Carter* (Westport, Conn.: Greenwood Press, 1994), 243–257.

5. Louis A. Warren, ed., "The Queen, The Emperor, The President," in *Lincoln Lore* (Fort Wayne: Lincoln National Life Foundation, 1956), 1404.

6. Abraham Lincoln, *The Collected Works of Abraham Lincoln*, ed. Roy P. Basler, 9 vols. (New Brunswick, N.J.: Rutgers University Press in association with the Abraham Lincoln Association, 1953–55), 4: 270, 271 (hereafter cited as *CWAL*).

7. Genevieve Foster, *Abraham Lincoln's World* (New York: Scribner's, 1944), 296.

8. Jasper Ridley, *Lord Palmerston* (New York: E. B. Dutton, 1971), 549–550.

9. *CWAL*, 7: 243.

10. J. O. Thorne and T. C. Kollocott, eds., *Chambers Biographical Dictionary* (Edinburgh: W & R Chambers, 1986), 1017.

11. Shelby Foote, *The Civil War, A Narrative*, vol. 3, *Red River in Appomattox* (New York: Vintage Books, 1986), 975.

12. Antonio J. Bermudez, Address delivered by Mr. Antonio J. Bermudez, Director General of Mexico's National Border Program, Juárez, Mexico, 1964, 1.

13. *CWAL*, 6: 27.

14. Carl N. Degler, *One Among Many: The Civil War in Comparative Perspective*, 29th Annual Fortenbaugh Lecture (Gettysburg, Pa.: Gettysburg College, 1990), 20.

15. Ibid., 18.

16. *CWAL*, 4: 317.

17. Ibid., 2: 323.

18. Ibid., 7: 93.

19. Ibid., 5: 388.

20. Thorne and Kollocott, *Chambers Biographical Dictionary*, 828.

21. Degler, *One Among Many*, 15.

22. Foster, *Abraham Lincoln's World*, 276.

23. *CWAL*, 8: 139.

24. Ibid., 139.

25. Julius W. Pratt, *A History of United States Foreign Policy* (Englewood Cliffs, N.J.: Prentice-Hall, 1960), 302.

26. Mark E. Neely, Jr., ed., *Lincoln Lore* (Fort Wayne: Lincoln National Life Foundation, January 1986), No. 1763: 2–3.

27. *CWAL*, 8: 78.

28. Ibid.

29. Alistair Cooke, *Alistair Cooke's America* (New York: Alfred A. Knopf, 1973), 218; James M. McPherson, *Abraham Lincoln and the Second American Revolution* (New York: Oxford University Press, 1991), 93–112.

30. Porter, "American Historians Rate Our Presidents," 16.

31. James G. Randall, *Dictionary of American Biography* (New York: Charles Scribner's Sons, 1933), vol. 6, pt. 1: 258.

Select Bibliography

———————————————— *Brenda J. Cox*

LEADERSHIP IN GENERAL

Arnhart, Larry. "Statesmanship as Magnanimity: Classical, Christian and Modern." *Polity* 16, no. 2 (winter 1983): 263–283.

Burns, James MacGregor. *Leadership*. New York: Harper & Row, 1978.

Davies, James C. *Human Nature in Politics*. New York: John Wiley & Sons, 1963.

Goodwin, Doris Kearns, and James MacGregor Burns. "True Leadership." In *The Rating Game in American Politics*, edited by William D. Pederson and Ann M. McLaurin, 213–234. New York: Irvington Publishers, 1987.

McPherson, James M. *Battle Cry of Freedom: The Civil War Era*. New York: Ballantine Books, 1988.

Miroff, Bruce. *Icons of Democracy*. New York: Basic Books, 1993.

Tuchman, Barbara W. "An Inquiry into the Persistence of Unwisdom in Government." In *The Rating Game in American Politics*, edited by William D. Pederson and Ann M. McLaurin, 197–212. New York: Irvington Publishers, 1987.

Wills, Garry. *Certain Trumpets: The Call of Leaders*. New York: Simon and Schuster, 1994.

THE PRESIDENCY IN GENERAL

Abbot, Philip. *The Exemplary Presidency: Franklin D. Roosevelt and the American Political Tradition*. Amherst: University of Massachusetts Press, 1990.

Abraham, Henry Julian. *Justices and Presidents: A Political History of Appointments to the Supreme Court*. New York: Oxford University Press, 1987.

The American Presidency: A Historical Bibliography. Santa Barbara, Calif. ABC-Clio, 1984.

Barber, James David. *Presidential Character*. 4th ed. Englewood Cliffs, N.J.: Prentice-Hall, 1992.

Cohen, Norman S. *The American Presidents: An Annotated Bibliography*. Pasadena, Calif.: Salem Press, 1989.

Davison, Kenneth E. *The American Presidency: A Guide to Information Sources.* Detroit: Gale Research, 1983.

DeGregorio, William A. *The Complete Book of U.S. Presidents.* New York: December Books, 1987.

Freidel, Frank. *The Presidents of the United States of America.* 12th ed. Washington, D.C.: White House Historical Association, 1989; distributed by Sewall.

Goehlert, Robert U. and Fenton S. Martin. *The American Presidency: A Bibliography.* Washington, D.C.: Congressional Quarterly, 1987.

———. *American Presidents: A Bibliography.* Washington, D.C.: Congressional Quarterly, 1987.

———. *The Presidency: A Research Guide.* Santa Barbara, Calif.: ABC–Clio, 1985.

Kane, Joseph. *Facts About the Presidents: A Compilation of Biographical and Historical Information.* 4th ed. New York: H. W. Wilson, 1987.

Koenig, Louis W. *The Chief Executive.* New York: Harcourt Brace Jovanovich, 1986.

Pederson, William D. *The "Barberian" Presidency.* New York: Peter Lang, 1989.

———, and Ann M. McLaurin. eds. *The Rating Game in American Politics.* New York: Irvington Publishers, 1987.

REFERENCE WORKS ON LINCOLN

Angle, Paul M. *A Shelf of Lincoln Books: A Critical, Selective Bibliography of Lincolniana.* New Brunswick, N.J.: Rutgers University Press in association with the Abraham Lincoln Association, 1946.

Elliott, Ian ed. *A. Lincoln: Chronology, Documents, Bibliographic Aids.* Dobbs Ferry, N.Y.: Oceana, 1970.

Kunhardt, Phillip, Jr., Phillip B. Kunhardt III, and Peter W. Kunhardt. *Lincoln, an Illustrated Biography.* New York: Knopf, 1992.

Lincoln, Abraham. *Lincoln on Democracy*, edited and introduced by Mario M. Cuomo and Harold Holzer. New York: HarperCollins, 1990.

Lincoln Encyclopedia: The Spoken and Written Words of Abraham Lincoln Arranged for Ready Reference. Edited by Archer Shaw. Westport, Conn.: Greenwood Press, 1980.

Matthews, Elizabeth W. *Lincoln as a Lawyer: An Annotated Bibliography.* Carbondale: Southern Illinois University Press, 1991.

Miers, Earl S. *Lincoln Day by Day.* Dayton, Ohio: Morningside Bookshop, 1988.

Neely, Mark E. Jr. *The Abraham Lincoln Encyclopedia.* New York: Da Capo Press, 1982.

Wills, Garry. *Lincoln at Gettysburg: The Words That Remade America.* New York: Simon & Schuster, 1992.

BIOGRAPHIES OF LINCOLN

Anderson, Dwight G. *Abraham Lincoln, the Quest for Immortality.* New York: Knopf, 1982.

Beveridge, Albert J. *Abraham Lincoln: 1809–1858.* Boston: Houghton Mifflin, 1928.

Bursey, L. Gerald. *Abraham Lincoln.* Popular Images of American Presidents. Westport, Conn.: Greenwood Press, 1988.

Charnwood, Godfrey Rathbone Benson. *Abraham Lincoln*, 3d ed. New York: Henry Holt, 1917.

Current, Richard N. "Lincoln Biographies: Old and New Myths." In *Arguing with Historians: Essays on the Historical and the Unhistorical*. Middletown, Conn.: Wesleyan University Press, 1987.

———. *The Lincoln Nobody Knows*. New York: McGraw-Hill, 1958.

Fehrenbacher, Don E. *Prelude to Greatness: Lincoln in the 1850's*. Stanford, Calif.: Stanford University Press, 1962.

Hanchett, William. *Out of the Wilderness: The Life of Abraham Lincoln*. Urbana and Chicago: University of Illinois Press, 1994.

Neely, Mark E., Jr. *Abraham Lincoln and the Promise of America: The Last Best Hope of Earth*. Cambridge, Mass.: Harvard University Press and the Huntington Library, 1993.

Oates, Stephen B. *With Malice toward None: The Life of Abraham Lincoln*. New York: Mentor Books, 1978.

Thomas, Benjamin P. *Abraham Lincoln: A Biography*. New York: Alfred A. Knopf, 1952.

Tice, George. *Lincoln*. New Brunswick, N.J.: Rutgers University Press, 1984.

OTHER WORKS ON OR BY LINCOLN

Borritt, Gabor S. *Lincoln and the Economics of the American Dream*. Memphis, Tenn.: Memphis State University Press, 1978.

Borritt, Gabor S., and N. O. Forness. *The Historians' Lincoln: Pseudohistory, Psychohistory, and History*. Urbana: University of Illinois Press, 1988.

Borritt, Gabor S., ed. *Lincoln the War President: The Gettysburg Lectures*. New York: Oxford University Press, 1992.

Braden, Waldo W. *Abraham Lincoln, Public Speaker*. Baton Rouge: Louisiana State University Press, 1991.

Bradford, Melvin E. "The Lincoln Legacy: A Long View." In *Remembering Who We Are*. Athens: University of Georgia Press, 1985.

Brooks, Noah. *Washington, D.C. in Lincoln's Time*. Athens: University of Georgia Press, 1989.

Cashman, Sean D. *America in the Gilded Age: From Abraham Lincoln to Theodore Roosevelt*. New York: New York University Press, 1988.

Cox, LaWanda C. *Lincoln and Black Freedom*. Chicago: University of Illinois Press, 1985.

Cunliffe, Marcus. "The Doubled Images of Washington and Lincoln. In *In Search of America: Transatlantic Essays*. Westport, Conn.: Greenwood Press, 1991.

Current, Richard N. *Speaking of Abraham Lincoln: The Man and His Meaning for Our Times*. Urbana: University of Illinois Press, 1983.

Davies, James C. "Lincoln: The Saint and the Man." In *The Rating Game in American Politics*, edited by William D. Pederson and Ann M. McLaurin, 297–335. New York: Irvington Publishers, 1987.

Donald, David. *Lincoln Reconsidered*. New York: Vintage Books, 1961.

Fehrenbacher, Don E. *The Leadership of Abraham Lincoln*. New York: John Wiley, 1970.

———. *Lincoln in Text and Context: Collected Essays*. Stanford, Calif.: Stanford University Press, 1987.

Ferguson, Robert A. "Lincoln: An Epilogue." In *Law and Letters in American Culture*. Cambridge, Mass.: Harvard University Press, 1984.

Findley, Paul. *A. Lincoln: The Crucible of Congress*. New York: Crown, 1979.

Foner, Eric. *A House Divided: America in the Age of Lincoln.* New York: W. W. Norton, 1990.

Glatthar, Joseph T. *Partners in Command: The Relationship Between Leaders in the Civil War.* New York: The Free Press, 1994.

Greenstone, J. David. *The Lincoln Persuasion: Remaking American Liberalism.* Princeton: Princeton University Press, 1993.

Grossman, A. R. "The Poetics of Union in Whitman and Lincoln: An Inquiry toward the Relationship of Art and Policy." In *The American Renaissance Reconsidered*, edited by Walter B. Michaels and Donald E. Pease. Baltimore: Johns Hopkins University Press, 1982.

Hill, Frederick T. *Abraham Lincoln as a Lawyer.* 2 vols. Albuquerque, N.M.: American Classical Collection Press, 1985.

Hofstadter, Richard. *The American Political Tradition: And the Men Who Made It.* New York: Alfred Knopf, 1948.

Holzer, Harold. "A Few Appropriate Remarks." *American History Illustrated* 23 (November 1988): 36–46.

Jennison, Keith W. *The Humorous Mr. Lincoln: A Profile in Wit, Courage, and Compassion.* Woodstock, Vt.: Countryman Press, 1988.

Johannsen, Robert W. *Lincoln, the South, and Slavery: The Political Dimension.* Baton Rouge: Louisiana State University Press, 1991.

Leuchtenburg, William E. "Most Americans Don't Know What Lincoln Really Represents," interview with Mario Cuomo. *American Heritage* 41 (December 1990): 59–62+.

Lincoln, Abraham. *The Collected Works of Abraham Lincoln.* Edited by Roy P. Basler. 9 vols. New Brunswick, N.J.: Rutgers University Press in association with the Abraham Lincoln Association, 1953–1955.

———. *The Collected Works of Abraham Lincoln*, 2nd supplement, 1848–1865. New Brunswick, N.J.: Rutgers University Press, 1990.

———. *Lincoln on Democracy.* Edited and introduced by Mario M. Cuomo and Harold Holzer. New York: HarperCollins, 1990.

———. *The Lincoln-Douglas Debates.* Edited with an introduction by Harold Holzer. New York: HarperCollins, 1993.

———. *Speeches and Writings 1832–1858.* New York: Viking Press, Library of America, 1989.

McPherson, James M. *Battle Cry of Freedom: The Civil War Era.* New York: Ballantine Books, 1988.

———. *Abraham Lincoln and the Second American Revolution.* New York: Oxford University Press, 1991.

Mitgang, Herbert. *Abraham Lincoln, A Press Portrait.* Athens: University of Georgia Press, 1989.

Neely, Mark B., Jr. *The Fate of Liberty: Abraham Lincoln and Civil Liberties.* New York: Oxford University Press, 1991.

Oates, Stephen E. *Abraham Lincoln, the Man Behind the Myths.* New York: New American Library, 1985.

Pauludan, Phillip S. *The Presidency of Abraham Lincoln.* Lawrence: University Press of Kansas, 1994.

Phillips, Donald T. *Lincoln on Leadership.* New York: Warner Books, 1991.

Randall, James G. *Lincoln the President: Last Full Measure.* Vols. 1–3. Chicago: Dodd, Mead & Co., 1955.

————., and Richard N. Current. *Lincoln the President: Last Full Measure*. Vol. 4. Urbana: University of Illinois Press, 1991.

Rietveld, Ronald D. *Lincoln's Views of the Founding Fathers*. Redlands, Calif.: Lincoln Memorial Shrine, 1992.

Simon, Paul. *Lincoln's Preparation for Greatness: The Illinois Legislative Years*. Urbana: University of Illinois Press, 1989.

Stevenson, James A. "American Voyages of Lincoln and Huck Finn," *Lincoln Herald* 90, no. 4 (winter 1988): 130–133.

Strout, Cushing. "America's Dilemma: Lincoln's Jefferson and the Irony of History." In *Making American Tradition: Visions and Revisions from Ben Franklin to Alice Walker*. New Brunswick: Rutgers University Press, 1990.

Strozier, Charles B. *Lincoln's Quest for Union: Public and Private Meanings*. New York: Basic Books, 1982.

Thomas, Benjamin P. *Lincoln's New Salem*. Carbondale: Southern Illinois University Press, 1987.

Thomas, J. L., ed. *Abraham Lincoln and the American Political Tradition*. Amherst: University of Massachusetts Press, 1986.

Wills, Garry. *Lincoln at Gettysburg: The Words That Remade America*. New York: Simon & Schuster, 1992.

Index

About the Editors and Contributors

BRENDA J. COX is a librarian at Louisiana State University in Shreveport. She received her M.L.I.S. from LSU in Baton Rouge in 1991. Her work has appeared in several books and the *North Louisiana Historical Association Journal*.

ETHAN FISHMAN is a professor of political science at the University of South Alabama. He holds a B.A. and an M.A. from the State University of New York at Binghamton and a Ph.D. from Duke University. His research deals with the application of traditional Western values to present-day American politics. Among his publications are *Likely Stories: Essays on Political Philosophy and Contemporary American Literature* (1989) and *Public Policy and the Public Good* (1991).

JOSEPH R. FORNIERI is a doctoral candidate in political philosophy at the Catholic University of America. He received his B.A. from the State University of New York at Geneseo and his M.A. from Boston College, where he was awarded a Bradley Foundation fellowship.

WILLIAM C. HARRIS is a professor of history and head of the history department at North Carolina State University. He holds a Ph.D. in history from the University of Alabama and has taught at Millsaps College. He has written five books on the Civil War–Reconstruction era, edited one book, and written numerous essays on the period. His biography of Williams Woods Holden of North Carolina won the Jefferson Davis Award in 1988 for the best book on Confederate history. He has completed a book-length manuscript on Abraham Lincoln and Reconstruction.

DAVID H. LEROY served as the first U.S. nuclear waste negotiator from 1990 to 1993. Previously lieutenant governor and attorney general of Idaho, he is now practicing law. The author of many professional treatises and articles, Leroy studies and collects materials related to Lincoln and colonization, Lincoln and the West, and Lincoln's early politics. He holds an LL.M. from New York University and a J.D. from the University of Idaho.

DAVID E. LONG holds a J.D. from Ohio State University and a Ph.D. in history from Florida State University. He is the author of *The Jewel of Liberty* (1994).

VINCENT J. MARSALA is a political scientist who received his Ph.D. from Louisiana State University in Baton Rouge. He is the author of *Sir John Peter Grant, Governor of Jamaica* (1972) and a contributor to numerous publications. He is a professor and dean at Louisiana State University in Shreveport.

WILLIAM D. PEDERSON is a political scientist who received his Ph.D. from the University of Oregon. He is the editor of *Great Justices of the U.S. Supreme Court* (1993), *Congressional-Presidential Relations in the U.S.* (1991), *Morality and Conviction in American Politics* (1990), *The "Barberian" Presidency* (1989), *Grassroots Constitutionalism* (1988), and *The Rating Game in American Politics* (1987). He received a 1994 Achievement Award from the Abraham Lincoln Association for organizing the first Lincoln conference in the Deep South and directing the first teachers' institute on Lincoln in the nation. He is a professor at Louisiana State University in Shreveport.

RONALD D. RIETVELD is a professor at California State University, Fullerton. He has been a student of Lincoln since the age of fourteen, when he discovered the last photograph of Lincoln in 1952 in the Nicolay papers of the Illinois State Historical Library. He received a B.A. from Wheaton College, a B.D. from Bethel Theological Seminary, and a Ph.D. from the University of Illinois, Champaign-Urbana. He has written extensively on Lincoln and nineteenth-century American history.

BROOKS D. SIMPSON received his Ph.D. in American history at the University of Wisconsin-Madison in 1989. He is a specialist in the Civil War and Reconstruction period at Arizona State University. Author of *The Political Education of Henry Adams* (1995) and *Let Us Have Peace: Ulysses S. Grant and the Politics of War and Reconstruction, 1861–1868* (1991) and coeditor of *Advice after Appomattox: Letters to Andrew Johnson, 1865–1868* (1987).

JAMES A. STEVENSON is an associate professor of history at Dalton College in Dalton, Georgia. He holds a B.S. in social science from Illinois State University, an M.A. in European history from Wayne State University, an M. A. in English literature from Georgia Southern University, and a Ph.D. in European history from the University of Wisconsin-Madison. He has published many articles about Lincoln.

FRANK J. WILLIAMS is an acknowledged leader of the Lincoln historical community in the United States. He was for twelve years president of the Lincoln Group of

Boston and now serves as president of the Abraham Lincoln Association. In addition, he lectures widely, serves on numerous Lincoln-related advisory boards and committees, and writes an annual report on Lincolniana for the *Journal of the Abraham Lincoln Association*. He was the principal organizer of several recent symposia, including "Lincoln and the American Political Tradition" at Brown University in 1984 and "Lincoln, the Law, and the Constitution" in 1987 for the fourteenth annual symposium of the Abraham Lincoln Association and the Illinois State Historical Library. Williams helped spearhead the publication of two books based on the Brown University conference and contributed an "Afterword" to *Lincoln on Democracy* (1990). Presently, he is working on a bibliography of every Lincoln work published since the last century.

ISBN 0-313-29359-7

90000>

EAN

9 780313 293597

HARDCOVER BAR CODE